D0082187

Dedicated to Artistic Directors everywhere
(in the hope they might give either of us a job)

SEE also: ATTITUDE and WHATEVER WORKS

Contents

DISCARDED

Acknowledgments

We would like to thank the following for permission to include quotations from their publications:

Extract from *Bedroom Farce* from *Three Plays* by Alan Ayckbourn published by Chatto & Windus. Copyright © 1989. Used in the United States by permission of Grove/Atlantic, Inc., and in the United Kingdom by permission of The Random House Group Limited.

Extract from *Present Laughter* from *Coward Plays 4* by Noël Coward published by Methuen Publishing Limited. Copyright © The Estate of Noël Coward.

Extracts from *Signpost to Murder* by Monte Doyle. Reproduced by permission of The Agency (London) Ltd, © Monte Doyle. First published by Samuel French. All rights reserved and enquiries to The Agency (London) Ltd. 24 Pottery Lane, London W11 4LZ info@theagency.co.uk

Extracts from *Picnic* and *Bus Stop*. Reprinted by permission of International Creative Management, Inc. Copyright *Picnic* © 1953 and *Bus Stop* © 1955 by William Inge.

Extract from *A Few Good Men*. Copyright © 1989 by Aaron Sorkin. Reprinted by permission of William Morris Agency, Inc. on behalf of the Author by special arrangement with Samuel French, Inc.

We would also like to thank Boston University's School of Theatre Arts and London's Royal Academy of Dramatic Art, for training us; William Germano at Routledge for inspiring us to write this book; and our friends for their insights: John Colclough (for his analysis of agents), Constantine Gregory (for the anecdote on accents), Hedli Niklaus (for factual details on radio acting), Kathleen Bishop (for practical costume advice), and Carolyn Jones (for all her valuable comments on the manuscript).

Introduction

This book is for actors who feel they are drowning in a sea of troubles and need a life belt.

This is also a book for actors who want to know more

About the craft of acting
About the techniques of acting
About *what* to do *when*

Whether you are starting off—the moment when you wonder if you really want to be an actor—or whether you are staring at the mirror wondering if you should continue, we designed this book to give you easy-to-understand articles full of facts and nuggets of information about how to tackle the realities of being an actor and of giving a good performance. This is not a book full of theoretical philosophies—there are many other books on the shelves that are concerned with those. We wish to tackle the practicalities.

We are not dealing with the details about how to lay out a resume or about which individuals to contact for various jobs, for that will vary from area to area and will change over time. No, we are dealing in this book with all those problems and the solutions to them, which are about the **craft** of acting.

We are writing jointly, but when we have a very different slant on a topic, or have a specific anecdote, then we identify which one of us is speaking.

The Actor Says:

My personal contribution to this book is based on continuous experience of being a professional actor since 1958. I have not only been employed to act, but have extensive knowledge of the trials and tribulations of being out of work and all that trying to get work entails. I have endeavored to cover the realities of being in the entertainment industry as well as the techniques required to produce the goods under some of the most difficult circumstances. Professional actors have nothing but themselves to sell, and only their bodies as a tool. Look after it (the body that is), you will need it to be in a healthy state, even in old age, if you are serious about being an actor full time and all your life: Good luck!

The Director Says:

Actors often come to me for advice, even though they are working with another perfectly good director. When asked why they come to me, the answer is refreshingly simple and flattering: "You give us answers we can understand, and notes that we can immediately put into practice." I know this book will do that for you too.

The modern actor cannot know when suddenly she will be catapulted from doing a day here and a day there in a series of little acting jobs to a long run in the theatre, a continual role in a television series, or a role in a significant movie that can change her acting situation forever. The actor's job is to be ready for it, and part of the job of this book is to prepare the actor for these possible eventualities.

When we need to choose between using the words *he* or *she,* we alternate from topic to topic to share them out. There is no relevance to the topic being addressed as to whether we use the male or female, simply an acknowledgment that there is no good word to use that is evenhanded between the genders.

How to Use This Book

Any book that has an alphabetical list of topics runs the risk of being difficult to navigate, because you the reader will not always know the name the authors have given to the particular article you are looking for. So the first thing to do with this book is to look up what you are interested in, to see if it has a heading attached to it.

If you cannot find what you are looking for under the alphabetical headings, then consult the Family Trees. The various topics are sorted into eight different Family Trees, which have been arranged into branches, twigs, and leaves. Go to the tree that covers the area of your search, and you can follow a path along the branches to get to the section you are interested in and to find the name of the article that will help you. You also can see the headings of the other topics that are close to the one you want. If the article relates to several different areas of this huge subject of acting, then we included it in a different Family Tree—wherever we think you will look for it.

At the bottom of each article you can see which Family Tree you are in, so you will know which associated topics are near by. We also give the exact branch/twig/leaf location for that subject.

Family Trees

The "Training" Family Tree

Training deals with all matters to do with becoming an actor, maintaining skills as an actor, and learning new ones. It has six main branches, with some twigs.

Tree: *Branches:*   *Twigs:*

Training

      Amateur dramatics

           Example: Mr. and Mrs. Noah fight

      Conservatories and drama schools

           Teaching acting

      Further training

           Radio acting

           Screen acting

      No training

           Be yourself (plus!)

           Fellow actors

           Jobs requiring acting skills

      Starting off

           Acting: What is it?

      University courses

           Qualifications

The "Getting Work" Family Tree

Getting work is the journey from first contact to actually landing the job, and has five main branches, lots of twigs, and four leaves.

Tree:	Branches:	Twigs:	Leaves:

Getting Work
    Agents
        Photographs
        Resumes
    Auditions
        Interviews
            Anecdotes and jokes
        Open auditions
        Over the top
        Readings
        Rejection
    Casting directors
        Commercial casting sessions
    It's not what it used to be
        Money is probably the answer
            Hierarchy
            Producers
        Never say no
    Typecasting
        Know your image
            Attitude
        Versatility

The "Homework" Family Tree

Homework is all the preparation you do at home, the results of which you take into the rehearsals or to the performances, and has six main branches, with lots of twigs, and a cluster of leaves that includes examples from plays to illustrate the points made.

Tree: *Branches:*   *Twigs:*   *Leaves:*

Homework
    Instinct versus intellect
        Don't give up
        Good and bad taste
    Journey
        Consistency
        Less is more?
            Example: Anna Christie and her dad
        Step-by-step
    Movement and gestures
        Example: Signs of the times
    Style
        Comedy and farce
    Text
        Example: Broadway versus Hollywood
        Gear changes
        Learning lines
        Let the words do the work
            Example: Brother and sister act
            Example: Lady Bracknell's handbag
            Example: Valuable verbals
            Example: You, thee — and the gold
        Opposites
            Example: Noël Coward on the phone
        Pauses
    Voice
        Dialects and accents
        Projection

The "Rehearsing" Family Tree

Rehearsing is what happens in the rehearsal room, if there is one, and how to maximize the benefits from this period. It has eight main branches, with appropriate twigs and four leaves.

Tree: *Branches:*   *Twigs:*   *Leaves:*

Rehearsing
- Commitment
  - Don't ask for permission
  - Drugs
- Improvisation
  - Role-play
- Mistakes
  - Don't give up
  - Forgetting lines
  - Illness
  - Punctuality
- Rehearsals (long, short, or none)
  - Directors
    - Notes
  - Discussions
  - Learning lines
  - Method acting
  - Step-by-step
- Technical and dress rehearsals
  - Costumes, wigs, and shoes
  - Crew
- Technique
  - Believability
  - Business (biz)
  - Gear changes
    - Example: Anna Christie and her dad
  - Opposites
  - Outside-in versus inside-out
    - Blowing your nose
    - Movement and gestures
  - Sex and violence

The "Performing" Family Tree

Performing is all that happens in a performance, and how to deal with the problems that come with appearing before those watching you — onstage or on-screen. There are four main branches, with some very important twigs and equally important leaves, including excellent examples.

Tree: *Branches:*   *Twigs:*   *Leaves:*

Performing
     Audience
             Good and bad taste
             Journey
                     Consistency
             Laughter
             Pauses
                     Example: Princely business
             Thinking
     Problems
             Battle of the sexes
             Breaking up (corpsing)
                     Example: Kate and corpsing
             Forgetting lines
     Technique
             Business (biz)
             Comedy and farce
                     Example: Kate and corpsing
             Eye-to-eye contact
             Less is more?
                     Example: Al and Bob's first meeting
             Over the top
                     Commitment
                     Example: Plunging in the deep end
             Projection
             Properties (props)
             Pulling focus
     Truth
             Believability
             Sex and violence

The "Style" Family Tree

Style refers to the differences in acting when confronted with scripts from different backgrounds. Period style is what you do differently when performing in plays written at an earlier time, and acknowledges the different types of presentation, such as for Restoration plays or for Shakespeare. Modern contemporary acting is here, as it is a style too. There are five main branches, with many twigs and leaves with examples to illustrate the various styles and their peculiarities.

Tree: *Branches:*   *Twigs:*   *Leaves:*

Style

       Medieval acting

              Example: Mr. and Mrs. Noah fight

       Shakespeare acting

              Shakespeare: First Folio

              Shakespeare: Prose or poetry

                     Example: The silence of the lads

              Shakespeare: Simple or complicated

                     Example: Brother and sister act

              Shakespeare: Verse

                     Example: Olivia's ends

                     Example: Princely business

              Shakespeare: What you call people

                     Example: You, thee — and the gold

              Shakespeare: Wordplay

                     Example: Valuable verbals

                     Let the words do the work

       Restoration acting

              Example: Mr. Horner is exactly that

       Melodrama acting

              Example: Signs of the times

[Next branch on page xxiv.]

The "Screen Acting" Family Tree

Screen acting is such an important part of the modern actor's life (and finances) that it gets its own tree. There are five main branches, with associated twigs and some nice leaves.

Tree: *Branches:* *Twigs:*   *Leaves:*

Screen Acting
    Auditions
            Casting directors
                    Commercial casting sessions
                    Photographs
                    Resumes
            Interviews
                    Anecdotes and jokes
            Readings
                    Text
    Screen cheating
            Eye-to-eye contact
            Properties (props)
            Screen reactions
                    Example: Al and Bob's first meeting
                    Example: Noël Coward on the phone
            Screen vocal levels
                    Dialects and accents
    Shooting and acting
            Editing and acting
            Film versus television
            Multicamera versus single camera
            Punctuality
            Stars
    Truth
    Typecasting
            Be yourself (plus!)
            Know your image
            Versatility

"The Team" Family Tree

The Team covers dealing with all the coworkers you will come across, including yourself. There are six branches, with a lot of twigs and important leaves.

Tree: *Branches:*   *Twigs:*   *Leaves:*

The Team
> Crew
> Designers
>> Costumes, wigs, and shoes
> Directors
>> Discussions
>> Don't ask for permission
>> Notes
> Fellow actors
>> Battle of the sexes
>> Hierarchy
>> It's not what it used to be
>> Stars
> Producers
> You (your other life)
>> Drugs
>> Jobs requiring acting skills
>>> Role-play
>>> Teaching acting
>> Qualifications
>> Rejection
>>> Attitude
>>> Illness
>>> Money is probably the answer
>>> Never say no
>>> Problems
> Whatever works

Acting: What Is It?

What indeed?

Well, it is exactly that, it is **acting**. It is not being, it is **pretending** to be. It is portraying a character so skillfully that the audience believes that you are going through all the emotions of the character to the point where it is convinced of the sincerity of what it is witnessing. The audience, however, always knows that you are an actor and that you know it is out there watching you, and that is the only truth about acting.

A lifesaver:

Sincerity is not always your friend.

You are going through a highly emotional scene, your voice starts to quiver and the tears come; you feel genuinely upset by the situation; if it shows too much, the stage audience gets worried in case you are losing control. This is **not** acting, for you have distracted your audience by your personal indulgence. The screen audience, however, is allowed to see the whole emotional thing, because it secretly knows that it is being shown only the really effective take, where the tears roll down in the perfect way.

The audience can well be moved to tears by the emotion of the character, without being concerned about the performer's emotional involvement. We have noticed how the audience does not always laugh when the actors are having a wonderful time corpsing.

SEE also: BREAKING UP (CORPSING)

The actor must be in total control at all times; the trick is to **appear** to be emotionally involved. There is a difference and the audience will sense it; audience members do not really want you to have a better time than they are having. After all, they are paying for it. For the screen, of course, the tears can as well be generated by the chemical tear stick as by the emotion.

The reason that audience members need and want a curtain call at the end of the evening is that they need to experience that wonderful change-over when they see before their very eyes the characters of the play reverting back to the actors who played them. Foolish indeed are the directors who deny the audience that very necessary cathartic act by finishing their productions with no curtain call. Again, the world of screen acting is different, for there can be no cathartic moment, and most of the audience leaves the theatre before the credits are shown.

To sum up what acting is, we offer the following:

All acting is cheating.

You need to use technique to recreate a character that is believable and real, night after night in the theatre and take after take in a film. It is your life belt:

Technique is your friend.

If you think that by becoming a professional actor you will feel wonderful each time you perform, cancel that thought right here and now. Instead, why not be pleased to create a wonderful moment for your audience and be proud of the technical way you did it?

An excellent actor is one who presents many more valid bits of information to an audience (about the situation, mood, characterization, etc.) than a merely good actor will. The methods used vary enormously from actor to actor, both in their preparation techniques and in the way they communicate all the good stuff to an audience. The techniques they use will vary from the arena of the stage to the challenge of the screen, but excellent actors will still be doing more for their audiences than their competitors will.

SEE also: METHOD ACTING and OUTSIDE-IN VERSUS INSIDE-OUT

First Family Tree:	Training
Branch:	Starting off
Twig:	**ACTING: WHAT IS IT?**

Second Family Tree:	Rehearsing
Branch:	Whatever works
Twig:	**ACTING: WHAT IS IT?**

Agents

What they can and cannot do for you.

An agent is like a car. It gets you from point A to point B with varying degrees of comfort. It needs to be paid for, taxed, insured, serviced, and supplied with gas, and then you have to drive it. It is always there when you want it, but it will not move on its own.

It would be nice to believe that once you have an agent, you can sit back and let her do the struggling, the constant looking out for opportunities, and the matching of your abilities to the parts that are on offer; someone to guide and mold your career the way you want it to be.

It would also be nice to win the national lottery or to be left a fortune by an obscure relative; well, they **are** all possible but all equally unlikely. An agent will, as a minimum, answer the telephone and negotiate money; anything else is a bonus (so do not expect it). An excellent agent will do more, but in this day and age she is often not given the time **she** wishes to give her clients a better service.

Agents have to exist, have to earn a certain income just to survive, so for a start they are into a different way of thinking about acting than their clients. We have found that when it ever comes to a choice between two jobs (and you are **very** lucky ever to be in a position when you have a choice), an agent will always—**your** agent will always—choose the job that by an amazing coincidence generates the most income for you and for the agent.

So if you want guidance for a career, if you want to grow as an artist in certain directions, **you** make the call, **you** make the decisions. Until you are a star, and can have an agent and a manager looking after you in great detail, agents will have so many people on their books that the individual touch is not possible to the degree that you or they would like.

4

It is at the starting point in your career that the proper agent can make a difference, because the industry is always looking out for the new face on the block, and it is worthwhile to find out who has the contacts in the areas where you feel happiest.

The Actor Says:

I have had at least a dozen agents in my career, and the thing that occurs to me now is that the agent you have when starting out is the one who has the most power to help you and guide you into the right area of work. I should have made greater efforts earlier on to find out who would capitalize on my comedic qualities.

So, although everyone might think they are extremely versatile and do not want to get pigeonholed, it is a much better idea to decide on either a type of character, and pursue that, or an area of work, and pursue that. Then find an agent who specializes in that particular field, with the right contacts, and work together to promote you. Once you are established and become better known, you can afford to branch out into other areas of work.

Agents tend to expect all their clients to be available at any time for interviews. Should you find yourself in the situation where you get very short notice for a casting session—such as you need to be there in an hour and a half—just say, "I'll be there." Even though you know it is impossible to make the time given, be positive with your agent and then work out how late you are likely to be. When you get to within twenty minutes of the appointment, call your agent with a really stunning and believable reason why you are likely to be late and let her sort it out with the casting director. An agent will be more sympathetic to a train stuck in a tunnel, a broken-down bus, or a minor accident than believing you are not able to go because of alternative work or family reasons—remember, the truth is not always your friend.

Just think for a moment: if all agents worked for all their clients the way the actor thinks they should, there would still be the same (small) number of jobs available and the same rejection rate.

Family Tree:	Getting work
Branch:	**AGENTS**
Twigs:	Photographs; Resumes

Amateur Dramatics

When you are not paid.

This is a wonderful ongoing practice and ever-present tradition that gives a great deal of pleasure to actors and audiences. In the UK amateur world, the person who gives the actors their moves, discusses the interpretation, and decides the set and lighting is known as the producer, even though he is in fact directing the play (and this also happens in some radio dramas as well). In the old days all actors were amateurs, only coming out to act for festivals and the wonderful pageant wagon plays. It was only around the time of Shakespeare that it became possible to earn a living as an actor, although the actors he wrote about rehearsing a play in *A Midsummer Night's Dream* were very obvious amateurs, with regular jobs elsewhere.

The Actor Says:
I was fortunate enough to be brought up in a city that sported three large professional theatres, and a main amateur company that still flourishes. I was a member of this company for five years, and I owe it a great debt, not just because of the opportunity it gave me to cut my teeth, as it were, by appearing in many of their quality productions, but because of the encouragement I received to go on and train for the professional theatre.

Amateur dramatics are often derided by professionals as full of poor or even bad actors and backstage backbiting, and there is probably a little truth in this, but there are some excellent amateur companies. They are a good place to start, to see if you really want to spend the rest of your life doing this sort of thing, and they are a good place to keep your talents up to scratch as you wait for your lucky break.

The problem with amateur work is the very reason it exists, which is for the actor to be seen. Very often, to be seen is more important for the amateur actor than to produce excellent work. One such amateur group in the United Kingdom had a theatre built to their own specifications—not everyone in the audience could easily see the stage, but they could all very easily see each other sitting in the auditorium. The performers are sometimes happier to be seen as themselves in a wonderful costume than to create the character who would actively choose to present himself in that way with that set of clothes.

However, if you decide that the professional life is not for you, there is no reason why you should not join such a group and spend your life playing good roles in plays that the profession can no longer afford to do (large-cast classics, for instance), while keeping a regular, well-paid job to support yourself and your family in a way that a great many actors who struggle to be professionals are not able to do.

Family Tree:	Training
Branch:	**AMATEUR DRAMATICS**
Twig:	Example: Mr. and Mrs. Noah fight

Anecdotes and Jokes

Make sure they have a good time meeting you.

It is always a good plan to have some jokes or anecdotes in hand when you go for an interview or audition, as it gives you a solid performance to fall back on if required.

There is a distinct skill involved here. Do not attempt to launch a joke unless you have an absolutely rock-solid punch line and know that you can recall it with relish. Jokes are often broken into three elements; in fact the magic number three is something you come across all the time in plots and texts. Plays were, for many years, performed in three acts, and there is something pleasing, even comforting, about delivering (and receiving) stories in three distinct chunks. The old Englishman, Irishman, Scotsman jokes were, and probably still are, very popular.

Anecdotes, as opposed to jokes, are usually of your own making and based on a real-life experience. Never worry that they have to be completely accurate. We have (alas) often inwardly yawned our way through someone's long yarn interspersed with, "No, wait a minute it wasn't Wednesday, it was Tuesday, or was it Thursday, anyway it doesn't really matter." No, it doesn't!

The Actor Says:
I often relate a real-life experience, but edit it, wildly, down to the basic three things: setting the scene; depicting the highlight; and timing the pay off. I never try to labor an anecdote with unnecessary trivia, but just get on with it to get to the pay off as quickly as possible. I often change some of the details (no one will know) to suit the situation and audience, but above all, I practice it and time it to perfection—I even rehearse it in the shower!

The really important thing to remember with an anecdote is that, like a joke, it must have a witty, strong, and surprising tagline. The tagline should be considered with great care and chosen deliberately word by word for maximum effect. Never preempt any word from a tagline—in other words, do not use important tagline words anywhere else in the story.

Here is a brilliant example by Michael Billington, the theatre reviewer of *The Guardian,* in his March 21, 2003 review of a production of *As You Like It* at Stratford-upon-Avon, where the Swan theatre has the audience placed on three sides of a raised stage. The reviewer talks of the director thus:

> *And, although [he] seeks to evoke the Forest of Arden through persuading the entire company to pose as standing elms, or bleating sheep, he crucially neglects the sightlines. Thus in the vital scene where Rosalind discovers the plethora of love-verses left by Orlando, I literally couldn't see the wooed for the trees.*

Being such a beautifully structured piece of writing, it is worth analyzing and noting that he is careful not to use either the word *wood* (Forest of Arden) or the word *trees* (standing elms) to produce the strong and witty punch line *wooed for the trees.* It is especially clever because it is obviously rooted in truth.

First Family Tree:	Getting work
Branch:	Auditions
Twig:	Interviews
Leaf:	**ANECDOTES AND JOKES**

Second Family Tree:	Screen acting
Branch:	Auditions
Twig:	Interviews
Leaf:	**ANECDOTES AND JOKES**

Attitude

How you come across to others— professionally and personally.

Why do you want to be an actor? Often actors have a talent to affect people's emotions from an early age. They have a gift for producing an effect on family and friends, and it is a natural progression for them to want to be an actor. Their attitude then toward performing will be set up as soon as they can walk. Others find that the urge to act comes much later in life, and they get their interest in acting from what they see, and this makes their attitude toward it all more of a desire than a need.

Either way, it is important to realize that your attitude will very much affect others, and it is only too easy to slip into a victimized or depressed mode. This is not helped when well-known, established actors are interviewed, and they say how much they love their work and how lucky they are to be paid to do something they enjoy so much. All very nice, but it gives the impression that an actor's life is and has always been like that. This is not true. Somehow, the more famous they are, the more they seem to forget the hard times, the disappointments, and the lonely and deeply uncomfortable times they have spent either trying to get work or doing the more lowly jobs when they started off.

All actors, no matter who you ask, will have tales of woe, rejection, humiliation, and panic; no one will have escaped these sinking feelings. We do not intend to depress you or put you off but simply intend to alert you to keep a positive attitude throughout what will inevitably happen should you launch into this most uncertain profession.

Your attitude then will be an important key to whether you will go through life constantly angry and sad at the cards you have been dealt or whether you recognize that you were never promised that it would be fair, and relish whatever comes your way. Yes, bad things will happen from time to time, but it is your choice whether you allow them to upset you greatly. Don't get upset at any aspect of an actor's life; after all as the old saying goes:

You knew that when you wrote in.

The Actor Says:

I often put myself into the shoes of a director or casting director, whether I am meeting them at an interview or at a party, and ask myself if I were they, how would I like the actor in front of me to come over? My personal anguishes are of no particular interest to them, since it may be that in their private lives they are having an even worse time than I am. I try to find an amusing topic that might encourage them to think of me positively for a suitable role, now or later.

Of course, you don't want to be a creep and agree with and praise everything your director and fellow actors say. You will want to speak up if something is wrong. But if they are looking for someone to play opposite a nervous or awkward actor, would your outspokenness prevent them from thinking of you for the role? A helpful and constructive attitude is a wonderful thing to have from a cast member, and being known for having this attitude is a great reputation to have.

SEE also: NEVER SAY NO

First Family Tree:	Getting work
Branch:	Typecasting
Twig:	Know your image
Leaf:	**ATTITUDE**

Second Family Tree:	The Team
Branch:	You (your other life)
Twig:	Rejection
Leaf:	**ATTITUDE**

Audience

Whom we all do it for—or should.

Everyone is, at some time or another, a member of an audience—the most important people in any theatrical situation, those who listen. An audience of one is enough when you are relating an anecdote or cracking a joke. The actor thrives on the audience's response, whether it is visible, audible, or spellbindingly silent.

Originally, in Shakespeare's day audiences went to the theatre to **hear** the play, hence the word *audience;* later, when scenery became more elaborate, the audience expected to **see** something special as well, but it was still referred to as an *audience.* Spectators watched sporting events and spectacular shows and so forth, so the primary function of an actor was, and still is, to tell a story and speak the text, whether good or bad (and not bump into the furniture!).

Audiences vary, of course. They can be children, foreigners, or people nodding off after a day's work (or a hefty meal), and they all show a different response to the performance onstage. The audience members can be all smiling like mad, but the actors will never hear them. It can be annoying to visit a friend backstage only to be told that the audience was "a bit sticky tonight" or "Oh, if only you'd been here last night—it was terrific." Well, we don't want to be told that the performance we watched was not the best; anyway, perhaps it was an almighty excuse for **their** not being so good that night!

Try to remember that no two audiences are ever alike and that no audience knows or cares about previous ones. The audience members are happy if they have been entertained—made to laugh or cry, think or fantasize— and feel disappointed if they have been bored or feel that they have wasted their money. They do not care if the actors are ill, unhappy, or distressed.

The element of surprise is **everything**. It is **boring** if the audience can predict what is going to happen next. There should be constant gear changes either in reactions or words or in the delivery of words that are not expected. Then you can take the audience with you on the journey. The audience must never get there first: that is theatrical or screen boredom. There is always a constant game between the audience members who are trying to second-guess the artists, and the performers (and writers and directors) who are trying to fool them.

SEE also: CONSISTENCY and GEAR CHANGES

Family Tree:	Performing
Branch:	**AUDIENCE**
Twigs:	Good and bad taste; Journey; Laughter; Pauses; Thinking

Auditions

Getting that job.

The main difference between stage and screen auditions is that for the stage those auditioning you are looking for potential—because they will be rehearsing with you and therefore need to see what you might come up with—but for the screen they are looking for results.

Stage Auditions

You will probably start with these. Don't be different: be good.

The Director Says:

I once auditioned more than three hundred actors in five days for a Shakespeare festival, and had to sit through seventeen Bastard speeches "Thou nature art my goddess." The last guy was so good, he got called back.

You see, all that advice about finding original audition speeches is from bored directors who want to see fresh speeches—oh, they have no intention of casting you because of them, but they would rather see an unsuitable actor doing an unknown speech than presenting a very familiar one. The real secret is to do a speech that suits you, one that shows off all your talents to the fullest. Then they will love you for your performance, not your choice of material.

The Actor Says:

My best audition ever, after which I was immediately offered a six-month contract, was the well-known First Fairy speech from A Midsummer Night's Dream. *I prepared the audition in great detail with wonderful business to suit my particular personality, playing the fairy as a distracted cleaning lady, and being messed about with by Puck. Throughout the piece the laughter was as encouraging as the subsequent offer was a delight.*

Do not start with an apology, for anything you say along the lines of "I have only just heard about the audition" or "I might not know all the lines" will just give you permission to fail. If you forget your lines, it will certainly be noticed, so to take out insurance in advance is not necessary or constructive.

SEE also: DON'T ASK FOR PERMISSION

The way you walk on and off the stage, or the space where the audition is taking place, is also part of your presentation, so practice that bit as well as the piece you are going to do. Practicing handshakes is also a good thing. (Well, you **are** going to do a lot of them, so make sure they are effective.)

Sometimes at the moment you walk onstage, those holding the auditions know they are not going to choose you—perhaps because you look too much like someone else in the cast—so do not insist on staying longer than they want you to. Actually, it is sometimes a relief for the auditioners when actors do **not** use up their full time allowance but leave earlier, for it allows them to take a bathroom break or get a cup of coffee.

Do not worry about doing a piece that has a beginning, middle, and end: they are not listening. What they do is watch the first bit of the audition, and then they are busy writing notes about you, maybe jotting down what you look like, and then they watch a bit more. To get involved with the entire piece—and to do this with everyone they are auditioning—would be quite a burden, so they tend to dip in and out of what you are presenting. Do not be sad if you think they are not watching every bit of your audition, because they are possibly not. They are taking notes and listening at the same time, but the good news is therefore that you do not have to finish it but can just do the parts that show you off to your best, and then you can stop.

Try to put yourself into the shoes of the auditioners, and so understand that they would prefer a short snappy piece to long wandering one. Most auditioners claim to get all they need from the first thirty seconds of an audition anyway—so this might be a case where less really **is** more.

Screen Auditions

Don't let the excitement stop you from being effective.

The pressures of a shoot are such that it can be difficult to give the actors a stream of creative notes, as the director is struggling to get the camera, tracks, lights, sound, design, makeup, costumes, and so forth all looking right. The director often has to assume that the actor will come up with the right goodies, and she gets to react to the performance only once she sees it on the screen. The actor then is **already** expected to deliver what is required, so that is what the auditioners are looking for in the audition.

The audition can often be just an interview, for the way you come across there is the way they imagine you will come across on the screen, so reading the script is often dispensed with, and the decision is made according to that impression (and, of course, the way you look).

Always perform at a screen audition as if you are being filmed in a big close-up. Your energy should be in your face, and your voice only be sufficiently loud enough to reach the imaginary microphone just above your head—**not** the person you are speaking to **or** the person who is auditioning you. The same very much applies to readings.

SEE also: SCREEN VOCAL LEVELS and TYPECASTING

First Family Tree:	Getting work
Branch:	**AUDITIONS**
Twigs:	Interviews; Open auditions; Over the top; Readings; Rejection

Second Family Tree:	Screen acting
Branch:	**AUDITIONS**
Twigs:	Casting directors; Interviews; Readings

Battle of the Sexes

Life is not the same for actresses as for actors (we must use "actress" for this topic).

Actors will always upstage actresses, in the most literal sense of the word.

The Director Says:

*All over the world, in all cultures and societies, I have found that when an actor and actress are together onstage, talking to each other on a proscenium auditorium, then the actor will always be about eighteen inches (about fifty centimeters) upstage of the actress, thus forcing her to be turned very slightly upstage every time she looks at him. They do not seem to be aware of this, so it is not a conscious decision—but they **do** it all the same. I suppose it is something to do with our inbuilt instinctive natures, because I see it happening everywhere.*

The Actor Says:

I don't find this such a problem, as most actors are taller than me, and so stand upstage of me automatically. In casting, the woman is always shorter than the man unless it is a comedy, so tall actresses (and short ones) had better develop their comedic qualities.

If you find this a problem, the solution is very simple. Actresses should either use the elbow technique or shuffle upstage themselves.

With this technique, when someone is not quite in the place he ought to be to receive your lines and your looks, then during your speech you take him gently by the elbow and propel him to the correct place on the stage. If you do it subtly enough, neither the audience nor the other actor notices what you are doing, but it does get the actor in the correct place. After some experience of the elbow technique, some fellow actors even start coming to

17

the correct place for those lines of yours that need someone downstage to receive them.

This also applies to many other situations, such as in a radio studio where the microphone must be shared between several artists. The actor will stand in front of the microphone for his lines and then, when the actress has her lines coming up, he might just stand there, and the polite actress just sort of squeezes herself in at the side, hoping he will notice and give her more space next time. The experienced actress will again use the elbow technique.

It is a well-known fact that salaries in all forms of acting are not equal, with men receiving the larger fees. Fight and complain, but do not expect it to be fair.

The Actor Says:

Then there is the question of what we call ourselves. I am an actress. I have always called myself an actress, and unless I change my sex, will continue to do so. I noticed a few years ago that I, and those of my gender, were being referred to as actors. Those advocating this change would give other examples such as doctors, barristers, vicars, teachers, plumbers, etc. where we don't need to define the gender, although we do regularly refer to them as female, woman, or lady doctor, barrister, plumber etc. to clarify things, because we want to know. I have often been asked before a medical examination whether I would prefer a female doctor to look me over. Why not a doctress? And even our Publisher asks that this heading be "The Actor Says."

*We certainly cannot identify gender by a person's name these days and, unlike the professions mentioned earlier, we do not do exactly the same job. On the whole, with a few camp exceptions, men play men and women play women. There **is** a difference. If there is **no** difference, why on earth do we have separate categories in awards ceremonies? Why shouldn't the best male and female artistes compete with each other for the acting Oscar? The current tradition, of course, makes sure that there are numerous categories, adding a selling point to the individual films, but if the roles are equally challenging, why shouldn't the sexes be equally competitive? And, have you noticed how the Best Actor Oscar invariably comes last? It's just a thought.*

Actors are sometimes very ready to give notes to actresses but not so ready to receive them. A slight error by an actress will be immediately pointed out and an apology expected, but when the man goes wrong it is often laughed off by him as perhaps an improvement on the performance.

Again, this is not fair—but it is what happens all over the globe, so work with it rather than kick against it.

The Director Says Again:

*I was talking about this to an actress, who told me that once when she was play-ing a maid in a comedy, she had some ridiculous business to do with a cushion and an alarm clock. One night (the director being long absent) her fellow actor didn't give her the cue line for her business, so she could not perform it. When she asked the stage manager what had happened, she was told that the other actor didn't like the business, so had decided to cut it, and she was powerless to do anything about it. I **know** what the director would have thought about his lovely produc-tion being changed in his absence, but also wondered what the reaction would have been if the roles were reversed and she had cut **his** business? Tantrums and bitterness? Messages to the management?*

SEE also: NOTES

First Family Tree:	Performing
Branch:	Problems
Twig:	**BATTLE OF THE SEXES**

Second Family Tree:	The Team
Branch:	Fellow actors
Twig:	**BATTLE OF THE SEXES**

Be Yourself (Plus!)

An important aspect of acting.

A lot of actors are accused of just being themselves—well, perhaps they needed to be. Perhaps that is why they were given the part in the first place. However, if you are typecast, you are expected to do more than just react the way you naturally would in those particular circumstances.

For example, if your character has to burst in to announce that the building is on fire, deep down the director will expect you not to do it the way you would in such an emergency but to do it in a way that also presents you—which is why he cast **you** in the first place. So if you are a person who naturally has a smile on your face, then your dramatic entrance is expected to be done with a smile; if gloomy is the attitude they get from your face and persona, then **that** is what he expects, coupled with the "Get out of here!" line.

In silent movies the actors found themselves being shouted at by the director through a megaphone. Why? Were they not good enough? Of course they were, but the tempo of filming needed things to happen faster than in real life, and so the director would encourage and guide the actors to be themselves—plus. Quicker changes happening more frequently—events being heightened from what they might be in real life—was what was needed for the silent screen. This approach works as well today as it did then: the very reason why you got the role can be the qualities and atmosphere that come from your being on the screen or on the stage.

Do not hide any personal flaw; use it. After all, the character you are playing must be used to it by now—otherwise you would have lines to say about being too short, speaking with a lisp, or having an inferior physique; whatever you think your flaw might be. To take your own values and quirks and exaggerate them will be to play into the very reason why they wanted you in the first place and make it even easier for you to act, for not only are you just being yourself but you are acting a version of yourself, a wonderfully technicolored version of you—plus. If **you** love the way you look and the way you come across, so will the audience.

No actor wants to be bad, so if you seem to be coming up with a bad performance, don't blame yourself, blame those who cast you in a role or production that obviously does not suit you. Rely then on your strengths, which are your own background, personality, and looks, and put **them** into the show.

SEE also: KNOW YOUR IMAGE

First Family Tree:	Training
Branch:	No training
Twig:	**BE YOURSELF (PLUS!)**

Second Family Tree:	Screen acting
Branch:	Typecasting
Twig:	**BE YOURSELF (PLUS!)**

Believability

It does not have to be real to look real.

Do not restrict yourself by reality. As far as acting is concerned, the following is your life belt:

The truth is not always your friend.

For example, there is a scene in Alan Ayckbourn's *Bedroom Farce* when Nick and Jan have a long stretch of dialogue while he lies on top of her on a double bed. The bed is set with the head upstage. Nick has been lying on the floor with excruciating back pain, and Jan has to lift him onto the bed and then fall over so that he lands on top of her for the sexually suggestive scene that follows. She wonders if he could be a gentleman and take the weight on his elbows and about how people seeing this would think they were doing what they had not been doing for ages. He is in pain and can concentrate only on his back spasm.

Now the logical and real thing would be for them to fall over at the foot of the bed and end up with their heads near the pillow, with him on top of her there, but the audience would then see only their feet during the subsequent dialogue. Or at the very least they should fall sideways onto the bed, but that would still make it difficult for the audience to see. How can we solve this problem?

Use the technique of what–how–now:

What do I want as a final result?
How can I achieve this, whatever the means?
Now make the result believable!

The Director Says:

*I found that the only way to get both their heads toward the audience at the front of the bed was for them to go upstage, for him then to throw her onto the bed, and jump after and on top of her. I waved aside the objections from the actors that what I wanted them to do was unrealistic—after all, they reminded me, he had a very bad back. We rehearsed so that she trod on his toes, and in the agony of hopping around, they fell onto the bed with their heads face to face correctly downstage. Oh, he did throw and leap, but we spent a merry afternoon making it **look** as if they had just fallen, and the scene played in front of the audience as well as it has ever gone. Believability came last.*

Funnily enough, on the screen actors will usually accept that they must look in the wrong direction as long as it looks all right in the camera but are loath to make the same wrong-seeming choice for their stage acting. The audience after all only sees the final result and does not judge you by the process you got there: that is reserved for acting classes!

When a director then says he does not believe you, it means that the moment is not coming across truthfully. It is your job then to solve this, and there are as many different ways of doing this as there are actors. Some actors will need to brush up on the text work, others on their background history and story, yet others on the **what–how–now** technique outlined earlier: whatever works to make the moment come across well, remembering that simple sincerity is often not the answer.

SEE also: SCREEN CHEATING

The Director Says Again:

Directing John Steinbeck's Of Mice and Men *I was horrified when the superb dead puppy made by the prop department completely distracted the audience when Lenny, as scripted, threw it across the stage on the first night. On the second night I substituted a sock stuffed with straw, which the audience completely accepted as a puppy. They were not, you see, being distracted by what they thought was a real dead animal.*

SEE also: OUTSIDE-IN VERSUS INSIDE-OUT

First Family Tree:	Rehearsing
Branch:	Technique
Twig:	**BELIEVABILITY**

Second Family Tree:	Performing
Branch:	Truth
Twig:	**BELIEVABILITY**

Blowing Your Nose

What is this doing in a book about acting?

In a performance, you decide your character has to blow its nose—maybe you wish to show that you are emotional or you want to do some gear-changing business. The problem is that you are in good health, and there simply is no mucus in your nose to expel with the appropriately satisfying sound, or at least not enough for many takes in front of the camera or the demands of eight performances a week.

The solution is simple: put a handkerchief to your nose and, using your lips, make a nose-blowing sound. To help the illusion, you can sort of glance at your handkerchief after it has received its load and slightly squeeze it as you put it away. Mission accomplished; those watching will think that you have blown your nose, and the truth of the moment has been maintained.

Of course, there was no truth there at all: at the heart of the moment was a lie. You were **not** blowing your nose; you were faking it, pretending, cheating, being untruthful: why, you were **acting** it, not experiencing it. Just like when you have to act a death scene.

Where does this leave those who claim that everything must be truthful? Where does it leave Method acting then? It is in its usual place: a great device that helps actors at certain moments; a useful teaching tool but not the start and end of all acting. If you have convinced the audience, does it matter how you got there?

SEE also: SEX AND VIOLENCE

First Family Tree:	Rehearsing
Branch:	Technique
Twig:	Outside-in versus inside-out
Leaf:	**BLOWING YOUR NOSE**

Second Family Tree:	Style
Branch:	Modern contemporary acting
Twig:	Method acting
Leaf:	**BLOWING YOUR NOSE**

Breaking Up (Corpsing)

What to do when you lose it.

Corpsing or breaking up is a form of laughter by the actors that must be mentioned and dealt with. It is when the onstage actor finds herself distracted by something that has happened that is not part of the action. Maybe another actor has deliberately tried to make her laugh, or something has gone wrong, or someone has said an unscripted word. The impulse to break up and come out of character can grow and become so strong it is impossible to hide it from the audience.

In the United Kingdom it is called *corpsing* because the character dies when the actor loses it, even for a few seconds. If you ever find yourself in this predicament, there are ways of dealing with it, but it is better to nip it in the bud if you can.

The Actor Says:

I have found there is one way to stop laughing, physically, providing you are not just about to speak. Simply press your elbows into your ribs and squeeze as much air out of your lungs as you can bear (without going red in the face), and you will find that the effort of breathing in again and filling your lungs with much needed air will make it impossible for you to laugh. If someone is deliberately trying to make me corpse, I get really angry and I find that works well to prevent me laughing, and soon works for them, too.

If however the breaking up is getting out of control, the best thing is to let the audience in on it and just have a good laugh. Now, this is very much easier in a comedy and, indeed, the audience may already have seen or heard the initial mistake that set you off in the first place.

If you are in the middle of a really dramatic play or a thriller, let's say, and something unexpected happens and you feel a corpse coming on, stamp on it immediately. It is fatal to allow such a thing to develop, and you could well be in deep trouble with your fellow actors, director, and management. In any event you must try to divert your thoughts to something else, preferably sad or serious, and discipline your brain as if your life depends on it. Maybe it does—you could get the sack!

The Actor Says Again:

*Once, in a West End production of a comedy, I was involved in the longest corpse I have even known; it went on for about fifteen minutes. There were six people onstage at the time and something absurdly silly and trivial happened that was only noticed by two of them (not me), but it set them off and infected us all in turn. (The obnoxious character had spat out his line, and actually sent some spittle to land on the other actor's cheek.) Every trick in the book was used to get through it: turning upstage and smiling with one side of the face; the emptying-the-lungs technique (which only I knew about); saying our lines absurdly loudly; you name it. When we finally got offstage we **all** fell to the floor, silently convulsed, in agony.*

There was an actor I knew in the audience that evening and I asked him if he had noticed the dreadful corpsing going on. Of course he had but, although he thought it was quite disgraceful at first because he didn't know what had caused it, he grew to enjoy it himself by the end of the scene. It was broad verbal comedy, so I suppose there were enough hilarious lines to support the terrible misbehavior.

So long as the audience can somehow share the joke, they don't seem to mind, as it is a truthful interaction. So if you find yourself in this dreadful dilemma, at least try to get the audience to understand why the actors are breaking up.

SEE also: LAUGHTER

Family Tree:	Performing
Branch:	Problems
Twig:	**BREAKING UP (CORPSING)**
Leaf:	Example: Kate and corpsing

Business (Biz)

The things you do to make your performance better.

When it comes to business of any kind onstage, you will need to practice again and again: simple things such as entrances and exits; opening and closing doors smoothly and without fuss; timing your exit line so that it exactly fits with walking to the door, opening it, turning toward whomever you are speaking to, delivering the line, then exiting. Very often it will be an important line, a plot line, or a laugh line, so practice until you feel the natural timing in your bones. This also can be done in a corner of the rehearsal room while waiting for your scene or, of course, at home.

You will need to practice the simplest of movements, such as touching the chair or sofa with the back of your leg before sitting down with composure or the intricate moans of an ardent lovemaking scene.

SEE also: HOMEWORK and SEX AND VIOLENCE

You might need a fight director or choreographer to direct a fight or fall. The following things can all be taught: how to fall; how to appear wounded by gunfire; or how to be strangled, suffocated, or dragged round the room by your hair. There are experts to help you achieve all things that are covered by technique, and make sure that you always look totally believable.

That is all practical business: things that need to be done and worked out in advance, especially comedy business. However, whatever you come up with in the way of added business that might not have been given to you directly by the writer should and must be rooted in the text. There should always be some hint in the lines that inspire a particular idea. Whether it is a costume, prop, or business, find the reason for it in the text.

SEE also: TEXT

Business should also take the time it takes—that is, you cannot write a personal check in one second, you cannot pour several drinks instantaneously, and you cannot sort out the money to pay a taxi driver while you are quickly leaving the vehicle. If you cannot do these practicalities in the time available, plan to change your business to things that you can manage to do, or start doing them early enough so that they can be completed properly—the audience always spots these cheats and does not like them.

The Actor Says:

I was once cast in the farce See How They Run. *I had appeared in a different role in a previous production, so I knew the play pretty well. In this production not only had the director done the play several times before, and was now playing a lead role as well, but the author was playing the Bishop. During rehearsals, every bit of business, intonation, and gesture given by previous performers were given to all of us—with the result that the whole production was labored. Each bit of business was obviously funny enough in its original outing, but crammed all together made it unmotivated, untrue—and therefore unfunny.*

As for physical extras, consider them by all means if you think they are justified, but be very economical. Once at drama school I added what could be regarded as "a funny walk" to my character. I had really hilarious dialogue, and I just found myself going up on the ball of one foot as I walked. It was no more than an affectation (or, more likely a painful corn), but it caused an extra titter every time I appeared. In the canteen one day, a young first term student was telling me how much he had laughed at my character, and my limp. "What limp?" I said, and got up and "funny walked" out of the room. He never forgave me.

You are often told to avoid some business because it is a cliché. Why is it so called? It is because it is often used. And why is it often used—because it works, and works well. So the advice should be to use clichés for biz, but use them in novel and interesting ways.

On the screen, business is often used to mask necessary technical matters, such as having to play a scene with your back to the other actor so that the camera can see both your faces. The director will ask one actor to deliver a speech while washing the dishes, working at a desk, or rearranging flowers; in fact, anything that can motivate the two actors not to look at each other and so allowing the camera a nice two-shot.

SEE also: EYE-TO-EYE CONTACT and PROPERTIES (PROPS)

First Family Tree: Rehearsing
Branch: Technique
Twig: **BUSINESS (BIZ)**

Second Family Tree: Performing
Branch: Technique
Twig: **BUSINESS (BIZ)**

Casting Directors

More important than you think.

Casting directors are used to bring in groups of actors for casting sessions for films, television dramas, commercials, and even theatre jobs. Sometimes the same person will deal with all these different areas of work, so you will need to get to know as many casting directors as you can. Building a good working relationship with them is not only wise but also essential. In this day and age, when directors no longer know in great detail about the increasing pool of potential actors, the casting director has become the key person. They are now the main conduit (or main barrier) between the actor and the job, so you will need to cultivate them and get them to know your work, for it is going to be a lifelong relationship.

There are contact books with casting directors listed in them, but to find the hot ones, watch the credits at the end of a current television drama or film. Write to each one who could legitimately use you in the near future. Introduce yourself and point out that if he could meet you, he will be able to assess your type and character more accurately. Send a photograph with a resume, and suggest that you will be delighted to come in and see him whenever he has a spare moment (you have to be in the same area for this bit to work). If you have heard nothing after a week, give his office a ring and mention your letter and your willingness to come in and see him. A reminder of your details (including any recent or upcoming performances) on a postcard every few months is a good idea; it all helps him to place you and update his records.

A little tip—if you want to be interviewed, but the casting people might not wish to have you travel hundreds of miles for the remote possibility of being suitable, then we suggest you invent a cousin or an aunt, and telephone the casting people and inform them that you are going to be in their area visiting relations and ask if it is possible to drop in for a chat.

If they say yes, book your travel arrangements and go to see them. (Even if you do have relations in town, you don't actually have to visit them after the interview.)

For commercials the clients will usually have a firm idea of the type of character they are looking for. The casting director will bring in about a dozen (sometimes many more) actors in that category. His lists will be divided into various features: age range, color (skin, hair, eyes, etc.), height, weight, straight, comedy, leading roles, character parts, special skills (driver, horse rider, musician, etc.), and others.

If a casting director can be sure that you will turn up on time, deliver the goods, and always be willing to do the silliest things at a casting session with aplomb, then he will be only too keen to bring you in again, even if you are not absolutely right for the part.

The Actor Says:

*There was one casting director who brought me in regularly, but for more than ten years of casting sessions with him I never got the job. When I mentioned this wryly one day, he said, "Oh, don't worry, Christine, you always give good value and the clients love you." Because of this, he continued to send for me, and eventually I **did** get the job!*

First Family Tree:	Getting work
Branch:	**CASTING DIRECTORS**
Twig:	Commercial casting sessions

Second Family Tree:	Screen acting
Branch:	Auditions
Twig:	**CASTING DIRECTORS**
Leaves:	Commercial casting sessions; Photographs; Resumes

Comedy and Farce

The craft behind getting laughs.

When looking through the listings for the West End or Broadway, you will see that shows are identified by some sort of description that helps the customers choose what they most want to see. The labels seem to be *play, thriller, drama, mystery, tragedy, comedy, farce, musical,* and so on. Further back one remembers labels such as *comedy drama, comedy thriller, light comedy, musical comedy,* and the like, which identified the piece even more specifically.

So why do shows fall into such distinct categories? And why do we need to have our expectations clarified before we book our seats? Some play titles, of course, give a completely misleading impression of what the play contains. We recall how a provincial theatre manager in England once booked a play called *Boys in the Band* in the belief that it was a musical! (For the uninitiated—it was an American play about Manhattan homosexuals.)

But we are dealing here with the difference between comedy and farce and how to **play** the difference. First of all, comedy is about character, and farce is more about types.

The Actor Says:

When I was at RADA I won a prize for Comedy of £3 (about $15 then) and a prize for "the best female performance in Comedy and Farce" of £5! The first part was that of a nun in a drama called Bonaventure. *The second character was a maid in a farce called* Rookery Nook. *So what, if anything, did I do differently?*

My nun had some amusing lines that suggested she was meant to be the light relief in an otherwise mysterious thriller. My job was to raise a few titters with my characterization being aware of the more serious content of the play. My maid on the other hand was a perfectly serious character in a ludicrous situation, with some nonsensical dialogue. I did embellish her with a distinctly funny walk that seemed to add to the audience's enjoyment, but my character found nothing amusing about her perfectly "normal" appearance and movements.

SEE also: BUSINESS (BIZ)

So we can say comedy is playing an intentionally amusing character in a normal situation and farce is playing a character very seriously in a ridiculous setup. It should be very easy to identify which is which, if it is not already on the play description. The dialogue alone will be a clear indication, and your fellow cast members and designer (we hope) will be in the right mode.

The Actor Says Again:

Sometimes I have been accused of going too far, and on these occasions I have tried to analyze exactly why this accusation has been made. I have a very expressive face, as do many actors who specialize in comedy, and when you have constantly been cast for your comic abilities, you can get a laugh by simply raising an eyebrow. It can be extremely difficult to cut back on natural expressions, and in most cases your reactions are exactly what is required. However, economy of expression can be equally effective and a deadpan look (a blank face) can get a big laugh. It gives the impression that you have not understood what has just happened, or you have not heard what has just been said. The laugh comes as you gradually realize what is going on and a slow knowing expression grows on your face. The danger comes when you have done a big, quick reaction and you go on changing your expression to try and extend and build the audience's response. This is referred to as mugging or milking the laugh, and can appear obvious and unsubtle, to say the least. I would like to think I was not guilty of this, but . . . maybe I lost the truth of the moment and my character appeared to be unbelievable.

SEE also: OVER THE TOP

The double take is something that enhances many a comedy or farce. This is when you look at something, look away, realize what you saw, and look back at it again. The speed with which you do this is the vital thing and determines the reaction you will get. It can be done so quickly that it is just an enhancement of the dialogue and is not intended to get a big reaction from the audience, or it can be a slower and (dare one say) bigger take, which should create an audible laugh. Then there is the slow burn, where you notice something fairly casually, carry on with what you were going to say, then (almost before uttering anything) turn slowly back to what you saw with a greater realization of its significance. A natural comic or farceur will be able to produce the double take without thinking about it, but if this does not come easily to you, practice doing it over and over again in front of a mirror.

There is one piece of business that occurs again and again in farce, and that is the stage trip. Of course, nobody should see it coming, least of all the actor, although if it is a running gag in the play, the audience will be anticipating it after a while, so you must work out how to fool them and surprise them again.

There is a little guideline that can be used in relation to a word, a line, a scene, a play, or a piece of business. It, of course, comes from the world of Method acting:

I want to—
In order to—
I am prevented by—
Therefore, I—

In relation to the stage trip you could use it this way:

I want to enter the room, in order to close the curtains, I am prevented by a book lying on the floor directly in my path, therefore I trip over it.

You must have "close the curtains" firmly in your mind when you enter the room. If you even think "trip" and indicate this to the audience, you lose the element of surprise. This simple device is the basis of all acting, but it is particularly helpful in comedy and farce when you are timing a bit of business or a laugh line.

Color is an all-important factor when it comes to comedy. It is very difficult to get laughs in black colors, whether you are surrounded by black curtains—as in "Sorry, no set, we can't afford it"—or wearing black clothes (unless, of course, the character is specifically required to be clothed that way).

The Actor Says Yet Again:

*I was playing a chatty next-door neighbor in a stage comedy, and chose a navy blue jumper and gray skirt. First night—no laughs! Help! I went to the dressing room, looked in the mirror, spotted the problem. Next performance—bright orange jumper. Loads of laughs! But here is a word of warning; if you decide to make a change of costume, **always** make sure the other cast members know before the show begins.*

SEE also: LAUGHTER

First Family Tree:	Homework
Branch:	Style
Twig:	**COMEDY AND FARCE**

Second Family Tree:	Performing
Branch:	Technique
Twig:	**COMEDY AND FARCE**
Leaf:	Example: Kate and corpsing

Commercial
Casting Sessions

Getting that advert that pays for your new car.

When a commercial is to go into production, a casting director is employed to get a pool of actors ready to be seen for the roles. She will go through her category files, or computer records, and choose up to a dozen or so actors for each role. She will then call the various actors' agents to book the chosen few for the casting session, and they in turn will contact their clients with the encouraging "I've got a casting for you."

We recommend you arrive at least ten or fifteen minutes before your call time, because you will be asked to fill in one or two forms and you might be given a script to study or a storyboard to look at. Always spend as much time as you need on the script and get familiar with it; even memorize the lines if possible. Leave the forms until after the session if necessary. You will probably meet up with actor friends in the waiting room—try not to engage in chat with them until you have read and absorbed the script. The forms will require you to give phone numbers (including your agent's) and measurements (in case you get the part). Always have these handy in a notebook if you cannot remember them, and update them when necessary. If you are unwilling to state your exact age, give a range of a few years on either side of the real thing, or just leave it blank.

If they want a photograph for their records, you should try not to stand square on to the camera but to turn your body to the right then look back at the camera over your left shoulder. It is amazing how much more flattering this is, and you can do it quickly and easily.

The casting director or her assistant will be at the session, and there will be a camera operator—that could be all! The actual director of the commercial might or might not be present. Remember that the client will have a very firm idea of the type she is looking for and will probably not recognize any of the actors who turn up. She has very little idea of what an actor's job is or the process you have gone through to get this far. She sometimes asks very naïve questions, which you should regard as very intelligent ones and answer them with the greatest of respect. Grovel, grovel—whatever works!

The Actor Says:

I was once in the middle of recording a scene with dialogue and business at a casting session, when the client's cell phone rang and he started a conversation. I had to stop since it was clearly being recorded with my audition, but I am convinced that he had no idea of the technicalities involved and how his thoughtlessness was ruining both his and my work.

The first thing you are usually asked to do is say your name and agent's name straight to camera, then turn to give left and right profiles. Sometimes they like a close-up of your hands or a full-length shot, or both. All of this you do willingly and cheerfully, but please don't add silly business or comments. It is simply to identify you.

When they ask what you have done recently, never make up credits— you could be found out—but you can slightly exaggerate things if recent credits are a bit thin on the ground. The question is usually asked so that they can get on camera the real **you** being as animated as possible, as they are not seriously interested in what you have done (would they recognize it anyway?); they simply want to see if your personality fits their requirements. Just as you have made some effort to dress according to the brief, it is also quite a good idea to bear in mind the type of character they are looking for and present that in your reply. Have a really good anecdote ready about a fairly recent job and spin it out for the amount of time they usually allow for general chat. This should be enough to fill the "Well, actually I've had rather a quiet year" slot!

If there is a script to look at, you will have an idea of the story line, but the person conducting the session will usually give you a brief synopsis of the situation anyway. Then on the command "Action!" you **act**. After a couple of takes, that's usually it.

SEE also: READINGS

The Actor Says:

When they say to me "Good-bye, thanks for coming in," I usually reply, "Not at all, thank you for seeing me" or "My pleasure." I don't think unnecessary crawling is appropriate at this time, after such a short session.

The Director Says:

I am always impressed when an actor says something on the lines of "I really enjoyed meeting you" or even "I would really love to work with you." I know it is just flattery—but you know, during a stressful day things like that go down really well.

It is slightly less advantageous if you are sent in with other actors, as a couple, or as part of a family, as you can be judged on group physical characteristics. You also might have to depend on the others being good at improvisation if that is what is asked for and being compatible with your style. If there are just two of you and you are asked to stand or sit side by side, try to get yourself on the other person's left side. You will then be on screen right, which is the strongest position (let's hope that they have not read this book too).

Please the director by being **technically** efficient. Do plenty of reactions but do not overproject vocally.

Bear in mind that the client (who will have the greatest contribution in casting the commercial) knows precious little about acting but is looking for the right type (the right look) to sell her product. She can see only what is on the screen at the audition, which includes the identity and chat bit, so put as much of the character as you can into those bits of the recording too. If the client is at the session, you should play the character all the time you are in the room. Difficult, but her imagination is often limited!

The more castings you go for, the more chances you have of being the right actor. If you do not get it, when you were "Oh, so right," it was probably for some quite trivial reason. In the end the person who gets the job is the person they wanted with the right look, and if it was not you, then it was not you. Lucky for somebody else (now **they** can get that new car!).

SEE also: PHOTOGRAPHS and RESUMES

First Family Tree:	Getting work
Branch:	Casting directors
Twig:	**COMMERCIAL CASTING SESSIONS**

Second Family Tree:	Screen acting
Branch:	Auditions
Twig:	Casting directors
Leaf:	**COMMERCIAL CASTING SESSIONS**

Commitment

It is better to commit than to prevaricate.

The Director Says:

I find a lot of actors are reluctant to commit to a performance, a moment, or a piece of business, in case it does not go down well with me, the director. They hold back until they can get a sense of how the land lies, and then gradually increase their level of performance over several rehearsals. I have found that the last one percent of commitment can often be 50 percent of the final wonderful performance—by pushing to the end, real excitements and values can be discovered. I tell my actors in rehearsal, "Just go further, and see what happens."

Actually, to be fully committed from the word go is a much better idea. For a start, the actor can immediately see—as can the director—whether it fits in, and what is far more important, the fellow actors can see and respond to it, and everyone gets much further on in the project with this approach than with the timid approach. A famous saxophone teacher told his students, "If in doubt about a note, play it loudly—then we will all **know** if it is right or wrong." A fully committed performance, if it is not appropriate, is easily spotted by the director, by your fellow actors—by you yourself. It is so much better to discover these things in rehearsal, where a deep level of performance can often make apparent just what is required, and in no time flat.

Also—and this is the tricky bit to believe—it is very easy to change a fully committed performance from one type to another. Actors have always worried that if they commit too soon, they will sort of get stuck in whatever they have come up with, but the opposite is true. It is actually quite hard to change a sort-of-there performance, and it is very easy to change a full-blown performance. For example, if you are fully committed to a

42

tongue-in-cheek performance, it is easiness itself to immediately change to a sincere one, if that is what is asked for in the rehearsal room.

Suppose you have to deliver a speech and the director wants you to end up standing on the table. It does not feel natural to you, so you ask not to do this until it feels justified. The odds are you will never get there, disappointing yourself and the director. A better solution is to leap up onto the table the first time it is suggested to you. It will feel odd, but by doing it with full commitment your acting talent will, over the rehearsal period, give you the truth of the build and give the director his finale on the table.

If you want to be committed but can't, do not blame it on a lack of energy. Your energy is always there, but there must be something blocking it, so find and remove the block. It is really quite exhausting to try to conserve energy, so just go with the flow.

The Actor Says:

Frankly, if a director asked me to jump on the table (even in younger days) and I thought it was a crass idea, I would do it so badly that he would immediately dismiss it with "looks ridiculous—forget it." And I'm not the only actor who uses this approach. I knew an actor who thought a certain speech should be in close-up, so when he realized it was being shot loosely, he kept forgetting his lines! (The lines returned when the shot changed to a close-up.)

Ideas are quite common—it is courage that is rare.

SEE also: EXAMPLE: PLUNGING IN THE DEEP END

First Family Tree:	Rehearsing
Branch:	**COMMITMENT**
Twigs:	Don't ask for permission; Drugs

Second Family Tree:	Performing
Branch:	Technique
Twig:	Over the top
Leaf:	**COMMITMENT**

Conservatories and Drama Schools

Training for professional acting.

Most of you will have undergone some training at such establishments, and we hope it was—or will be—a happy and fruitful time for you. A drama school or conservatory is a very valuable time spent in the company of others who also want to be actors, so make good friends and keep them, for these are the people who will help you throughout your career. Who knows—some of them might become writers, producers, or directors!

The dangers of such training are that your audiences for the most part are friends and colleagues (even rivals!), and the notes and responses you get can be very deceiving.

After a while in the acting profession, the only people who worry about a conservatory or drama school training are those who did not have one.

It might seem strange that those months or years spent in a conservatory training should not count for more, but working actors, while acknowledging the value of the classes they took and the opportunity of giving a variety of performances, often feel that their real training came out of their work in the professional theatre, performing to an audience of strangers. In the opposite camp, even successful actors who never attended any formal training feel that something is missing, that they are not really proper actors.

Well, they **are** proper actors if they entertain and create wonderful characters, and the training everyone gets is always adjusted in the light of experience. Most of these establishments have a philosophy, a series of *musts* that they have attached to their acting training. Each of them is useful and valuable in their own way, in that they have a certainty, but there is no real must in the world of acting, and all *musts* have to bend to the reality of what is asked of the actor.

The Director Says:

I was asked by the students of a training program in Chicago how to reconcile what I was telling them about the instant acting required on the screen with the forty-page biographies that they had to produce for each character they portrayed at school. I pointed out that were they to be successful in screen acting, the problem would be solved by there being no time at all for such wonderful dossiers.

The Actor Says:

Read this book—save the fees!

We have noticed that when actors have had a specific training, they hold on to the theories they were taught then in acting class, even though in later life their professional experience has guided them in other directions. It is as if they are embarrassed to betray their first teachers, so they talk with reverence about acting the way they were first taught—and then go on to put into practice all they have learned from experience. The moral? Listen by all means to others, but be careful to observe if they actually put into practice what they preach, or if they are holding on to some of their own training commandments.

SEE also: WHATEVER WORKS

Family Tree:	Training
Branch:	**CONSERVATORIES AND DRAMA SCHOOLS**
Twig:	Teaching acting

Consistency

Not always a good thing.

To be consistent runs the risk of being predictable, and to be predictable can lead to being boring, and that is not good. Of course, everyone wants their heroes to be the same as they always were, but that does not mean they also have to be completely consistent.

Deep down, the audiences either at home watching the screen or out watching in a larger forum want their actors to take those risks that they themselves are unwilling or unable to take—so our heroes must have impossible love affairs, take impossible physical risks, and generally live that dream life that the audiences fantasize about. In a word, the audiences are mostly consistent in their own work and play, and watching actors is their night off, when they want them to be different.

So in rehearsal try new and different things, as these can open up the role for you. These decisions will not necessarily be seen, so you can really experiment and take risks, knowing you are doing it so that your eventual audience will get a performance as varied and interesting as it can be.

SEE also: INSTINCT VERSUS INTELLECT

However, in performance, different rules do apply. In a play with any sort of run, the actors are expected to do the same thing on the same line—every time. Many actors jibe at this, but it is what the industry wants. The trick is then to get all your variations in by the first night, or for the first take. For the screen, once a moment is set, the actors are required to be consistent because all the different shots are taken of that moment, and consistency with your wonderful variations is the name of the game.

Stars of the movie world are, however, exempt from these strictures and are allowed to do very different things for each take. In fact, one of the hallmarks of a great movie actor is that she is willing to put into the camera a whole range of performances, so that the director or editor has many more choices when crafting the final film together. Make sure your director knows you are capable and willing to do this, if she should wish to go for another take.

SEE also: LESS IS MORE?

First Family Tree:	Homework
Branch:	Journey
Twig:	**CONSISTENCY**
Second Family Tree:	Performing
Branch:	Audience
Twig:	Journey
Leaf:	**CONSISTENCY**

Costumes, Wigs, and Shoes

How to use them to improve your performance.

Just as you can be recognized at a distance by your friends because of the clothes you choose to wear, so should any character you play inhabit its clothes in the same way. Study clothes carefully to gather what character would want to look like this or want to feel like that when wearing those clothes.

Actors are invariably at the mercy of designers and costumiers. How often has an actor carefully worked out a piece of business or an idea for his character, only to find that the set (or even costume) makes this impossible or at the very least incredibly difficult? Because the actor only fully gets in tune with the part after some study and rehearsal, the results of this ought to be reflected in the costume, and that is where you should work with your designers to achieve harmony between image and performance.

The Actor Says:

*I was playing a maid once in a farce set in a country vicarage. I asked wardrobe for a little cotton apron, a half-style one that ties round the waist, perhaps with a little pocket, for serving the afternoon tea. At the only dress rehearsal just hours before the first performance, I was presented with a brightly colored, full-length plastic apron featuring a picture of a large beer bottle, something I felt to be totally inappropriate for the character, the scene, and the play. It not only totally upstaged my performance but the play itself, during my appearance in that scene. I found something more suitable in a charity shop the next day and wore that for the rest of the run. The designer never spoke to me again and, as he had been in that theatre for a long time and had a great deal of influence, I never **worked** there again either.*

An actor ruefully pointed out recently, as he looked at a costume and design that were completely opposite to what he, after his research and study, thought his character would look like, "These days the actors' imagination is an increasingly underused resource."

When giving information to the wardrobe department, always be current with all your measurements and **never lie about your size.** When you turn up for your fittings, it is embarrassing if they have got the costume in the size you said you were and you try to squeeze the size you actually are into it. Always wear underwear at a fitting (men especially take note!), as the clothes you are trying on might have to be returned to the store if they are not suitable. When dealing with advance information to the production team, always make sure you have informed them if you have any allergy or sensitivity to a particular makeup. If you have any such allergies, it is wise to bring some suitable makeup with you. You should also take your own base and powder if you have any unusual skin tone, to make sure you will always be looking your best.

You might be challenged with a ten-foot train to maneuver or with corsets, wigs, tights, high-heeled shoes, long gloves, sword belts, buttons and buckles, high collars or ruffs, heavy hats or crowns, and so forth, so make sure that the problems they present are tackled early on and not left to the dress rehearsal. Get a facsimile of the clothes as soon as possible, so that you can incorporate into rehearsals any character input from the costume. In particular, try to wear the shoes as soon as possible, because different types of shoes make you walk in different ways.

The Director Says:

I can often tell when watching a play which of the female actors wore jeans during rehearsals. They stride about the stage in their dresses, or even worse period frocks, with no connection between the clothes and their movements. I counter this by always asking actors in rehearsal to wear a close approximation of their costume at all times, and particularly to get the right sort of shoes and walk in them all day too. If any of the actors are to wear wigs, then I ask them to wear close-fitting hats, so that they can get used to the pressure they will feel when their wigs turn up.

If you are in a long run, it is unlikely that the shoes will last the whole time. Ask the designer to purchase a matching pair (or matching the pair that you already own that fit you well), and alternate them with your own until they are comfortably broken in. If you are wearing your own clothes, please make sure they are clean. It is amazing how well a ring round the collar or a stain will show up on the new high-definition cameras that are rapidly coming into our business.

The reason the various armies of the world march in different ways is because their distinctive uniforms put varying pressures on them and the way they must move. The German army's goose step is a direct result of soldiers' wearing boots with no give in the ankle, so the soldier has to throw his foot forward to move. The British army marches the way it does because the soldiers have to wear heavy boots, so they stamp loudly as they turn a corner. Just as you would wear such a uniform in rehearsals to get used to it, so should you replicate whatever you will be wearing in performance, whether it is a tight-fitting costume, an enormous wig, or strange clumpy shoes. If the final costumes are available to wear in rehearsal, wear them, so you can break them down to look as if they have belonged to your character over a period of time.

SEE also: MOVEMENT AND GESTURES

We are often very annoyed at a performance when an actor wears very noisy shoes, and the dialogue is sometimes even drowned by this clatter (this is equally annoying in rehearsals, too). You can easily avoid this by gluing felt to the soles and heels of the offending shoes.

First Family Tree:	Rehearsing
Branch:	Technical and dress rehearsals
Twig:	**COSTUMES, WIGS, AND SHOES**

Second Family Tree:	The Team
Branch:	Designers
Twig:	**COSTUMES, WIGS, AND SHOES**

Crew

They help you—appreciate them.

The Technical Crew

(For the stage there are the stage management, lighting, sound and flying operators, and stagehands. For the world of screen, you must add those who deal with continuity, those pushing and operating the camera, and all the special effects whiz kids.)

You get the applause and the praise. If anyone is to be congratulated for a film or a stage play, it is the actor. She is the one everyone sees, and perhaps wants to be. And how do you feel about the technicians, and much more important, how do they feel about you?

As the world of entertainment gets ever more complicated, whether you are working on the stage or on the screen, the technical requirements are growing all the time. The simplest theatrical event seems to include a whole lot of projections, bits of film, complicated scene changes, and the like, and as for film, it is a wonder the actors can ever perform, given that for some of the time they are playing to an invisible character who will be computer generated in good time, but after the actors have had to commit themselves to their performances.

The technicians of a piece are now as vital as the performers, and they are your coworkers. Appreciate them and find out how you can make their jobs easier, and in return they will make your performance seem better. Do you want to look as good as possible? The camera operator can give you favorable extra hints as to shadows and angles if the camera departments are part of your thoughts and you have made it clear you are happy to work with them to achieve a good result.

Actors often forget that the technicians want to do a good job as much as you do, and just as you want an excellent performance to be seen, so do they want an excellently composed shot, a wonderful sound mix, or a really smooth scene change to be experienced by the eventual audience. Ask your technicians what they like about actors and what they dislike—learn their names! Working with them will make sure that in an emergency they will all be pulling for and not against you.

Mind you, some of them do have a pejorative view of actors, referring to them as "warm props," but this is probably because they will work more weeks a year in that theatre or on that set than you, and so they look at you as usurping their territory, rather than the other way around. However they treat you, you still have to work positively with them.

The Artistic Crew

(This includes the choreographer, musical director, fight director, makeup staff, and vocal coach; make sure the lighting cameraman and camera operator are on your artistic list.)

These are artists in their own right, and they should be treated as such. They have to do what they feel is right within the framework, time, and money given them, so they are often highly pressured. Understanding their problems and restrictions will allow you to work better with them, and they with you. And that means that you will look better in the show than if you have had a constant running battle with some of them. Their work must be closely allied to that of the director, and just occasionally you have to tread a narrow line between two conflicting demands on you.

The musical director is probably going to influence you during the run more than your director, because she will be in the pit every night, conducting the musicians and cueing you into your song (or even singing your lines if they happen to go from your head).

As for the musicians, there is only one thing to say: they will play too loudly. They always do, and the sound engineers seem to be on their side—so be prepared to belt out your songs over a competing orchestra and amplification system. This is because they are artists in their own right and they want to make sure that though they are (usually) unseen, they will be heard while you are being seen.

First Family Tree:	Rehearsing
Branch:	Technical and dress rehearsals
Twig:	**CREW**

Second Family Tree: The Team
Branch: **CREW**

Designers

How to make sure that what they do doesn't spoil what you do.

Many more stage shows are directed by the designer than most directors will admit. The designer—set, costumes, makeup, props—will be working on a production well before the actors, and usually before the cast are even engaged for that project. The look of a particular character, the way he will come across, is therefore decided before the actor has been able to make his own contribution to the process, and this leads to a lot of heartache and conflict.

An actor we know accepted the part of Lady Macbeth only as long as she did not have to wear black—she had a strong belief that the character as written by Shakespeare was not a dragon queen but a real person with human feelings and failings. The director reluctantly agreed. When her costume finally arrived just before opening night—it **was** black, to go with the production concept. Too late to get it changed, she had to go onstage projecting an image that was completely opposite to what she had done with her rehearsals and preparation.

It is essential therefore to find out at the earliest opportunity exactly what is planned for the design of your costume, wig, makeup—anything that reflects your character's personal taste and attitude, so that either you can adjust your performance to fit what has been decided to be your image or you have a chance to get it altered to what you are producing for the performance. You also need to check that your planned moves and business are actually possible on the set that you will be working on; you know the details of the doors and stairs; and that if needed there will be space offstage for a fast prop pick-up, or for doing a very quick costume change.

The Actor Says:

The set design can often prove a hazard, especially when timing is everything. I was recently playing a maid in a comedy and had thirty entrances and exits through the same door. Looking at the set design on the first day of rehearsals, my heart sank when I noticed that my door had been placed at the back of a deep and steeply raked stage. I also noticed that there was a rostrum half way upstage—a split-level room—which I would have to maneuver thirty times!

I managed the business with a lot of extra practice, and I always rehearsed going up the rostrum step in the rehearsal room, even though it was not there. Timing the exit lines was the trickiest problem, and a good deal of cheating was required, as I could not just go to the door, deliver my line, and then exit.

SEE also: BUSINESS (BIZ)

In the screen world the designer, or art director, is more removed from direct contact with the actor, and the costume designer is just as often buying clothes as designing them and having them made from scratch. You can often be asked if you have any suitable clothes (and you can get paid if they use them!), so it is a good plan to build up a wardrobe of clothes and especially shoes that can be just the right thing for a shoot. Your own shoes can be a great comfort when shooting a complicated sequence, rather than trying to break in an unfamiliar pair, and a long run in the theatre can benefit greatly from your using your own footwear.

The makeup designer will be in charge of the way you look (and obstinate actors have been known to go to the bathroom and adjust the image that has been given them to one they feel is even more appropriate). Because the makeup chair is the last thing an actor will visit before the set, the makeup department receives all the final insecurities that actors have (and cunning directors will make sure to pick up all the gossip from that area—so this is sometimes a way of getting your concerns to the director, without making it look like a complaint).

Family Tree:	The Team
Branch:	**DESIGNERS**
Twig:	Costumes, wigs, and shoes

Dialects and Accents

A potential pitfall.

A dialect is a complete variety of sounds, grammar, and words that fit a particular region, period, or class. An accent is usually just a difference of pronunciation. When they are used, especially on-screen, it is usual to find a native speaker to take on the burden of being convincing in a regionally based dialect or of having a distinct accent. You should be aware that if it is **not** native to you, then it will change your acting—and not always for the better.

Sometimes it might be tempting to add little mannerisms to your character that are not indicated in the text, and you feel an extra embellishment would help things along. For instance, if you choose to do an accent or dialect that is not your natural one, your energies will go into **that** aspect of the role and your acting can go out of the window. Be careful that you always have a powerful acting reason for that accent or speech defect.

The problem with an accent is not, in fact, learning the new sounds, tunes, and stresses; it is being completely willing to give up your own individual familiar sound and take on the verbal signals that indicate that you are from a different place or time, or both. Because most people are proud of their roots, some even passionately so, taking on someone else's sounds can lead to problems.

The Actor Says:
It always bothered me, when watching old war films, that the Germans spoke English to each other with a German accent. Why would they? Then I met up with an actor friend who doubles as the dialogue coach on films and had been working with an all British cast playing Nazis. They had been rehearsing for some time with strong German accents, as required by the director and producers,

*but rebelled just before filming began as they thought it sounded fake and terrible. Brought in as an instant trouble shooter, my friend made a brilliant decision. He told them to speak carefully in a very articulated manner, ignoring all contractions in words like "don't," "it's," "they're," and to use **no accent at all**. This transformed the way they acted, as it also gave them a good sense of period. They said "do not," "it is," "they are," sounding as if they were trying to speak "perfect" English, and the illusion was that they were speaking naturally in German.*

For many years, American actors had a struggle to put on a convincing British accent, partly because they were unwilling to accept being part of the class system that is at the root of the British sound. It is only now that actors such as Gwyneth Paltrow and Renée Zellweger can be confident enough to give up their "all men are equal" American accents to convincingly play class-ridden Brits.

Do be careful, however, that the effort of putting on an accent does not make you speak louder than you should. This is particularly important for screen work, where many good performances have been ruined when the actors' use of an accent that was not their own pushed them into being too theatric—being too loud.

First Family Tree:	Homework
Branch:	Voice
Twig:	**DIALECTS AND ACCENTS**

Second Family Tree:	Screen acting
Branch:	Screen cheating
Twig:	Screen vocal levels
Leaf:	**DIALECTS AND ACCENTS**

Directors

Love them or hate them—
they will always be there.

The good news is that there are some wonderful, thrilling, and truly creative directors around who will encourage you and want the very best you can give. On the other hand there are some dreary, ineffectual, and totally unhelpful ones. Most likely yours will be somewhere in between.

There could be a number of reasons why you got the job, and it might not always happen that the director chose you. Maybe you are a member of a company and she is freelancing and you were, therefore, cast in advance. You simply do not know at first what the background is, but if things start to go a little wrong and you sense that it is not going to be a smooth ride, then you need to work out why.

Because actors in the theatre are mainly chosen by the director, they feel beholden to them and keep a certain reverence to secure the possibility of working with them again. You never feel that arguing with the director will lead to any conclusion that will favor the actor, and it could lead to a permanent animosity.

Therefore, our advice is as follows:

Always agree with the director (at first!).

If you need to disagree, then phrases such as "That's a wonderful idea, but my lines are not quite indicating that; I wonder if you can help me?" can be brought into play. If you really feel that the director is on a completely opposite tack to the way you see your character, then you have to fight your corner, but in the most tactful way possible. Smile, beam even, and agree as far as you can—find any fragment of her argument to praise, but point out your dilemma and ask her to try to come up with a helpful solution.

SEE also: NEVER SAY NO

Usually, if you have really studied your part and found the basic logic and realism in the lines **and** are able to theatricalize this at early rehearsals, the chances are that the director will leave you alone and concentrate on some other poor soul who has not been so clever and does not yet have a handle on her character.

It takes a great deal of skill to end up doing the business **you** want to do, but the trick is to make it look as if the director suggested it in the first place. If you try lots of different ideas, including the director's and any other suggestions floating around, it will be easier to pluck out the best one (which, you hope, just happens to be yours!).

The Actor Says:

Recently I was in a stage play and my character was required to clear a breakfast table with no other people onstage. In the script I was given, there was nothing in the stage instructions to cover what would be about a two-minute scene. There was, however, in a different version of the play, a suggestion that she sings a certain song in a "loud raucous voice." The director had made it very clear that the author's word was sacred and showed no sign of flexibility during the early rehearsals. I felt that the song was a must—otherwise I would be alone, in silence, doing some rather boring business. So I waited until the third rehearsal and just hummed the song "accidentally." He stopped me briskly and chastised me for not going far enough. "Well, if you're going to hum, why not sing the words? What sort of voice do you have?" etc. So, I got my song and, as it so happens, an exit round every night!

However the director treats you, your job is to create the best character out of the lines and business given to you by the author, who is more important than you or the director, and to work alongside your fellow actors amicably to produce the best possible entertainment for the audience members. They are, after all, the most important people in the building—remember?

The Director Says:

Directing a television trial scene, and after the first take when she showed nothing on her face as her character listened to the judge passing sentence, I asked *the actor to let a whole range of emotions cascade over her face for the second take—and promised that I would not use any inappropriate ones in the editing. She replied loudly, "Oh, you want shit acting," to which my only response was to say, "Yes, shit acting—Action!" and to place her on the list of people I will **never** want to work with again.*

Don't forget, directors spend most of their time in rehearsal (of actors or of cameras) and appreciate those who help such rehearsals to be enjoyable. **They** only really get to perform in front of you—so appreciate and admire their performance.

Many of the screen directors (unlike their stage equivalents) have never acted and do not have an insight into the craft of creating and developing a character, let alone the experience of performing it. They look at the screen and direct what they see there—so if you feel you are being treated like a piece of the scenery, well, that is how some of them regard you. Concentrate on being the most cooperative and useful piece of furniture you can be, and remember that the director is seeing the truth only as shown on the screen: if it looks good, it is good; if it looks bad, it is bad. Your feelings will not come into it at all.

First Family Tree:	Rehearsing
Branch:	Rehearsals (long, short, or none)
Twig:	**DIRECTORS**
Leaf:	Notes

Second Family Tree:	The Team
Branch:	**DIRECTORS**
Twigs:	Discussions; Don't ask for permission; Notes

Discussions

Make sure all that time round the table is worth it.

Discussions can be a lot of fun, as everyone can sit around and talk—and talk and talk. The good talkers get stuck in and dominate, and the talkers who are not as good let them get on with it. After a suitably long period, you get back to practical working on the show.

One small problem—has the play improved at all? Has understanding what is going on or developing a larger sense of the context in which the action is happening improved the performances? The problem is that nearly all directors think it does, because this is what they would need were they actors. For the most part they are not, just as the script consultants and literary and performance critics are not actors—and what they feel is essential for themselves is not always necessary for the performers they are working with or writing about. The moral is to not be disheartened if you feel you are not contributing as much to the discussions as others and to make sure that you always put into your performance some results of those times round the table—take notes!

In the time it takes for a nice discussion to happen, the actors could have gone through the scene three or four times in different ways, and then everyone would know which version worked best. The varied rehearsals would have released many good things to put into the acting. Discussions (alas) are often a substitute for actually getting down to working out what to do, how to share it with the audience, and how to make it truthful and believable, so do not yourself extend them beyond what is valuable to your performance.

What is interesting is that long group discussions are much less known in the screen world, where there is usually not the time or the opportunity for all the actors to get around and chew the fat for a while on a particular aspect of the piece being done. Often, the actors in modern films have only

61

a sketchy idea of what is going on, and the premiere is a real revelation as to what it was they had been working on.

Acting is doing, and doing it in front of an audience or a camera. If a snag is hit, if there is an impasse that cannot be resolved, **then** a discussion can be of great help, but it should be a matter of last resort, not a first approach.

How should you the actor deal with these inevitable discussions? Enjoy them by all means, but also try to relate whatever is talked about to what you are actually going to do—remember, the audience cannot be sent little notes as to what you all discovered sitting round the table. They can get it only through your acting.

First Family Tree:	Rehearsing
Branch:	Rehearsals (long, short, or none)
Twig:	**DISCUSSIONS**
Second Family Tree:	The Team
Branch:	Directors
Twig:	**DISCUSSIONS**

Don't Ask for Permission

You're an actor—so act!

You might worry that your ideas will not be accepted, that someone will reject your new thoughts as silly or irrelevant. This fear leads to actors taking out insurance—by only half doing an idea until they get permission to do the full thing. This means that if the idea is rejected, then only a bit of the idea has been rejected, and the artist can continue to rehearse without loss of face or status.

This is profoundly wrong, as doing this makes the idea vague, ill defined, and even more likely to be rejected than if it were acted out in all its glory, relishing the new contributions. After all, rehearsal is a place for trying things out, but if you ask for permission first, the natural instinct of a director can be to reject it.

Even if he is the most open of directors, your asking can be seen as an indication that you are not really sure about it, and he will often decide that it will be better for you to do what you had done before. By just doing it, everyone at the rehearsal—you, your fellow actors, the director—can sense immediately whether the new idea works, and you have avoided the dreaded discussions that can reduce the imaginative input from actors.

The audience is having a night out, at the theatre or cinema. Audience members have spent a lot of their day being safe: not telling their boss or a customer what they really thought about them or doing what was expected of them rather than what they wanted to do or even knew would be best to do. They have lived through the usual pattern of a day's work.

Then they see you: are you repeating the day they have already had, or are you taking risks? After all, speaking in public is listed as one of the main fears that ordinary people have—and here you are doing it for a living!

The risk takers are always admired and loved, and that applies as much to an actor as to a sports star. You are acting on behalf of the audience, and when a choice comes up of playing safe or taking a risk, why not take that risk? Even if it does not completely come off, it is more exhilarating for them (and for you) than turning out the expected performance that is forgotten the moment the audience members leave and wonder where they have left the car. Sinking or swimming can be just the thing that inspires you and entertains them.

Just as you did not ask for permission to be an actor (we hope), you should not ask for permission to come up with the ideas and thoughts that made you want to be an actor in the first place. It is your job to present thoughts and reactions, and if you know you will not be asking for permission, then the ideas will flow more easily.

SEE also: DON'T GIVE UP

First Family Tree:	Rehearsing
Branch:	Commitment
Twig:	**DON'T ASK FOR PERMISSION**

Second Family Tree:	The Team
Branch:	Directors
Twig:	**DON'T ASK FOR PERMISSION**

Don't Give Up

Have confidence in yourself.

If you come up with an idea, don't reject it because you think it is wrong or silly but trust that it popped into your mind for a good reason. Don't give up on your instinctive choices but instead find ways of putting them into the performance.

The Director Says:

Whenever actors try to say something, but lose it underneath a giggle, I always make them do whatever it was they were struggling to say. It is obvious that their instinct wants to come up with something, but their intellect censors it as silly, so they giggle as they say it.

A female actor playing the messenger for me in Timon of Athens *giggled at one point, but then refused to say why. Eventually I persuaded her to say what was on her mind and she came up with "tap dancing." Even I thought that was silly, but nevertheless I made her do it and that's why, on opening night, she brought the house down as her tap dancing shoes gave her and the audience a wonderful galloping horse. Her instinct was obviously better than my intellect.*

Conversely, if you are told to cut something out, don't. Instead, replace it with something else. After all, there must have been a reason why you came up with the original idea, so changing it to something else acknowledges that there is something that needs to be theatricalized. Just cutting things out leads to empty and unfulfilled acting, so change rather than delete.

The Authors Say:

We were worried that readers of this book would not be able to find the exact topic they wanted if they did not know its title, but our first suggestion for a complicated index system was turned down by our long-suffering Publisher. We came up with a different suggestion, which met with the same response—as did the next one, when he suggested we leave it out altogether as it would only confuse everyone. Finally, our Family Tree system arose, which met with his approval, and our belief that we must find a solution. We never thought of deleting the idea—we just kept coming up with different versions.

There must be a reason why you became an actor—**are** an actor—and that is that deep down you feel you have something to offer, something inside you that is of worth to the world of performing. That is the something that spurs you to make a certain move, to do a certain piece of business, or to decide on a particular characterization. All these decisions are important.

The problem is that most acting (until or unless you occupy stellar heights) is filtered through a whole range of other people, starting with the director, often passing through the producer, and maybe even touching on those who raised the money for the project in the first place. They will all want to influence you as to what you do, for the creative impulse is a very seductive one, and many others will want to share in it—even going so far as to claim credit for it.

Your job as an actor is to realize that your initial impulse is of value. If it is rejected, do not let go of it but come up with an adaptation. If they also do not want that, do not give up, do not ignore your own impulse, and come up with another adaptation of the idea. There **must** be a good reason why your brain came up with it in the first place, and it is a waste of talent if it just disappears at the first suspicion that it might not be fully accepted.

Treat every impulse of yours as a valuable note from your subconscious to you, suggesting an approach and instinctive response that should be respected—by you, if not by all your coworkers. In particular, notice whenever you make a ridiculous suggestion with a laugh, because the laugh is your conscious mind trying to prevent a "stupid" idea from coming out; your subconscious has had a really neat insight and is struggling to get it through your personal censor.

SEE also: DON'T ASK FOR PERMISSION and REJECTION

First Family Tree:	Homework
Branch:	Instinct versus intellect
Twig:	**DON'T GIVE UP**

Second Family Tree:	Rehearsing
Branch:	Mistakes
Twig:	**DON'T GIVE UP**

Drugs

Pluses and minuses.

Acting has always been associated with drugs. In the old days, of course, this was alcohol, and nowadays it is more potent brews.

There must be a reason for this, and one reason is the wild difference between the actor in rehearsal, moment by moment creating new ideas and thoughts, new bits of business and moves, and the actor in an eight-performances-a-week straitjacket, with a stage manager reporting to the management every time an actor wanders even slightly from the moves in the prompt book.

A burst of creativity is all too soon replaced by following the railway tracks. People become actors for the creative moments, and so can take to their various drugs to blast out their memory, so to speak, and get back to the seat-of-the-pants type of acting that happens in the rehearsal room. So given that it is an impulse to get back to risky acting, find ways of varying your role that will not throw your fellow actors but will give you the variations and challenges that at the very least will be easier on your purse than any outside stimulants.

The Director Says:

I have noticed that in rehearsal it is usually possible to spot those actors that were high the previous night on chemical drugs—as opposed to those who just got drunk. Taking drugs seems to remove the anger that is such an essential part of acting—the anger that you are not better; that you are not doing as well as you could. The actors who get high after a rehearsal tend not to progress overnight. They turn up at the next rehearsal at exactly the same point where they left it—whilst the others, including the drinkers—have let their natural anger at not being better bring them to an advanced stage emotionally and intellectually compared to where they were the day before.

Some drugs can elongate apparent time and others can speed it up, so if you are high and your fellow actor is not, then you will be on different time scales, which makes good acting between you very difficult.

Neither alcohol nor chemical drugs are to be encouraged, but it is wise to know the different effects they have on your acting. And as for smoking and your lungs—well, can you imagine a violinist deliberately scraping his hands on a cheese grater or a ballet dancer walking barefoot across glowing embers?

First Family Tree:	Rehearsing
Branch:	Commitment
Twig:	**DRUGS**
Second Family Tree:	The Team
Branch:	You (your other life)
Twig:	**DRUGS**

Editing and Acting

Why it is important to know what goes on in the edit suite.

The moment an actor sits in front of an editing screen and carefully watches what is going on, and in particular which take is preferred to another one, is the moment her screen acting improves.

The British actor Ian McKellen noted that he was puzzled why everyone except him seemed to be whispering their lines when he was acting in the filmed version of Trevor Nunn's stage production of *Macbeth*. He went into the editing room and then realized that they were all doing screen performances, and he was still doing his successful stage performance, which came across as just shouting. We noted his more recent whispered performance as Gandalf in the film *The Lord of the Rings*, as it showed how well he has learned his lesson.

SEE also: SCREEN VOCAL LEVELS

The editor is not there to be fair or to give each actor an equal opportunity on-screen; the editor is there to make the best possible drama. If the best moment is one of yours, then the editor will cut to you even if someone else is speaking. And if that someone else is doing something more interesting than you are, when you are speaking, then the editor will stay on her face, and yours will float down onto the cutting-room floor.

The Actor Says:
I was playing a small part in a British situation comedy once—a nice little scene but it was not relevant to the main storyline in that particular episode. I hadn't considered it significant enough to tell my family, and wasn't able to

*watch it myself. So, when my brother rang to say he had just seen my name in the credits but had not seen **me** in the show I was somewhat mystified, as I had seen my filmed sequence slotted into the recording, and enjoyed the studio audience's reaction. It turned out that the show was overrunning and something had to be edited out—so my performance got the chop. Fair enough, but because they couldn't edit my name from the credits, each time it was shown, a repeat fee continued to wing its way to me!*

The edit is where you can notice that if you had reacted before you spoke on the take, the editor can cut to the shot of you immediately; to have started to speak and then put some expression on your face on the take will encourage the editor to stay on the previous speaker, and cut to you only when you are halfway through your speech.

You will also notice that the key to good screen acting is not just to do little reactions but to keep on doing them: to be, as it were, like cigarette smoke in a room, always changing, always moving, but in little exciting ways.

SEE also: SCREEN REACTIONS

Family Tree:	Screen acting
Branch:	Shooting and acting
Twig:	**EDITING AND ACTING**

Example: Al and Bob's First Meeting

Those giants of Method—they must have done less with their reactions!

Because we can't include a DVD with this book, we have done the next best thing and noted down all the reactions that went on between Al Pacino and Robert De Niro during the first time in film history they played a scene together. It is in Michael Mann's *Heat*, with Pacino and De Niro playing a detective and a crook, respectively, and this is also the first time these characters have met in the film. The following is an analysis of the beginning of the scene, and we have noted down how long it was before each spoke—and an approximate description of what reactions they did **before** speaking.

PACINO:

[3½ seconds] Flickers eyes right and left twice; takes a breath

DE NIRO:

[2 seconds] Takes a breath; makes small hand gesture

PACINO:

[1½ seconds] Moves head up and down

DE NIRO:

[2 seconds] Makes small grimace

PACINO:

[1½ seconds] Moves hand

DE NIRO:
> [4 seconds] Flickers eyes left and right

PACINO:
> [1½ seconds] Opens mouth a little

DE NIRO:
> [½ second] Nods

PACINO:
> [2½ seconds] Nods; flickers eyes right

DE NIRO:
> [2 seconds] Looks up

PACINO:
> [4½ seconds] Nods; turns head looking right

DE NIRO:
> [1½ seconds] Flickers eyes left

PACINO:
> [2 seconds] Makes small smile

DE NIRO:
> [3 seconds] Nods; grimaces; flickers eyes left

PACINO:
> [1 second] Turns head

DE NIRO:
> [6½ seconds] Looks down; turns head; works lips

PACINO:
> [2 seconds] Turns head; looks right

DE NIRO:
> [1½ seconds] Nods; flickers eyes left

PACINO:

[1 second] Makes small head movement

DE NIRO:

[3 seconds] Flickers eyes left; takes breath

PACINO:

[7 seconds] Nods; flickers eyes right; looks back; then right again

Go on—try it yourself. Do those reactions for that length of time, especially the one that lasts for 7 seconds. Are you surprised just how much you (and so they) are doing?

Was it "Less is more" here? Were the actors holding good continuous eye-to-eye contact? Were they picking up their cues? Not a bit of it, especially when you compare it with the same scene done by different actors in Michael Mann's earlier film *L.A. Takedown* (of which *Heat* was a remake), where the two actors hold continuous eye contact and come in briskly with their lines. It can easily be seen that the stars of the screen are very confident in taking their time, creating little bits of business, and doing lots of reactions, all to let the audience into their thoughts and giving them valuable insights into their characters.

SEE also: EYE-TO-EYE CONTACT

First Family Tree:	Performing
Branch:	Technique
Twig:	Less is more?
Leaf:	**EXAMPLE: AL AND BOB'S FIRST MEETING**

Second Family Tree:	Screen acting
Branch:	Screen cheating
Twig:	Screen reactions
Leaf:	**EXAMPLE: AL AND BOB'S FIRST MEETING**

Example:
Anna Christie and Her Dad

How much more you can do with so little, when using gear changes.

In Eugene O'Neill's *Anna Christie,* there is a key scene where Anna meets her father for the first time in fifteen years. Chris is a poor seafarer and has not seen his daughter since she was five years old. He has received a letter from her saying that she is coming to see him. Unknown to him, Anna was seduced by a cousin in the family she was brought up with. She is now a fully developed girl of twenty, but she is run down in health and plainly shows all the outward evidences of belonging to the world's oldest profession.

Chris has been told Anna is in the bar, and she knows he will soon be before her. He hesitates before going through the door, and then when he goes into the bar he is in awe of what he takes to be her sophisticated clothes. He nervously avoids her first glance where she takes in what he is dressed like, and he talks to her as if to plead for understanding. The following is the script as it appears in the printed version:

CHRIS:

Anna!

ANNA:

[Acutely embarrassed in her turn.] Hallo—father. She told me it was you. I yust got here a little while ago.

Picture the scene—Anna is sitting at a table when her father comes in. She glances up at him and he speaks. After a little pause, she replies. The audience has noticed his reaction to her clothes, some reaction on her face before she speaks, and his reaction to her words. Nice use of "Less is more," as the actors stick to their sincere intentions.

Now look at the scene another way, using **gear changes**. Oh, there were some nice gear changes when Chris dithered over whether to open the door, but see what **else** can be found in this tiny scene.

Anna is sitting with her back to the door, so when her father comes through the doorway, she cannot see him. He then can see her, and the way she is dressed.

GEAR CHANGE FOR CHRIS
He did not think she would be dressed that way.

GEAR CHANGE FOR CHRIS
He admires and likes the clothes.

GEAR CHANGE FOR CHRIS
He loses the courage to speak.

GEAR CHANGE FOR CHRIS
He gets the courage to speak: "*Anna!*" Anna is concentrating on her drink, when she hears her name.

GEAR CHANGE FOR ANNA
She automatically puts on her working-girl expression, and turns to face the speaker. She turns back.

GEAR CHANGE FOR ANNA
She recognizes that it is her father. She turns to him again to study his dreadful clothes.

GEAR CHANGE FOR ANNA
She turns back with her reaction to how poor the clothes are.

GEAR CHANGE FOR ANNA
She puts on a dutiful daughter expression on her face. She turns to her father: "*Hallo—father.*" He was expecting a rebuke over his clothes.

GEAR CHANGE FOR CHRIS
His daughter is speaking to him.

GEAR CHANGE FOR CHRIS
Can he now talk some more to her? Give her a fatherly kiss?

GEAR CHANGE FOR CHRIS
He decides to walk down and talk to her. They can now see each other's face. She is trying to be nice.

GEAR CHANGE FOR ANNA
Will he understand how she earns a living?

GEAR CHANGE FOR ANNA
She is the dutiful daughter again: "*She told me it was you. I yust got here a little while ago.*"

GEAR CHANGE FOR ANNA
She realizes she has slipped back into using her father's Swedish accent.

Lots of gear changes, and lots more subtext and extra information for the audience to see and enjoy and to understand the play and the characters even better. Yes, **more** is so much better for all concerned.

First Family Tree:	Homework
Branch:	Journey
Twig:	Less is more?
Leaf:	**EXAMPLE: ANNA CHRISTIE AND HER DAD**

Second Family Tree:	Rehearsing
Branch:	Technique
Twig:	Gear changes
Leaf:	**EXAMPLE: ANNA CHRISTIE AND HER DAD**

Example: Broadway versus Hollywood

Same author, different mediums— different scripts?

The screen script needs to be different from a stage one, and the best way to see this is to compare like with like. Aaron Sorkin wrote *A Few Good Men* as a stage play, and after a successful run there, it was made into a film. He wrote the screenplay, so what differences did he make to the script for its Hollywood outing, to be directed by Rob Reiner? The structure was altered, and of course there were many more location shots. The dialogue was in the main the same, but it was condensed somewhat, as this same scene between Sam, Jo, and Kaffee (the three naval lawyers defending the accused) shows in the two versions:

Broadway's *A Few Good Men* by Aaron Sorkin (1989)

SAM:

I'm gonna go call my wife. I'll meet you later.

Sam starts to exit.

JO:

Why do you hate them so much?

This stops Sam in his tracks.

SAM:

> They beat up on a weakling, and that's all they did. The rest is smoke-filled, coffee-house crap. They tortured and tormented a weaker kid. And it wasn't just that night, read the letters, it was eight months. And you know what? I bet it was his whole life. They beat him up, and they killed him. And why? Because he couldn't run very fast. I'm off duty now, don't ask me to be pals with these guys.

JO:

> Sam, do you think the argument we're going to make on Monday is legally sound?

SAM:

> I think the argument we're going to make on Monday is morally reprehensible.

KAFFEE:

> I'm not a judge, Sam. I'm not a jury, and I'm not a prosecutor. That makes me the one person in the room who is *honor bound* to do things which are morally reprehensible. [*A long silence. Kaffee stands and puts his case on the table.*] All right, everybody take the night off.

Hollywood's *A Few Good Men* by Aaron Sorkin (1992); Director Rob Reiner

We are reprinting the stage version, blacking out those bits that do not appear in the film version and adding shot descriptions. The rest of the lines are more or less the same:

Three-shot of Jo, Sam, and Kaffee:

SAM:

> I'm gonna go call my wife. I'll meet you later.

Sam crosses shot; contain the three-shot:

> *Sam starts to exit.*

JO:

Why do you hate them so much?

This stops Sam in his tracks.

SAM:

They beat up on a weakling, and that's all they did. The rest is smoke-filled, coffee-house crap.

Tight shot of Sam:

They tortured and tormented a weaker kid. And it wasn't just that night, read the letters, it was eight months. And you know what? I bet it was his whole life. They beat him up, and they killed him. And why? Because he couldn't run very fast. I'm off duty now, don't ask me to be pals with these guys.

JO:

Sam, do you think the argument we're going to make on Monday is legally sound?

SAM:

I think the argument we're going to make on Monday is morally reprehensible.

Over-shoulder shot, favoring Jo and Kaffee:

KAFFEE:

I'm not a judge, Sam. I'm not a jury, and I'm not a prosecutor. That makes me the one person in the room who is *honor bound* to do things which are morally reprehensible. [*A long silence. Kaffee stands and puts his case on the table.*] All right, everybody take the night off.

With a stage version, the audience participates with the actors to let the atmosphere and events be defined by the words. In the film version, with the camera slyly observing the action, the actors rely more on their own persona as characterization. There are fewer words to say, as the little looks and expressions on the screen would be invisible in the theatre, where the words have to do the work.

Broadway's and Hollywood's *Amadeus* by Peter Shaffer

Peter Shaffer wrote the successful stage play *Amadeus,* and when he did the screenplay in consultation with the director Milos Forman, there were many changes made to the structure for, as Forman said, all theatre is stylistic, including the language, but for film you have to start with real scenery and so the script must change. The changes made from the stage to the screen versions are very apparent in the scene where Mozart's wife Constanze, desperate for money, has agreed to return to Salieri's apartment at night, in return for which he, as court musician, will help with Mozart's promotion.

In the stage version, presented in London and New York between 1979 and 1981, each has five speeches as they meet, she offers herself to him, he rejects her with contempt, and she physically attacks him. Salieri has twenty-eight words to say; Constanze has forty-seven. The scene, with its explicit stage instructions as to how she hitches her skirt up, is unchanged in the revised 1998–99 stage version, also presented in London and New York.

In the film version, as finally edited and released in 1984, much less is spoken, as the story is told with many shots and with close-ups of Salieri watching Constanze remove her clothing before he violently rings the bell and brings the encounter to a close.

Although Constanze speaks about the same number of words in both versions, Salieri's twenty-eight words on Broadway are reduced to just **four** for the screen. Each actor has much more to do with their reactions to each other, in their silences, looks, and business, than with the words they exchange. Constanze shows him the flash of flesh above her stockings in the stage version, but she becomes completely topless in the filmed version. Her attack on him onstage changes to her hurling a candelabra at the door he has just exited by in the film. On-screen, the words no longer do all the work; the pictures are also very much part of the story.

First Family Tree:	Homework
Branch:	Text
Twig:	**EXAMPLE: BROADWAY VERSUS HOLLYWOOD**

Second Family Tree:	Style
Branch:	Modern contemporary acting
Twig:	Screen acting
Leaf:	**EXAMPLE: BROADWAY VERSUS HOLLYWOOD**

Example: Brother and Sister Act

Simple or complicated, what different attitudes do they get from their words?

In the language of Shakespeare, the difference between simple and complicated language tells the actors what is going on. This also applies to modern scripts, where we know the simplicity of "Would you like a cup of tea?" implies a very different emotion than "Can I wine and dine you?"

The following, from *Measure for Measure,* is a good example of how language changes from the simple to the complicated. The novice nun must tell her brother that she will not save his life by sleeping with the judge:

CLAUDIO:

Now sister, what's the comfort?

ISABELLA:

Why,
As all comforts are: most good, most good indeed,
Lord *Angelo* having affairs to heaven
Intends you for his swift ambassador,
Where you shall be an everlasting leiger;
Therefore your best appointment make with speed,
Tomorrow you set on.

CLAUDIO:

Is there no remedy?

ISABELLA:

> None, but such remedy, as to save a head
> To cleave a heart in twain:

CLAUDIO:

> But is there any?

ISABELLA:

> Yes brother, you may live;
> There is a devilish mercy in the judge,
> If you'll implore it, that will free your life,
> But fetter you till death.

CLAUDIO:

> Perpetual durance?

ISABELLA:

> Aye just, perpetual durance, a restraint
> Through all the world's vastidity you had
> To a determin'd scope.

CLAUDIO:

> But in what nature?

ISABELLA:

> In such a one, as you consenting to't,
> Would bark your honor from that trunk you bear,
> And leave you naked.

CLAUDIO:

> Let me know the point.

He is direct and to the point, but all her speeches are complicated (as if she were avoiding telling him the simple news that he is to die). Interestingly, as the scene progresses, he then gets more complicated in his language, and she gets more simple:

CLAUDIO:

> Aye, but to die, and go we know not where,
> To lie in cold obstruction, and to rot,
> This sensible warm motion, to become
> A kneaded clod; and the delighted spirit
> To bathe in fiery floods, or to reside
> In thrilling region of thick-ribbed ice,
> To be imprison'd in the viewless winds
> And blown with restless violence round about
> The pendant world: or to be worse than worst
> Of those, that lawless and incertain thought,
> Imagine howling, 'tis too horrible.
> The weariest, and most loathed worldly life
> That age, ache, perjury, and imprisonment
> Can lay on nature, is a paradise
> To what we fear of death.

ISABELLA:

> Alas, alas.

The changes between the two forms of language help the actors to see where the changes in the thinking are, and by following them, they can quickly get the scene to work and act it the way it was intended by the Bard. Modern authors will do the same, and you should avoid acting a simple speech in a complicated way or taking out insurance by saying a very complicated one in a simple sincere way.

First Family Tree:	Homework
Branch:	Text
Twig:	Let the words do the work
Leaf:	**EXAMPLE: BROTHER AND SISTER ACT**

Second Family Tree:	Style
Branch:	Shakespeare acting
Twig:	Shakespeare: Simple or complicated
Leaf:	**EXAMPLE: BROTHER AND SISTER ACT**

Example:
Kate and Corpsing

When one is dying to laugh—but it will kill the play.

Dealing with your wish to laugh can be tricky.

The Actor Says:
One of the hardest moments I had onstage was also one of the best. I was in Alan Ayckbourn's Bedroom Farce, *playing Kate. In one scene Malcolm, her handyman husband, has made a dressing table for her. It is still offstage.*

> *Banging from the hall.*

MALCOLM:

> [*Off.*] Get in, you bastard, get in, will you? [*More banging and a final crash.*]

> *Malcolm staggers in, bleary and disheveled.*

KATE:

> Have you done it?

MALCOLM:

> Give me a hand in with it, will you?

KATE:

> [*Jumping out of bed and following him off.*] Oh, right, I'm dying to see it.

Malcolm and Kate carry on the dressing table. It is a lop-sided mess. They set it down. Kate steps back.

The theatre carpenter had made this brilliant piece of furniture, and every night as soon as we carried it on the audience laughter built, first at the furniture itself, and then at my reaction to it. I, as Kate, was seeing it for the first time and had to show a mixture of pride and horror. It's the sort of reaction you could milk forever, but you know you have bigger laughs to come, so you have to stem the flow—I made it clear I had a line to say.

KATE:

Oh. Yes . . . yes . . .

MALCOLM:

Well, it's—not quite right but . . .

KATE:

It's very nice. I like the drawers. [*She pulls one out. It is stuck.*]

MALCOLM:

Hang on, hang on, don't force it.

He pulls at the drawer without effect. He tugs at it. He wrestles with it and finally delivers it a mighty blow with the flat of his hand. The drawer opens.

MALCOLM:

I'll ease them a little in the morning.

KATE:

It's very handsome.

MALCOLM:

Not bad.

At this moment the audience's laughter always increased as I was trying to look at the sloping tabletop, and bending my head in line with the slant. The laughter built to an almost hysterical level, but I knew I had this hilarious line to follow, and I could hardly stop my face from twitching into a grin. It was agony—and the last thing I should do, but in a way I felt that the audience would understand my dilemma.

KATE:

I'm just a bit worried things might roll off the end.

A huge, huge laugh from the audience. There had to be a long pause, but we also had to let the play continue, and my fellow actor had to bring the audience down with his line, so he made a big gesture.

MALCOLM:

Roll off the end?

KATE:

With it being a bit on the slant.

By this time everyone in the building was pretty hysterical, including us, so it was a question of taking a very deep breath and ploughing on with the dialogue being said extra loud.

MALCOLM:

Well, it's got to be finished off. It's got to be sanded down yet.

KATE:

Oh, I see. Well. Well done.

So, although I lost control sometimes, it was a magical moment of theatre that everyone could enjoy to the full, and we used all our techniques to deal with the delights and the problems of laughter.

SEE also: LAUGHTER

Family Tree:	Performing
Branch:	Problems
Twig:	Breaking up (corpsing)
Leaf:	**EXAMPLE: KATE AND CORPSING**

Second Branch:	Technique
Twig:	Comedy and farce
Leaf:	**EXAMPLE: KATE AND CORPSING**

Example:
Lady Bracknell's Handbag

What's that doing here? (It's all in the words.)

It is wise to remember that every single word that is written for an actor to speak has been **chosen** by the author; chosen very carefully in some cases. Even what appear to be badly written lines have, nevertheless, been chosen to be uttered by you, the actor. Just occasionally authors do not see a joke, innuendo, or pun they have written, but any script bears further scrutiny even though you think you have uncovered absolutely everything.

Consider the following (now famous) dialogue from Oscar Wilde's *The Importance of Being Earnest:*

LADY BRACKNELL:

Now to minor matters. Are your parents living?

JACK:

I have lost both my parents.

LADY BRACKNELL:

To lose one parent, Mr. Worthing, may be regarded as a misfortune; to lose both looks like carelessness. Who was your father? He was evidently a man of some wealth. Was he born in what the Radical papers call the purple of commerce, or did he rise from the ranks of the aristocracy?

JACK:

I am afraid I really don't know. The fact is, Lady Bracknell, I said I had lost my parents. It would be nearer the truth to say that my parents seem to have lost me. . . . I don't actually know who I am by birth. I was . . . well, I was found.

LADY BRACKNELL:

Found!

JACK:

The late Mr. Thomas Cardew, an old gentleman of a very charitable and kindly disposition, found me, and gave me the name of Worthing, because he happened to have a first-class ticket for Worthing in his pocket at the time. Worthing is a place in Sussex. It is a seaside resort.

LADY BRACKNELL:

Where did the charitable gentleman who had a first-class ticket for this seaside resort find you?

JACK:

[Gravely.] In a handbag.

LADY BRACKNELL:

A handbag?

JACK:

[Very seriously.] Yes, Lady Bracknell. I was in a handbag—a somewhat large, black leather handbag, with handles to it—an ordinary handbag in fact.

LADY BRACKNELL:

In what locality did this Mr. James, or Thomas, Cardew come across this ordinary handbag?

JACK:

In the cloakroom at Victoria Station. It was given to him in mistake for his own.

LADY BRACKNELL:

The cloakroom at Victoria Station?

JACK:

> Yes. The Brighton line.

LADY BRACKNELL:

> The line is immaterial. Mr. Worthing, I confess I feel some-
> what bewildered by what you have just told me. To be born, or
> at any rate bred, in a handbag, whether it had handles or not,
> seems to me to display a contempt for the ordinary decen-
> cies of family life that reminds one of the worst excesses of
> the French Revolution. And I presume you know what that
> unfortunate movement led to? As for the particular locality
> in which the handbag was found, a cloakroom at a railway
> station might serve to conceal a social indiscretion—has prob-
> ably, indeed, been used for that purpose before now—but it
> could hardly be regarded as an assured basis for a recognized
> position in good society.

The Actor Says:

*When cast as Lady Bracknell I, like so many actors before me (and since), had
the daunting task of uttering the immortal words "A handbag?" made famous by
Dame Edith Evans in the 1952 film. She put great emphasis on the word quiv-
ering upwards in tone, and the director decided on a big close-up of her mouth,
which gave weight to the exaggeration. So, I looked at the script very carefully for
possible clues to help me cope with this nightmare moment.*

*I noticed that the only exclamation point came after the word "Found!" and
I realized it was not so much the handbag that did for Jack, but where it was
found. I got the feeling that if it has been found on the steps of Buckingham
Palace, Lady Bracknell might have considered that socially acceptable, but the
cloakroom at a railway station was beyond the pale, and that's the crux of the
scene. So the fact that she goes on to inquire as to the locality of the handbag
seemed to me to override the simple "A handbag?" line, and I glanced at my own
bag, which helped me to say the word with puzzlement rather than outrage.*

It was as if, even after discovering what her nephew was found in,
there was still room for the possibility of Lady Bracknell's understanding
his dilemma. You will also note that in her summing up, the disgrace of

the railway station cloakroom is paramount in her dismissal of him as a prospective match for her daughter.

It is from working these problems out at home that you can bring solutions and ideas into the rehearsal room, and you will be expected to do this completely for the screen. The more famous you become, the more you will be expected to bring to the acting feast.

Family Tree:	Homework
Branch:	Text
Twig:	Let the words do the work
Leaf:	**EXAMPLE: LADY BRACKNELL'S HANDBAG**

Example:
Mr. and Mrs. Noah Fight

Family quarrels in the medieval style.

Imagine that you are in a small town square on a feast day, and a wagon trundles into view. Local amateur actors, some of whom you recognize as the men who dye your clothes, jump out of the wagon, put some furniture on the bare boards of the narrow truck, draw up a curtain, and start acting. You gather round with your friends and neighbors, cheering and shouting ad libs at the actors, and joining in the debate about whether it is the husband or the wife who is in the right. Everyone has a wonderful time for this form of pageant wagon theatre.

The following is from the anonymously written *The Wakefield Noah* (where traditionally the Dyers Guild presented the story of the Deluge). Noah is trying to tell his wife about God's wish for him to build an ark (we have put definitions of the difficult words at the end).

GOD:

> Noah, to thee and to thy fry
> My blessing grant I;
> Ye shall wax and multiply
> And fill the earth again,
> When all these floods are past and fully gone away.

NOAH:

> Lord, homeward will I haste as fast as that I may;
> My wife will I ask what she will say,

Exit God.

And I am aghast that we get some fray
Betwixt us both;
For she is full techy,
For little oft angry;
If anything wrong be,
Soon is she wroth.

Then he goes to his wife.

God speed, dear wife, how fare ye?

WIFE:

Now, as ever might I thrive, the worse I thee see.
Do tell me belife, where has thou thus long be?
To death may we drive or live for thee, for want.
When we sweat or swink,
Thou does what thou think;
Yet of meat and of drink
Have we very scant.

NOAH:

Wife, we are hard stead with tidings new.

WIFE:

But thou were worthy be clad in Stafford blue;
For thou art always adread, be it false or true.
But God knows I am led, and that may I rue full ill;
For I dare be thy borrow,
From even unto morrow
Thou speaks ever of sorrow:
God send thee once thy fill!
We women may wary all ill husbands.
I have one, by Mary that loosed me of my bands!
If he teyn I must tarry, howsoever it stands,
With semblance full sorry, wringing both my hands for dread.
But yet other while,
What with game and with guile,
I shall smite and smile,
And quit him his mead.

NOAH:

> We! Hold thy tongue, ram-skit, or I shall thee still.

WIFE:

> By my thrift, if thou smite, I shall turn thee until!

NOAH:

> We shall assay as tight. Have at thee, Gill!
> Upon the bone shall it bite.

WIFE:

> Ah, so, Marry! thou smites ill!
> But I suppose
> I shall not in thy debt
> Flit from this flet!
> Take thee there a languet
> To tie up thy hose! *[Striking him.]*

This is good knockabout stuff, played out front to the audience, with everything shared and commented on. Notice what the wife comments to the audience about. She obviously expects the women there to agree with her.

You need to know certain medieval words: *belife* = speedily; *swink* = labor; *Stafford blue* = be beaten blue; *borrow* = pledge; *wary* = curse; *teyn* = is troubled; *quit him his mead* = pay him his due; *ram-skit* = sheep diarrhea (an insult); *flet* = floor; *languet* = rope.

From these early medieval plays to Peter Quince and his mechanicals, in Shakespeare's *A Midsummer Night's Dream*, rehearsing in a forest, amateurs have always been an intrinsic part of theatre, and they are a good place for certain plays with prohibitively large casts to still have an outing in front of an audience and for the actors to have an audience to play to.

First Family Tree:	Training
Branch:	Amateur dramatics
Twig:	**EXAMPLE: MR. AND MRS. NOAH FIGHT**

Second Family Tree:	Style
Branch:	Medieval acting
Twig:	**EXAMPLE: MR. AND MRS. NOAH FIGHT**

Example:
Mr. Horner Is Exactly That

Restoration immorality.

The Restoration period had actors and audiences locked together in a celebration of sexuality and licentiousness, all a result of the sudden lifting of the previous puritanical government's strict moral guidelines, and the restoration of power to the lords of the land, and of the theatres to their audiences.

The following is from William Wycherley's *The Country Wife*, in which Mr. Horner has convinced the townsfolk that he is impotent and therefore is safe to be left alone with their wives (but of course he was using this as an excuse to tumble as many of them as he could):

LADY SQUEAMISH:
> But where is he?

SIR JASPER:
> He's in the next room with my wife.

LADY SQUEAMISH:
> Nay, if you trust him with your wife, I may with my Biddy. They say, he's a merry harmless man now, e'en as harmless a man as ever came out of Italy with a good voice, and as pretty, harmless company for a lady, as a snake without his teeth.

SIR JASPER:
> Ay, ay, poor man.

> *Reenter Mrs. Squeamish.*

MRS. SQUEAMISH:

> I can't find 'em—Oh, are you here, grandmother? I followed, you must know, my Lady Fidget hither; 'tis the prettiest lodging, and I have been staring on the prettiest pictures—

> *Reenter Lady Fidget with a piece of china in her hand, and Horner following.*

LADY FIDGET:

> And I have been toiling and moiling for the prettiest piece of china, my dear.

HORNER:

> Nay, she has been too hard for me, do what I could.

MRS. SQUEAMISH:

> Oh, lord, I'll have some china too. Good Mr. Horner, don't think to give other people china, and me none; come in with me too.

HORNER:

> Upon my honor, I have none left now.

MRS. SQUEAMISH:

> Nay, nay, I have known you deny your china before now, but you shan't put me off so. Come.

HORNER:

> This lady had the last there.

LADY FIDGET:

> Yes, indeed, madam, to my certain knowledge, he has no more left.

MRS. SQUEAMISH:

> O, but it may be he may have some you could not find.

LADY FIDGET:

> What, d'ye think if he had had any left, I would not have had it too? for we women of quality never think we have china enough.

Even today, some audiences find this a little too saucy for comfort, but the author was simply addressing the thoughts and ideas of those who paid to come in and what they wanted to be entertained with. The play was as current then as a Sam Shepard play is today.

Family Tree:	Style
Branch:	Restoration acting
Twig:	**EXAMPLE: MR. HORNER IS EXACTLY THAT**

Example:
Noël Coward on the Phone

How opposites give the play a better start, or a reaction a better effect.

Using opposites can really bring out meaning and add a lot of comedy, as this start to Noël Coward's play *Present Laughter* shows. At curtain up a pretty girl dressed in pyjamas enters a famous actor's drawing room:

Garry Essendine's studio in London. The furnishing is comfortable, if a trifle eccentric. When the curtain rises it is 10:30 a.m. The studio is rather dim as the curtains are drawn. Daphne Stillington comes out of the spare room. She is a pretty girl of about twenty-three or four. She is wearing a man's dressing gown and pyjamas. She wanders about until she finds the telephone and then, almost furtively, dials a number.

DAPHNE:

Hallo—hallo! Is that you Saunders? Can I speak to Miss Cynthia? . . . all right I'll hold on . . . hallo . . . Cynthia darling, it's Daphne . . . yes . . . are you alone? Listen I'm you know where . . . Yes I did . . . No he isn't awake yet . . . There's nobody about at all . . . No, in the spare room, I've only just got up I'm not dressed or anything . . . I can't go on about it now someone might come in . . . If anybody rings up from home will you swear to say that I stayed with you . . . Darling you promised . . . In that case say I'm in the bath or something . . . Yes, as soon as I'm dressed in about an hour I should think . . . Of course . . . I can't wait to tell you . . . All right.

She puts down the telephone. Miss Erikson enters.

DAPHNE:

> *[A trifle nervously.]* Good morning.

MISS ERIKSON:

> *[Betraying no surprise.]* Good morning.

The scene seems to play itself, but there is so much you can do with it, setting up the style of the play, the humor of the situation, and the fact that the audience members are going to enjoy themselves, if you use opposites all through Daphne's phone call:

> *She dials a number.*

SET UP THE OPPOSITE:

> Assume that the person answering is your friend, and smile:
> *"Hallo—hallo!"*

DO THE OPPOSITE:

> Be disappointed that it is only Saunders the butler:
> *"Is that you Saunders?"*

SET UP THE OPPOSITE:

> Assume that Cynthia is right next to the telephone:
> *"Can I speak to Miss Cynthia?"*

DO THE OPPOSITE:

> Be annoyed that you are going to have to wait:
> *". . . all right I'll hold on"*

SET UP THE OPPOSITE:

> Think that it is only Saunders again, with a downbeat:
> *". . . hallo"*

DO THE OPPOSITE:

> Break into a big smile that it is your friend at the other end:
> *". . . Cynthia darling, it's Daphne"*

SET UP THE OPPOSITE:

> Be angry she does not recognize your voice:
> "*. . . yes*"

DO THE OPPOSITE:

> Be excited that you are about to reveal that you stayed the
> night with the Great Man:
> "*. . . are you alone? Listen I'm you know where*"

SET UP THE OPPOSITE:

> Be hurt that she does not believe you:
> "*. . . Yes I did*"

DO THE OPPOSITE:

> Be superior because you have intimate knowledge of the
> Great Man:
> "*. . . No he isn't awake yet*"

SET UP THE OPPOSITE:

> Be suggestive that the Great Man is an intimate of yours:
> "*. . . There's nobody about at all*"

DO THE OPPOSITE:

> Be regretful at having to confess that you did not spend the
> night with him:
> "*. . . No, in the spare room, I've only just got up I'm not dressed
> or anything*"

And so on. This technique works with all scripts, as you can inform
and entertain the audience by using opposites. It is especially useful for
screen work, where the editor might very well take advantage of all your
reactions and use them—and the opposite reaction always works very well
when you wear your screen reaction life jacket: *React before you speak.*

First Family Tree:	Homework
Branch:	Text
Twig:	Opposites
Leaf:	**EXAMPLE: NOËL COWARD ON THE PHONE**

Second Family Tree:	Screen acting
Branch:	Screen cheating
Twig:	Screen reactions
Leaf:	**EXAMPLE: NOËL COWARD ON THE PHONE**

Example:
Olivia's Ends

How verse helps you to understand
what is going on.

Take the following speech by Olivia from *Twelfth Night* when she is asking
the priest to tell everyone about her marriage to Sebastian:

OLIVIA:

> Father, I charge thee by thy reverence
> Here to unfold, though lately we intended
> To keep in darkness, what occasion now
> Reveals before 'tis ripe: what thou dost know
> Hath newly past, between this youth, and me.

Many actors will approach it from a sense of what the speech is about
and will follow it according to the punctuation only, speaking it approxi-
mately as follows:

OLIVIA:

> Father, I charge thee by thy reverence here to unfold,
> though lately we intended to keep in darkness,
> what occasion now reveals before 'tis ripe:
> what thou dost know hath newly past,
> between this youth, and me.

However, a lot of time and trouble was taken by one William Shakespeare to write it all in verse, and you should follow a simple but significant rule, an absolute lifesaver:

When acting verse, choose the last word of a line.

When you are doing this, a totally different speech emerges, as you create the character who **wants** to choose these particular words (we have put the last word of each line into bold):

OLIVIA:

> Father, I charge thee by thy **reverence**
> Here to unfold, though lately we **intended**
> To keep in darkness, what occasion **now**
> Reveals before 'tis ripe: what thou dost **know**
> Hath newly past, between this youth, and **me.**

The choice goes to the end of the line, and it changes the sense and Olivia's attitude. It sometimes happens that actors are told to run lines on (or enjamb them), but as you can see, this then stops you from receiving all the good information from the Master himself that he put into the end of each verse line.

The choice can of course be done in different ways, emphasis being the usual one, but you can also choose with pitch, tone, pace—why, the choices are yours, the clues are Shakespeare's.

Family Tree:	Style
Branch:	Shakespeare acting
Twig:	Shakespeare: Verse
Leaf:	**EXAMPLE: OLIVIA'S ENDS**

Example:
Plunging in the Deep End

Well, how would *you* do these speeches?

We have talked of commitment and of it being impossible to go over the top, and the dangers of being consistent, so in this section we present examples from different playwrights of what they can demand of you, the actor. We also suggest that these are good ways of trying out and confirming working from the outside-in, and you can judge how far you could go with this and with using the various other techniques we have mentioned in this book.

Sally's climactic confrontation in the Monte Doyle play *Signpost to Murder* needs great contrasts and big gear changes:

SALLY:

> Think back to that night. You've quarrelled—violently. She is in the bathroom—you can hear the water running—your head is pounding with rage. Even from the bathroom she continues to shout at you. She screams insults—her voice grates on you—it is hateful—vicious—and it seems to vibrate in your body, until you feel you can't stand it any more. You must have silence, silence, at any price. You run to the bathroom—she screams at you again and again—you take her throat in your hands—you must stop that voice—you tighten your grip—you bang her head against the taps—again and again—and again . . .

You get the same sort of desperation, and need the same sort of commitment and variation, for this speech by Rosemary in William Inge's *Picnic:*

ROSEMARY:

You said you were gonna marry me, Howard. You said when I got back from my vacation, you'd be waitin' with the preacher. Where's the preacher, Howard? Where is he? *[Grabbing his arm and holding him.]* Come back here, Howard. I'm no spring chicken either. Maybe I'm a little older than you think *I* am. I've formed my ways too. But they can be changed. They *gotta* be changed. It's no good livin' like this, in rented rooms, meetin' a bunch of old maids for supper every night, then comin' back home alone. *[She grips him by the arm and looks straight into his eyes.]* You gotta marry me. *[Desperate.]* Oh, God! Please marry me, Howard. Please . . . *[She sinks to her knees.]* Please . . . please . . .

William Inge also gave meaty speeches to male actors. Dr. Lyman confesses he had lecherous thoughts about his young friend in *Bus Stop,* and the actor is challenged to make this as extreme and as believable as the author intended:

DR. LYMAN:

It takes strong men and women to *love* . . . *[About to fall, he grabs the back of a chair for support.]* People strong enough inside themselves to love . . . without humiliation. *[He sighs heavily and looks about him with blurred eyes.]* People big enough to *grow* with their love and live inside a whole, wide new dimension. People brave enough to bear the responsibility of *being* loved and not fear it as a burden. *[He sighs again and looks about him wearily.]* I . . . I never had the generosity to love, to give my own most private self to another, for I was *weak.* I thought the gift would somehow lessen *me.* Me! *[He laughs wildly.]* Romeo! Romeo! I am disgusting!

You will need your technique about you (especially the use of opposites) to get all the delights from John Galsworthy's speech for the mother Mrs. Gwyn in his play *Joy,* as she berates her daughter. A small hint for this speech—don't just make her angry all through, let her instantly swivel from anger to misery to disgust; we promise you—if you do it believably, it will not be over the top:

MRS. GWYN:

> Ashamed? Am *I* to live all my life like a dead woman because you're ashamed? Am I to live like the dead because you're a child that knows nothing of life? Listen, Joy, you'd better understand this once for all. Your Father has no right over me and he knows it. We've been hateful to each other for years. *Can* you understand that? Don't cover your face like a child—look at me. *[Joy drops her hands, and lifts her face. Mrs. Gwyn looks back at her, her lips are quivering; she goes on speaking with stammering rapidity.]* D'you think—because I suffered when you were born and because I've suffered since with every ache you ever had, that that gives you the right to dictate to me now? *[In a dead voice.]* I've been unhappy enough and I shall be unhappy enough in the time to come. *[Meeting the hard wonder in Joy's face.]* Oh! you untouched things, you're as hard and cold as iron!

And, finally, a deeply committed speech for the men, again from Monte Doyle's *Signpost to Murder,* and more extremes of passion and variety needed from the actor playing Roy:

ROY:

> *[Hoarsely.]* Sally—when I'm free—I'll find David. I'll find him, and bring him here—I'll prove that . . . *[He checks.]* Why are you looking at me like that? I know that look. Gentle and tolerant—I saw it often—in that place. You don't believe I can clear myself, do you? Do you? You're humoring me. *[He catches her arm.]* You think I am insane. Twenty-eight days together, inseparable—there's hardly a thought of mine you haven't shared—and yet you still believe that I'm . . . Oh, God! *[He stops, horrified.]* I've clung to my sanity, like a life-belt. If I let go now—I'll go under. You want me to admit that I'm a murderer. That I killed Ruth.

All these speeches change wildly from the start to the end—there is no consistency here. You need emotional recollection and sheer technique to get you through them and to present to your audience the joys of a deeply committed performance and a fulfilling experience for those who paid to come in. Is it possible to go over the top with any of them? Just you try it!

SEE also COMMITMENT and CONSISTENCY and OPPOSITES

First Family Tree:	Performing
Branch:	Technique
Twig:	Over the top
Leaf:	**EXAMPLE: PLUNGING IN THE DEEP END**

Second Family Tree:	Style
Branch:	Modern contemporary acting
Twig:	Outside-in versus inside-out
Leaf:	**EXAMPLE: PLUNGING IN THE DEEP END**

Example:
Princely Business

Keep going until the Bard says stop!

A long speech is difficult to do, and we believe that Shakespeare helps his actors in a soliloquy by telling them where the pauses are, and so when to do some business.

Take for example this famous speech:

HAMLET:

> Oh what a rogue and peasant slave am I?
> Is it not monstrous that this player here,
> But in a fiction, in a dream of passion,
> Could force his soul so to his whole conceit,
> That from her working, all his visage warm'd;
> Tears in his eyes, distraction in's aspect,
> A broken voice, and his whole function suiting
> With forms, to his conceit? And all for nothing?
> For *Hecuba*?
> What's *Hecuba* to him, or he to *Hecuba*,
> That he should weep for her? What would he do,
> Had he the motive and the cue for passion
> That I have? He would drown the stage with tears,

As you can see, there is a lot of regular verse (lines that are iambic pentameters, or variations of them—did you spot the Alexandrine?), until there is a line of just two words:

For *Hecuba*?

So this is the place to stop, put in some stage business, do **something** to acknowledge that Shakespeare has quite clearly told you to stop for a bit.

These ideas were first floated clearly in an out-of-print book by a translator, who wondered what to do about the broken lines he came across in the text. He came to the conclusion that they were, in fact, indications of a pause. Naturally, if Shakespeare knows how to tell you to pause, then if he does **not** tell you to pause, do not. Just get on with it, and find to your delight that it plays just perfectly.

The Director Says:

I went to see a production of Hamlet, *where the prince was played by Michael Maloney, whom I have worked with on text in the past. At the moment in the play when he got to "For Hecuba?" he jumped straight into the open grave, then popped his head up for his next line:*

> *What's Hecuba to him, or he to Hecuba,*

The audience loved it, and afterwards I asked him why he had done it. He replied that he remembered me saying that a half line was a pause for business, so he decided to dive out of the audience's sight into the trap. It worked wonderfully well as a piece of theatre—and came from pausing when Shakespeare tells you to.

Oh, you wanted to know which was the Alexandrine? It was the line immediately after the pause:

> What's *Hecuba* to him, or he to *Hecuba*.

(There are twelve bits in the line, or six *di-dums*!)

SEE also: BUSINESS (BIZ)

First Family Tree:	Performing
Branch:	Audience
Twig:	Pauses
Leaf:	**EXAMPLE: PRINCELY BUSINESS**

Second Family Tree:	Style
Branch:	Shakespeare acting
Twig:	Shakespeare: Verse
Leaf:	**EXAMPLE: PRINCELY BUSINESS**

Example:
Signs of the Times

Entertaining nineteenth-century melodrama.

Taken from the last moments of *A Tale of Mystery*, by Thomas Holcroft (1824), the detailed instructions show how much of the play had to be done with gestures, with well-recognized signs for established emotions, for the unsophisticated audience members just wanting a brief respite from their day's hard labors.

MICHELLI:
> Welcome! A thousand times welcome!

SELINA:
> Ten thousand thanks to the savior of my father!

MICHELLI:
> Your father, sweet lady?

SELINA:
> Oh yes! discovered to me by his mortal enemy.

MICHELLI:
> The monster Romaldi?

SELINA:
> *[Dejectedly.]* Alas!

MICHELLI:
> For your father's sake, for your own sake, welcome both.

ROMALDI:

[Half from the door.] I heard my name!

MICHELLI:

[Leading them to the door, just as Romaldi advances a step.]
Come. I have a stranger—

SELINA:

[Seeing Romaldi, shrieks.] Ah!

FRANCISCO:

[Falls back and covers his eyes, with agony.]

MICHELLI:

How now?

Romaldi retires.

SELINA:

'Tis he!

Music of terror etc.
*Francisco putting his hand towards her mouth, enjoins her silence
with great eagerness. Michelli, by making the sign of biting his right
hand, asks Francisco if it be Romaldi. Francisco turns away without
answering. Michelli denotes his conviction it is Romaldi, and hastily
ascends to cross the bridge in search of the archers, Francisco entreats
him back in vain. Romaldi, in terror, enters from the house, presenting his pistol. Francisco opens his breast for him to shoot if he pleases.
Selina falls between them. The whole scene passes in a mysterious and
rapid manner. Music suddenly stops.*

ROMALDI:

No! Too much of your blood is upon my head! Be justly re-
venged: take mine!

*Music continues as Romaldi offers the pistol: which Francisco
throws to a distance, and entreats him to fly by the valley. Romaldi
signifies the impossibility, and runs distractedly from side to*

side: then after Francisco and Selina's entreaties, ascends to cross the bridge. Met at the edge of the hill by an Archer: he is driven back; they struggle on the bridge. The Archer's sword taken by Romaldi; who, again attempting flight, is again met by several Archers. Romaldi maintains a retreating fight. Fiametta, Bonamo, Stephano, Montano, and Peasants follow the Archers. Francisco and Selina, in the greatest agitation, several times throw themselves between the assailants and Romaldi. When the combatants have descended the hill, Romaldi's foot slips, he falls, and Francisco intervenes to guard his body. By this time all the principal characters are near the front. The Archers appear to be prepared to shoot, and strike with their sabers; when the entreaties and efforts of Francisco and Selina are renewed. The Archers forbear for a moment; and Francisco shields his brother. The music ceases.

SELINA:

Oh, forbear! Let my father's virtues plead for my uncle's errors!

BONAMO:

We all will entreat for mercy; since of mercy we all have need: for his sake, and for our own, may it be freely granted!

The curtain falls to slow and solemn music.

THE END

It must have been great fun in that old darkened auditorium, sitting with a mass of shouting and jeering people, watching performers acting out the simple moralities of the time. Why, it must have been like watching a modern soap opera on television (without the shouting!). It certainly was the forerunner of those silent movies that played to the same sort of audiences and influenced modern cinema so much.

First Family Tree:	Homework
Branch:	Movement and gestures
Twig:	**EXAMPLE: SIGNS OF THE TIMES**

Second Family Tree: Style
Branch: Melodrama acting
Twig: **EXAMPLE: SIGNS OF THE TIMES**

Example:
The Silence of the Lads

See the effect of the change from prose to poetry.

In Shakespeare's *Antony and Cleopatra* there is the famous scene where Enobarbus talks of the glories he has just seen. It starts off in prose, with all the lads joining in, but when it comes to describing Cleopatra, then Enobarbus for the first time in the play changes from speaking in prose to speaking poetry, and the others no longer join in but listen in silence:

MECENAS:

    Welcome from Egypt sir.

ENOBARBUS:

    Half the heart of *Cæsar*, worthy *Mecenas*. My honorable friend *Agrippa*.

AGRIPPA:

    Good *Enobarbus*.

MECENAS:

    We have cause to be glad, that matters are so well disgested: you stay'd well by't in Egypt.

ENOBARBUS:

    Aye sir, we did sleep day out of countenance: and made the night light with drinking.

MECENAS:

> Eight wild boars roasted whole at a breakfast: and but twelve
> persons there. Is this true?

ENOBARBUS:

> This was but as a fly by an eagle: we had much more mon-
> strous matter of feast, which worthily deserved noting.

MECENAS:

> She's a most triumphant lady, if report be square to her.

ENOBARBUS:

> When she first met *Mark Anthony*, she purs'd up his heart
> upon the river of Sydnus.

AGRIPPA:

> There she appear'd indeed: or my reporter devis'd well for her.

ENOBARBUS:

> I will tell you,
> The barge she sat in, like a burnish'd throne
> Burnt on the water: the poop was beaten gold,
> Purple the sails: and so perfumed that
> The winds were lovesick.
> With them the oars were silver,
> Which to the tune of flutes kept stroke, and made
> The water which they beat, to follow faster;
> As amorous of their strokes. For her own person,
> It beggar'd all description, she did lie
> In her pavilion, cloth of gold, of tissue,
> O'er-picturing that Venus, where we see
> The fancy outwork nature. On each side her,
> Stood pretty dimpled boys, like smiling cupids,
> With divers-color'd fans whose wind did seem,
> To glove the delicate cheeks which they did cool,
> And what they undid did.

Eagle-eyed readers will have noticed that there are two delightful half lines where Enobarbus can take a pause and relish in what he has just said or torment his listeners until he decides to carry on. This arrangement of the lines is taken from the First Folio—modern editors, alas, usually run the two half lines together.

The change from the one type of speaking to the other is a huge note for the actor—and a very useful one too, especially when your character changes from one to the other in the same scene.

Family Tree:	Style
Branch:	Shakespeare acting
Twig:	Shakespeare: Prose or poetry
Leaf:	**EXAMPLE: THE SILENCE OF THE LADS**

Example:
Valuable Verbals

Now you can know the difference between a metaphor and a simile (and other goodies).

Looking at the wordplay in a Shakespearean scene can give the actors useful information about how to play it, because in the absence of proper rehearsals back in the days when the plays were written, the writer-director had only these means of influencing his actors. At the very least, he had to have a fail-safe way of communicating with the many different boy actors who would be taking over the female roles over the years as their elders' voices broke. These same insights into verbal complexities should also be applied to modern scripts, wherever you find them.

In each case, the wordplay brings to the actor's attention something specific, and we have marked them by putting them in bold.

Alliteration (Lady Anne in *Richard III*):

> If ever he have wife, let her be **made**
> **More miserable** by the death of him,
> Than I am made by my young Lord, and thee.

Assonance (Anthony in *Julius Cæsar*):

> O pardon **me**, thou **bleeding piece** of earth:
> That I am **meek** and gentle with **these** butchers.

Clever words (Viola in *Twelfth Night*):

> O time, thou must untangle this, **not** I,
> It is too hard a **knot** for me t'untie.

Double entendre (Miranda in *The Tempest*):

> *(Miranda is talking to the first eligible young man she has ever met,
> and the word "die" can also mean orgasm; "the bigger bulk" could be
> either his or hers; and "cunning" sounds awfully like "cunny"—the
> Elizabethan word for something rude.)*
> At mine unworthiness, that dare not offer
> What I desire to give; and much less take
> What I shall **die** to want: but this is trifling,
> And all the more it seeks to hide itself,
> **The bigger bulk it shows.** Hence bashful **cunning**,
> And prompt me plain and holy innocence.

Metaphor (Greene in *Richard II*):

> Alas poor Duke, the task he undertakes
> Is **numbering sands**, and **drinking oceans dry**,

Midline endings (Jaques in *As You Like It*):

> (We identified the midline endings with an **M** in the margin.)

> All the world's a stage,
> And all the men and women, merely players;
> They have their *exits* and their entrances,
> And one man in his time plays many parts,
> **M** His acts being seven ages. At first the infant,
> Mewling, and puking in the nurse's arms:
> Then, the whining schoolboy with his satchel
> And shining morning face, creeping like snail
> **M** Unwillingly to school. And then the lover,
> Sighing like furnace, with a woeful ballad
> **M** Made to his mistress' eyebrow. Then, a soldier,
> Full of strange oaths, and bearded like the pard,
> Etc.

Repeated words (Angelo in *Measure for Measure*):

> **What's this? what's this?** is **this** her fault, or mine?

Rhyme (Richard in *Richard II*):

> Forget, forgive, conclude, and be **agreed**,
> Our doctors say, this is no time to **bleed**.

Separations (Richard in *Richard III*):

> (between "glorious" and "summer" and between "this" and "son")

> Now is the winter of our discontent,
> Made glorious summer by this son of York:

Simile (Demetrius in *A Midsummer Night's Dream*):

> These things seem small and undistinguishable,
> Like far-off mountains turned into clouds.

You still can't sort the metaphors from the similes? Here is the easy way, talking about someone else's opinion:

> "That **is** a pile of doo-doo." METAPHOR
> "That is **like** a pile of doo-doo." SIMILE

Scripts for commercial products are notorious for being loaded with assonance and alliteration, let alone metaphor and simile and rude double meanings—why, with these experiences the modern actor is **completely** equipped to tackle Shakespeare!

First Family Tree:	Homework
Branch:	Text
Twig:	Let the words do the work
Leaf:	**EXAMPLE: VALUABLE VERBALS**

Second Family Tree:	Style
Branch:	Shakespeare acting
Twig:	Shakespeare: Wordplay
Leaf:	**EXAMPLE: VALUABLE VERBALS**

Example:
You, Thee—and the Gold

The changes between what you call people show the changing emotions.

Shakespeare also tells actors how to let the words do the work by using the difference between the words *you* and *thee*. A good example of this is the scene between Antipholus and his servant Dromio, from the play *The Comedy of Errors*. Antipholus is in fact talking to the twin of his servant, who does not know what on earth he is talking about.

When the words *thou, thy, thine,* or *thee* are used by Antipholus, the words for intimate or quiet speaking, we have put a **T** in the margin; when it is the more formal or loud *you* or *your*, we put a corresponding **Y**. Because Dromio always uses *you* or *your*, we do not put his marks in.

S. ANTIPHOLUS:
  Y Stop in your wind sir, tell me this I pray?
  Y Where have you left the money that I gave you.

E. DROMIO:
    Oh sixpence that I had a Wednesday last,
    To pay the saddler for my mistress' crupper:
    The saddler had it sir, I kept it not.

S. ANTIPHOLUS:
    I am not in a sportive humor now:
    Tell me, and dally not, where is the money?
  T We being strangers here, how dar'st thou trust
  T So great a charge from thine own custody.

E. Dromio:

> I pray you jest sir as you sit at dinner:
> I from my mistress come to you in post:
> If I return I shall be post indeed.
> For she will scour your fault upon my pate:
> Methinks your maw, like mine, should be your cook,
> And strike you home without a messenger.

S. Antipholus:

> Come *Dromio*, come, these jests are out of season,
> Reserve them till a merrier hour than this:
> T Where is the gold I gave in charge to thee?

E. Dromio:

> To me sir? why you gave no gold to me?

S. Antipholus:

> Y Come on sir knave, have done your foolishness,
> T And tell me how thou hast dispos'd thy charge.

E. Dromio:

> My charge was but to fetch you from the mart
> Home to your house, the *Phœnix* sir, to dinner;
> My mistress and her sister stays for you.

S. Antipholus:

> Now as I am a Christian answer me,
> Y In what safe place you have bestow'd my money;
> Y Or I shall break that merry sconce of yours
> That stands on tricks, when I am undispos'd:
> T Where is the thousand marks thou had'st of me?

E. Dromio:

> I have some marks of yours upon my pate:
> Some of my mistress' marks upon my shoulders:
> But not a thousand marks between you both.
> If I should pay your worship those again,
> Perchance you will not bear them patiently.

S. Antipholus:

    T Thy mistress' marks? what mistress slave hast thou?

E. Dromio:

> Your worship's wife, my mistress at the *Phœnix;*
> She that doth fast till you come home to dinner:
> And prays that you will hie you home to dinner.

S. Antipholus:

    T What wilt thou flout me thus unto my face
    Y Being forbid? There take you that sir knave.

E. Dromio:

> What mean you sir, for God's sake hold your hands:
> Nay, and you will not sir, I'll take my heels.

> *Exit E. Dromio.*

Antipholus switches to the *thy* mode when actually asking about the money and where it is, and back to the *you* mode when he shows his anger with Dromio. It seems he dare not be too angry or abusive until he finds out exactly where his money has got to. At the very end when Antipholus hits Dromio, he changes to the *you* mode.

The switches show the actor when the gear changes happen, when to shout, and when to be quietly persuasive, and this change from using the word *you* to the word *thy* is always significant in the works of Shakespeare.

Alas, too many actors treat the words as if they are the same, which they patently are not. The different words you call people demand different thoughts, and this applies across the whole spectrum of scripts.

First Family Tree:	Homework
Branch:	Text
Twig:	Let the words do the work
Leaf:	**EXAMPLE: YOU, THEE—AND THE GOLD**

Second Family Tree:	Style
Branch:	Shakespeare acting
Twig:	Shakespeare: What you call people
Leaf:	**EXAMPLE: YOU, THEE—AND THE GOLD**

Eye-to-Eye Contact

Not the absolute necessity you thought.

A lot of actors, if in trouble and drowning in the sea of confusions, stick to being sincere. A lot of actors are wrong.

Being sincere and staring into the eyes of a fellow actor is not always the solution. For a start, it does not really imitate nature, because you very rarely do this when facing another. Your eyes dart all over the place. Second, the angle at which an audience watches you, either up on the stage or through the changing angles of a camera, means that eye-to-eye contact cannot always be the best way to communicate with the audience. Eye-to-eye contact can, in fact, be the enemy of realism in acting.

To lose yourself in another's eyes is a good way to avoid what else you could be doing with your acting. Just to be sincere is to show your fellow actor, and your audience, only the surface of what you mean, and therefore you can be missing out on the subtext.

Although it might **feel** right and truthful to stand side on to the audience and look another character straight in the eyes, all the audience sees are two profiles. The audience cannot tell what each character is really thinking. So finding a reason to turn away from the other character means that you not only show the audience what you really feel but also release your fellow actor to do the same thing for his character.

The eye-to-eye contact can, of course, be very effective for brief moments, but if it is held for too long the audience will be unable to see changes and inner thoughts and so will start to feel uninvolved. The audience might well temporarily switch off.

The Actor Says:
When I trained at RADA in the 1950s, the Method was not taught in England, indeed it was barely talked about or understood. Being "in the moment" was

not a known phrase. Since becoming aware of its meaning, I totally understand it and confess that I have enjoyed it on occasions—and a very nice feeling it was—but it would happen purely by accident and I would come offstage thinking "that was great, I really felt good in that scene." The bubble could often be burst by someone commenting on how "that scene didn't go so well, I thought," and I would know that I had been indulgent and not totally aware of the effect of the scene as a whole.

It is an interesting debate. Frankly, there has to be an awareness of being onstage—in a play—at all times. Part of your brain knows that it's make-believe and is ready for all eventualities such as a prop not being set or somebody else losing his lines (drying).

On-screen, the tyranny of eye-to-eye contact defeats even the most determined director, as some actors cling to the mistaken belief that if only they can look into their fellow actor's eyes, they will be seen to be truthful and real. The rush of a shoot can be so pressured that these unfortunate actors take refuge in a device that not only makes them less effective but also dubs them uncooperative and difficult. To be able to cheat your eyes round to the camera, and to do it in a way that appears truthful and motivated, is one of the marks of a really useful (and successful) screen actor.

The Director Says:

I have had an actor in tears, as she insisted on glaring into the other person's eyes, even though this took her away from the camera lens, and so in my contained two-shot her eyes could not be seen. Her tears were because she knew that she was not doing what I wanted, but she really felt a deep need to keep to this unnatural practice. Unnatural because in real life, of course, we do not hold other people's eyes for a long time unless we are lovers—or amateur actors. I think I placed her in the latter category.

Actually, we have been a little unkind here, as eye-to-eye contact **can** be maintained if you want it. For the camera to see your and the other actor's faces, the director will often place you standing slightly behind another character, but you want to talk to him while having eye-to-eye contact. The good news is that you **can** look at the other person's eyes—from behind—as long as you imagine that his skull and hair are made of glass and that you can see right through his head. This is your life belt:

You maintain eye-to-eye contact by looking through the back of his skull.

The director is happy, because this now allows the camera to see both sets of eyes, and you are happy to keep that wished-for contact. The cheat is simply one of having a head made of glass.

SEE also: METHOD ACTING and WHATEVER WORKS

First Family Tree:	Performing
Branch:	Technique
Twig:	**EYE-TO-EYE CONTACT**

Second Family Tree:	Screen acting
Branch:	Screen cheating
Twig:	**EYE-TO-EYE CONTACT**

Fellow Actors

How to cope with (and learn from) these essential other people.

Harmony and friendship are the ideal way to work together with your fellow actors. There is no doubt that they are a lifeline, both onstage and offstage. You rely on them for cooperation when acting alongside them and for friendship throughout your life. All professional actors will have a gang of actor friends that they can share experiences, stories, and in-jokes with.

The Actor Says:

*I well remember getting to know an actress who had recently married a friend of mine. One of the first things she asked me was "Who are your mates?" We exchanged names of close chums (all in the business) and found we had many amusing anecdotes in common apart from the endless tales of glory **and** woe connected with mutual people and events.*

It is no accident that actors often call each other "darling." This is perhaps because they cannot remember each other's name, since they will also be calling them by the name of the character they are playing. It is also an acknowledgment that they consider themselves close friends already, even though they might have just met each other. Many who enter the business after years of training admit they learned more from their fellow actors once they started acting than from all those years of classes.

The Director Says:

I once worked with an actor who, whenever one of her fellow actors forgot a line (or dried), she would always take the blame for it herself, saying that she must have given the feed line the wrong way. It took me a while to realize that she was *in fact using this as a way of constantly making herself better—and by taking the blame, she kept the rehearsals happy as she skillfully plied her craft. And you know, just occasionally, it **was** her fault that the other actor could not come up with the right line.*

Nobody wants to give a bad performance, so if a fellow actor is headed that way and it affects you, try to work out why she is going in such a direction, rather than just blame her and consider it is her fault you are not better. Sometimes it might even be your fault, by the way you are feeding her her lines, for example.

When acting with a fellow actor, you can find it effective to "come in under" with your speech, rather than always topping her. However, do not let this become a habit, so that you **always** undercut her speeches with your own—it is a technique that works only when used very sparingly indeed. If she comes across better, then so will you.

You also never know which other actor can affect your future prospects by her contacts and opinion of you. Why not get everyone a cup of coffee? How about adopting the philosophy that you will treat other actors the way you want to be treated? (Especially when you have become well-known and famous.)

The Actor Says Again:

I went backstage once after a show. A great friend was playing in it, but I was reluctant to visit as it was a disastrous musical, still in previews. In her dressing room an announcement came over the Tannoy calling the whole cast in at 10:00 the following morning to completely restage a big number with a new choreographer—I heard the wails and cries that went up from all the other dressing rooms. I was distressed for my friend and her colleagues, and as I left the stage door with tears in my eyes, a man also visiting came up to me and said, "Never mind, dear, I thought you were wonderful." Obviously anyone weeping would presumably be a member of the cast, and as a fellow actor he had wanted to support me, just as I had done the same for my friend.

SEE also: GETTING WORK

When working with your fellow actors on a script, work out what your other role in the play might be apart from the character you are playing: the way you fit in in the whole production. If you are in a supporting role, then be supportive, not competitive, with the main characters. It is all a matter of working together as a team to get the most compatible results and mutually entertaining performances.

SEE also: NOTES

For screen work the relationship between the actors is much more fragmented, as some might not ever meet each other, even if they have scenes together. Some actors will grab each other to run lines in their trailers or the communal area; others will not want to run their lines at all so that they can keep a type of spontaneity for the camera. Your job is to deliver what it is your audition promised you could do and to fit in with whatever is going on, especially the regulars on the set.

There is also the problem that the raw material you use for your acting is the very thing that people keep most private: their emotions. This will mean that at certain times, on certain jobs, your acting colleagues will, in a strange way, be closer to you than your partner is (in film they solve the problem by pointing out that "on location doesn't count!").

First Family Tree:	Training
Branch:	No training
Twig:	**FELLOW ACTORS**

Second Family Tree:	The Team
Branch:	**FELLOW ACTORS**
Twigs:	Battle of the sexes; Hierarchy; It's not what it used to be; Stars

Film versus Television

Or what you do differently when acting for the big or small screen.

When the television industry first started to present dramas, it just put its cameras in front of a stage performance and filmed what it saw, unlike film, which had a whole series of different shots to help convey the story and emotions. Over the years it has been a long journey of bringing the two media closer and closer, so the differences now are more technical than artistic.

A film can be made today and the director and crew may not be sure at first whether the result will be shown on the big or small screen. Even if they are making it for the big screen, the dreaded straight-to-video option (or DVD these days) can still ensure it is seen only on the small one.

The first difference between turning a script into a movie and making it to be shown on television, when using a single camera, is in the time taken. The demands of television will insist that a crew bring home anything from five to fifteen minutes of finished material from each shooting day. A major movie will get anything from two minutes down to a few seconds, as they set up their complicated shots and sequences. The difference in the amount to be shot in a day affects you directly, as the number of lines to be learned, digested, and performed will be hugely more for the small screen than the big screen.

Interestingly, the rehearsal time will probably be the same (none), even though the budgets will be vastly different. Films will tend to be on location, whereas television tends to go for the studio.

Because the small screen does not show so much so well, small screen dramas tend to be shot with much closer shots, with a greater use of the close-up and extreme close-up. As long as you are responding to the size of shot correctly, it will not change your results, but it will need to be looked out for. The television show also will do less coverage; that is, fewer options covering a sequence, so that you will need to nail your performance from the beginning, as there might in fact be no other shot covering that particular moment.

The most obvious compromises are made in the dressings and particularly the lighting, where a television production team just will not have the time to light your face as well as the more traditional film production team will, so you should be more aware of shadows and finding your light.

Films need a lot more postproduction and, in particular, much more replaced sound, as the production team struggles to reproduce the natural sounds you made in the studio with their Foley and Dolby effects. You will have to loop; that is, match a new voice to the filmed face, as a necessity of replacing the dialogue. You can use this as a last opportunity to improve your performance.

Television uses more multicamera techniques, but even here the film world is starting to copy it, with certain scenes now being simultaneously shot with two cameras so as to get the mid shot and the close-up at the same time.

SEE also: MULTICAMERA VERSUS SINGLE CAMERA

Family Tree:	Screen acting
Branch:	Shooting and acting
Twig:	**FILM VERSUS TELEVISION**

Forgetting Lines

Make it a positive.

Forgetting lines is not always a bad thing in rehearsal; in fact, it can be a really useful clue from you to you. As long as you have spent some time learning the lines, then you know them, and you are not so much forgetting the lines as choosing not to remember them.

And why would you so choose? Well, that is the interesting bit, for if you assume that there is always a **good** reason for forgetting lines, then you can use this moment to refresh a part, to go to the core, because the lines going from your head means something is not right. Either those particular lines do not fit the character you have created (so it is a note that you should change the character) or the lines conflict with something inside you, and this is a note for you to sort out those thoughts and those reasons why the lines refused to come out.

Drying or losing your lines during a performance is the actor's nightmare! It is a rare actor who has never dried (completely forgotten what to say next). Let us deal with the reason first. It could be that you did not have enough time to learn the lines thoroughly and there is simply too much to cram in. So if you know that the rehearsal period is extremely short and you have the script in advance, do not hesitate to start learning your lines. There is no substitute for learning them early.

Do not make the excuse, which is somewhat old-fashioned nowadays, that you cannot learn your lines until you have begun rehearsals and got your moves. Another excuse is that the script might be changed once the director has made certain production decisions, or he is still working on the final draft: anything to avoid the appalling task of committing lines to memory. Well, just imagine that moment in the future when you are standing onstage—and **nothing!** It's that moment in the dream when you are standing in the wings, you hear your cue, and you have no idea what your first line is. You wake up wondering why on earth you had not learned your lines: you wasted time day after day. Were you just hoping you would know them?

Let us suppose you are onstage in front of the audience and you dry. There might be a prompter in the wings who will bang out the line for you. There might be a fellow actor who happens to know what you should say next and whispers it to you. You might be able to improvise enough to get yourself out of the scrape, but if none of these aide-mémoirs are available, something will occur to somebody and the play **will** continue, but **whew!** Hot-making moments such as this will leave you a gibbering wreck, and the chances are you will not dry so badly ever again. One little trick is to write down a difficult word on a handy prop or even on the palm of your hand. Another trick is to make a word association in your mind. Another is to use the alphabet and use it to remember lists, for example.

The Actor Says:

I was playing once in three-weekly repertory and dried badly on the second Saturday matinee. There was total silence, everyone, including me, froze. After what seemed like two hours (but was probably about five seconds) I came out with a mouthful of totally unintelligible gibberish. We draw a veil over the next few moments as the other actors tried desperately to cope with this ridiculous situation. I had no more trouble with this line during our final week until the last Saturday matinee when I dried again in exactly the same place—but this time I had the key word inked onto my palm.

Another device is the time-honored practice of having pages of your script in different parts of the set, hidden in books, or even taped up on the invisible side of the scenery.

The Director Says:

A very tall actor friend confessed to me that when in previews for a musical, the lyrics for his song were changed at the last moment, so he wrote them on the stage. In performance he found that, not wearing his glasses, he couldn't read them standing up, and so sank to his knees for the words of the new verse. The director congratulated him on a very interesting interpretation, and I suspect in the same circumstances I would have done the same. We directors love actors who come up with interesting innovative bits of business.

In this day and age, theatres often have no place for a prompter, and actors have to cope whichever way they can if the lines go. There is an increasing use, especially by older actors, of the earpiece by which an offstage person can say the lines into a microphone for the actor to repeat on stage.

SEE also: LEARNING LINES

First Family Tree:	Rehearsing
Branch:	Mistakes
Twig:	**FORGETTING LINES**

Second Family Tree:	Performing
Branch:	Problems
Twig:	**FORGETTING LINES**

Further Training

Should you go to classes and workshops?

Once you are a professional actor, that is, once you have actually been paid to do some acting, you then have the problem of keeping your abilities and talents finely tuned. A lot of actors go in for further training, which is admirable, if they genuinely want to improve their skills. They can expand their knowledge and experience by training in areas that they are not sure about, such as screen acting or radio work.

What is not so useful is when actors take further training as a substitute. Receiving a fee to act for a paying audience is the real thing, so when actors pay to take further training and use this to act for other trainees, it might not be so beneficial to their acting. They run the risk of getting sucked into a mutual support system, where actors sit around and talk about each other's acting. This soon changes into their acting to please their fellow actors, or worse still to please their tutor.

The Director Says:

Watching students at the Actors Studio in New York doing everything in order to get good reviews from their fellow actors, I suspected a lot of the exercises and experiences the actors went through to prepare their roles were more to do with being able to boast about them in the feedback session afterwards, rather than a genuine exploration of creating the character. Excellent work comes out of that environment, but it also has its share of self-indulgent acting as well.

A lot of acting teachers do fine work with their students, of course, but never forget that there is a charge, and so some teachers have a wish for you to continue training with them for their own benefit, not necessarily yours. Running acting classes is, after all, a business.

136

Actors are not guiltless, because some of them sign up for wonderful courses but have no desire to learn from their distinguished teachers. They just want to be able to put the famous names on a resume, as if they had worked for them professionally.

Classes are a wonderful way to improve and to keep you in touch with the industry, but you should not get stuck too long on one phase or get into a situation where you have to spend months or years trying to achieve some mythical level of acting nirvana.

Family Tree:	Training
Branch:	**FURTHER TRAINING**
Twigs:	Radio acting; Screen acting

Gear Changes

A very valuable tool.

When does your character change? There must be moments when a new piece of information is learned, a new situation develops, or your character comes to a new conclusion. These are moments of gear change, and yet actors often find ways of staying the same, of being consistent.

In rehearsal and performance it is often possible to justify a character's staying the same after one such moment, but it is very disappointing to the audience if it happens that way. The moments of gear change are the interesting moments, the ones when the audience can see and experience something happening.

Instead of hiding the changes, relish them, indulge in them, **share** them with the audience with great happiness, whether it is a large moment on stage where every last member of the audience can understand that something wonderful has happened or a big moment on screen when the audience can sense that an idea has occurred to the face on screen, that a reaction has registered in a clear and unambiguous way.

A criticism is often given that the audience can "see the wheels turning round." This is perhaps the very reason that people have come to see the performance—so that they **can** experience all the changes. The criticism probably means that the actor has insufficiently motivated the gear changes, and so he appears obvious and untrue rather than as giving a believable sequence of thoughts following from the current situation.

Never come onstage with an attitude already taken, with an expression already on your face. Enter and then let the audience see the changes within you as your thoughts change. All the great playwrights do this, so stop to think out what gear changes you can share with your audience that your author has prepared for you.

This is even more true of screen acting, where the tiny changes in your face to show changes of thought are just what delights audience members, as they feel privileged to observe secret information about what your character is thinking. In a close-up do not start with an attitude or emotion but let it grow on you as you speak (Jack Nicholson is an absolute master at this technique), so the audience can travel with you on your emotional journey.

SEE also: SCREEN REACTIONS

In real life, whenever a change happens, people tend to change their physical attitude: the office manager who removes his spectacles just before telling you he is letting you go; the friend who drops his shoulders and hangs his head before confessing to having cheated you; the stranger who uncrosses her legs before indicating she would like to get to know you better. It happens in real life all the time—make sure it happens in your acting life as well.

SEE also: CONSISTENCY

First Family Tree:	Homework
Branch:	Text
Twig:	**GEAR CHANGES**

Second Family Tree:	Rehearsing
Branch:	Technique
Twig:	**GEAR CHANGES**
Leaf:	Example: Anna Christie and her dad

Getting Work

Buckle down, keep at it— don't wait for that phone call.

Getting work is a job in itself, and you should put time aside each week to work on this aspect of your career. When starting out, and well into your career, never assume that other people in the entertainment industry know who you are. Make contact with casting directors particularly, because they hold the key and open the doors for most work either on the screen or on the stage. Most theatres these days employ people to help with the casting; maybe they get in a freelancer for that one particular show, so getting yourself known to all the well-known casting directors is essential.

The Actor Says:
I was given a good piece of advice some years ago, and that was to send out regular postcards to casting directors. This means that they don't have to open a letter but see immediately that you are actively keeping in touch and updating them with your details or latest credits. I have also found that printing my name at the top of the card and attaching a sticker photograph plus a short message and my agent's telephone number keeps it short and businesslike. I also try to think of something witty or topical, as well as informative, which might raise a smile and brighten their day. I have been known to send up to two hundred cards at a time, resulting in an immediate increase in interviews, and very often one job!

So much of the work you will get depends on luck and on their thinking of you just when the job comes up, so that card could arrive at exactly one of those moments. It **has** happened.

Which photograph should you send out: the large one to casting directors or the small one on your postcards? From your session with your photographer, you have a number of pictures from which to make your final selection. Most actors will choose up to seven or eight different shots in varying poses and changes of clothes, and so forth, but you will probably end up using only one or two as your favorites. You will put one photograph in any actors' directory you have access to, and it is a good plan to use the other as a contrast to send out to people.

Things are rapidly changing since the Internet came into being. For one thing, the old-fashioned process of personally sending large photographs to all and sundry is not only unnecessary but also a terribly costly business. The good thing is that an agent can send instant pictures to a casting director who has a printout on her desk when you turn up for the interview. In fact, your photographer can take an image of you and put it through the computer to your agent, who can make comments on it before any decision is taken to print it. It reduces the number of prints enormously, because you will have been able to make adjustments and choices on the spot.

SEE also: PHOTOGRAPHS

Keep in contact with those people who you know like your work, especially those who trained with you and who might have gone on to be writers, directors, producers—even **casting directors.** That friendly contact over the years can pay dividends. It is a very **bad** idea to call them on the telephone, especially at home, unless you know them extremely well and can regard them as a friend. Who knows what they might be doing the moment you call?

Make up your own database where you can record who has seen you in what, who has interviewed you when, and whom you wrote to. You should carefully record whenever a casting director has sent you for a job (and what the result was, if you got called back, and so forth), so you will have a record of which casting directors know that you can at least get to the stage of being considered. These will be the ones you will regularly keep in contact with. Your database will allow you to give any new agent a complete list of all your personal contacts, for her to exploit as well as she can.

We recommend you make regular theatre and cinema visits—it is surprising how many actors don't find this interesting—for not only do you see some extraordinary acting from which to learn but you will be seen as being interested in the current acting world and be able to discuss all the latest performances with your interviewer when going for your next job. Find the financial means somehow. It is part of the "Getting work" process.

Some people hate to go round backstage after a show, especially if they have not particularly enjoyed it, but the actors **in** the show love it (as a rule), so do make the effort. No need to stay long, but the actors will appreciate the time you took and who knows what other people you might bump into? Again, do not be pushy, but **be seen.**

If, of course, you hated the show, there is no point in going round, unless you have a very close friend in it; then it is **essential.** Your friend really needs to see you. Having braved it backstage on such an occasion, there are several favorite expressions—such as "Congratulations!"; "How about **you,** then?"; "It was lovely to see you on stage"—that can be used to cover your embarrassment. Insulting other people is not the wisest choice of words at this stage, no matter how ghastly you thought the set, direction, or music, because you cannot be sure who is listening at the keyhole or who will be told of your comments; just stick to praising your friend.

SEE also: FELLOW ACTORS

It is not always financially possible to throw dinner parties on a lavish scale, but having little groups round for drinks with nibbles from time to time should not be beyond your pocket. These are the ideal occasions to include friends who are also part of the job network. If you do this on a regular basis, then you will (surely) be invited out, too. Do not push too hard in any direction, but just be sociable.

The Director Says:

*At a party or get-together, don't ignore us directors. At one such gathering, a drunk observer wondered if I didn't despise all those actors making an effort to say hello to me. The reply was easy—if I didn't want actors to approach me, I wouldn't go to such parties! Don't hog our attention, though; make sure that we know you are there, and then let **us** decide if we want to talk to you further or not. Nothing is worse when, being unemployed oneself, a pushy out-of-work actor angles for work from you.*

Family Tree:	**GETTING WORK**
Branches:	Agents; Auditions; Casting directors; It's not what it used to be; Typecasting

Good and Bad Taste

Do you have it?

Throughout this book we are urging you to let go, to try new things, to give your inner instincts full reign, and now we come to this topic, where we will ask you to hold back. Is this a contradiction? No, there **is** such a thing as good taste.

Something done with bad taste is something done just for effect or to shock, annoy, or just get a belly laugh. It is rooted not in the character or situation but in the wish to be noticed or to be personally appreciated. So really, bad taste is just bad acting. These are moments that stand out as chosen by the person playing the role, rather than something his character would want and need to do, and they come across as bad taste.

SEE also: OVER THE TOP

The Actor Says:

I was working with an actor on Angelo's "What's this? what's this?" speech from Measure for Measure *and at the beginning he just clutched his crotch—crude and not very funny—but when I got him to glance downwards,* **maybe** *looking at the floor or* **maybe** *looking at the bulge in his trousers, it was both believable and funny.*

SEE also: SEX AND VIOLENCE

Just as there is a difference on the screen between the full bloody violence in all its gore and shots that imply the violence without indulging in it, so in acting there is a difference between being completely explicit, which allows for only one interpretation, and being implicit, which allows the audience members to create some of their own images and ideas.

143

In other words, a double entendre (that is, it has another quite clean meaning) would be in good taste, but a single one (with only one crude meaning) would be in bad taste.

SEE also: EXAMPLE: MR. HORNER IS EXACTLY THAT and SHAKESPEARE: WORDPLAY

First Family Tree:	Homework
Branch:	Instinct versus intellect
Twig:	**GOOD AND BAD TASTE**

Second Family Tree:	Performing
Branch:	Audience
Twig:	**GOOD AND BAD TASTE**

Hierarchy

Beware: there are different sorts.

There are two hierarchies that you will immediately come across: the hierarchy of stardom (or at least of being quite well-known) and the hierarchy of the importance of the part you are playing (you will get to the third hierarchy of money when more established in the profession). Both these will affect the way you are treated and the degree of importance that the others will attach to your comments.

The first hierarchy is the one we all know—how we all stand around and laugh at whatever the star says and notice how the project revolves around whatever she wants. The audience has come to see that particular luminous body—or will be coming to the local multiplex to do so—and it is only right and natural that she should get all the attention.

The problem arises if your part is actually larger than that of the star or is even an important part to play in the project. Do not be surprised to find one morning that your best lines and bits of business have mysteriously gone over to the better-known actor. Do not be surprised to find that a scene that was all about you gets rewritten to be all about—you've guessed. This is the way of the money world.

SEE also: STARS

The other hierarchy has to do with your role in the piece, and if it is a subservient one, such as a maid (a short one?), do not be surprised if the other actors take on their character's personalities and order you to get the coffees at break time. Do not be hurt if your suggestions are treated as less important than those given by the lady of the manor, even though her role might in fact be less important than yours.

The last hierarchy has to do with money, and here it gets tricky. Because many actors demand that their agents get them top dollars, and it is possible for only one person to achieve that, it has been known for the management to negotiate with the actors in a certain order, so at the time they can promise one actor top salary, just before granting it to another one a little while later. It is of course common practice to pay male actors more than female actors, as it is common practice (and rightly so) for them to make a fuss about it. Keeping silent on what you are paid is usually only to the advantage of the management.

The Actor Says:

*I was asked to take over the part of "Mrs. Silly Cuckoo" in a children's stage show. The original actor was **better known** to the potential audience than I was, so the management decided not to change the billing outside the theatre. The joke was that my bird costume and huge beak meant that no one could tell the difference—although there was certainly a difference in our salaries. It could have been anyone inside there, but they felt they needed the better-known name on the credits.*

SEE also: PRODUCERS

First Family Tree:	Getting work
Branch:	It's not what it used to be
Twig:	Money is probably the answer
Leaf:	**HIERARCHY**

Second Family Tree:	The Team
Branch:	Fellow actors
Twig:	**HIERARCHY**

Homework

Private study is your secret weapon.

There is an old theatrical saying: the best part of any job is the moment you get it; from then on it's downhill all the way. To prevent this from happening to you, make sure you are fully prepared for the rehearsals, and **that** means doing your homework. Many actors waste the time before the job begins, fondly imagining that it will all come out right in the rehearsal period (if there is one), and arrive at the theatre or on set shockingly unprepared.

The Director Says:

I was recently directing a feature film, where one of the characters had to play an imaginary guitar. Imagine my surprise when he did it really badly for the camera rehearsal, and when I inquired, it turned out that he did not know how to play a guitar. He had had the script for months, but had made no effort to learn or practice guitar playing. When asked why, he said he had assumed someone would tell him if he needed tuition on guitar playing. I wonder if I will ever use him again?

You can never do too much homework, as you will not know what is required of you until you start work, and by then it will be too late to learn that accent, ride that horse, drive that truck, whatever. Get yourself ready for whatever skill the profession might demand from you, and get good at it **before** it is needed. Becoming more skillful is a very acceptable and enjoyable way of spending your time when not acting. And research into the background of the part, the period, and the people will give you a great store of knowledge to feed on during your homework.

At the 2003 Academy Awards ceremony, Peter O'Toole, who had been nominated seven times in previous years, was awarded an Honorary Oscar. During the montage of his films showing on the screen he said,

> *I've never talked about acting in my life **but**, any good actor will tell you that the common denominator is **private study** for months, if necessary, so every nuance, every phrase is considered and thought out well in advance.*

There speaks a man who knows!

The Actor Says:

When working privately in my own home, I put the other characters in imaginary places as if onstage. I was quite certain that all actors did this, so I was surprised when I came across an actor who found this an almost impossible thing to do. She was going over her part with me, and couldn't play to another character unless someone was actually standing there, so restricting herself to just going over her lines before rehearsals began.

Privately acting out your possible moves, working out your business, and even timing your laughs are very much the usual ways of preparing for a role.

SEE also: EXAMPLE: ANNA CHRISTIE AND HER DAD and EXAMPLE: LADY BRACKNELL'S HANDBAG and EXAMPLE: NOËL COWARD ON THE PHONE

Family Tree:	**HOMEWORK**
Branches:	Instinct versus intellect; Journey; Movement and gestures; Style; Text; Voice

Illness

What it (and being pregnant) means to an actor.

All illnesses are accidental, or all illnesses are chosen by the recipient. Which do you want to believe in?

We believe that our bodies will often speak to us through our illnesses, so if an illness (or even an accident) incapacitates you, always work out what it is you are prevented from doing by this illness or accident. Then spend some happy hours pretending to yourself that that is in fact what your body wanted, otherwise it would not have got ill (or had that accident).

The Director Says:
Directing As You Like It *abroad, the actor playing Rosalind started to lose her voice in the week before opening, and I realized that I had not been treating her as the star the way the locals would (as a Brit I had been unaware of the significance of her previous credits). Heaps of praise and attention turned out to be the best medicine, and her voice rang out loud and clear on the first night.*

You will find over time, weird as it might sound, that most of your illnesses do in fact contribute to your well-being by preventing you from doing certain things, even though at the time you were devastated by not being able to take up that job, travel out to that other city, or meet up with that person. And even if it is all indeed an accident, by pretending it is what your body wanted, you will be able to extract good from what might otherwise have been a bad situation.

Always listen to your body, and take a rest when it tells you to. As an artist you have, as your raw materials, a voice and a body to work with. Look after them the way a musician would look after her Stradivarius, for there is no replacement possible. This effort can influence things such as whether you should continue smoking, for example, when you will need your voice and lungs for a good many years, and need them to be flexible and capable of whatever demands might be made of you in the future.

Technically, being pregnant is not being ill, but it does change you, and not just in enlarging ways. Pregnant actors tend to greatly reduce the risks they take in preparing a performance, especially in rehearsal, and although this is understandable, it can be worrying to the production team if they were relying on the usual up-front performance. If acting when pregnant, then, realize that this could be an influence, and be careful not to let the instinct for reduced risk-taking affect your normally sparkling acting.

First Family Tree:	Rehearsing
Branch:	Mistakes
Twig:	**ILLNESS**

Second Family Tree:	The Team
Branch:	You (your other life)
Twig:	Rejection
Leaf:	**ILLNESS**

Improvisation

Having fun (but not always rehearsing the play).

"Let's do an Improv!" goes the cry, and the actors hurry to their places, looking forward to losing themselves in their work and having an enjoyable time. Improvisations can be a wonderful part of preparing a role, as long as you are clear what you are doing and what you want from it.

Not all actors are equally good at it, or even enjoy it. Some only really blossom at it when they are in front of an audience and have to improvise lines to cover a mistake (often not their own) that needs to be compensated for if the audience is not to lose the plot.

The Director Says:

A quick tip here—don't do this in a Shakespeare play. I have had a whole production grind to an embarrassing halt, when one actor was a bit late coming onstage, the other actor then thought he would do a brilliant cover up by asking "Where hast thou been?" and the oncoming actor then completely lost it as he tried to improvise an answer—in iambic pentameters! No—if you have a prompter, use the prompter!

Improvisations are used so much in training that it is important to remember that they are not always the necessary thing in professional work, where the time would probably be better spent in rehearsing the play. The important parts of preparation, such as working out moves, planning bits of business, and making sure that there are no bits of the play that are still vague and not nailed down, are the sorts of things an actor often wishes he had done when faced with a dress rehearsal for which he feels unprepared.

Make sure then that acting out the minute details of a whole day in your character's life will have visible results in your ultimate performance.

The Director Says Again:

I trained in a Method school in America, and came back to the United Kingdom with a whole armory of devices—improvisations to help the company relate well with each other, improvisations to establish the family unit, etc. It did not take me long to realize that professional working actors already did those things that my improvisations were designed to do—it was only amateur actors and trainee actors who really needed them.

The danger with using your own words is precisely that you will get a character and attitude from them, and then have to apply these to the author's words. This can work very well indeed with modern contemporary plays but falls down the further you move away from modern language to that of people fifty, one hundred, or of course four hundred years ago. Again, be careful that you attach your performance to the words and that the discoveries and ideas you get from the improvisations are not imposed on the written character but used to reveal extra insights into it. Remember—you can't improvise someone cleverer or wittier than you are! That is why improvisation techniques do not work so well on classic texts.

The rehearsal time is precious, and as long as each moment is a creative one pushing onward to the final result, then all will be well. Finding out why this particular improvisation is being done will enable you to make sure it contributes to your creating the very best character you can for your potential audience.

Creating a whole play out of improvisations is a very well-established technique, giving good results. It is noticeable, however, that if you write down all that is said, even in the most successful improvisation, only about a quarter of the words will finally make it to the end product; in other words, it is a very unpressured type of acting.

And what of shows that are entirely improvised in front of the audience? Magic, if they are genuinely doing that and not just picking out those ideas to do that match what they already know they can do. Improvisations are powerful tools, and when well used they can be really valuable, but you have to know when to use them and when not.

Often in work outside professional acting, such as role-play, which demands a performance from you, the very art of improvisation comes into its own. The actor is expected to master a brief, make certain points, and still come across as truthful and believable. The actor who prepares well, and first and foremost does what is required by the exercise and then adds his own slant and quirks, will be the person who gets reemployed, which is a very good way to pay the bills **and** stay tuned in to the world of performing.

Improvisation—a wonderful tool if used in the right place but a potential distraction from the job in hand in the wrong place.

First Family Tree:	Rehearsing
Branch:	**IMPROVISATION**
Twig:	Role-play

Second Family Tree:	Style
Branch:	Modern contemporary acting
Twig:	Method acting
Leaf:	**IMPROVISATION**

Instinct versus Intellect

The battle of the senses!

There are some actors who achieve great results purely by instinct, and others who approach a part with intellectual discussion and endless debate, bringing scholastic knowledge and background research to the rehearsal process. Each actor, in her own way, can produce a wonderful performance, and there is no universally accepted better way to approach a part. The intellectual can be accused of time wasting by the instinctive actor, but the audience will probably have no idea how each actor had approached her part, and even if they did, (in all probability) will not care!

Trust your instinct! How often is that heard in the rehearsal room and in the studio? If you feel like doing it, then do it, particularly if you think of something silly to do. There is always a danger that your intellect will be over-eager to prevent you from doing something interesting. Conversely, if you feel, instinctively, that something is wrong, fight your corner, but be very tactful in the way you do this.

SEE also: WHATEVER WORKS

Everyone has a little gremlin on their shoulder that tells them not to do things: "Do not take a risk, do not go out on a limb, do not do what your heart tells you to do—be logical." Actors have to learn to get rid of their gremlin, or at least not listen to its seductive whine of safety and boredom. It is often better to do what your heart, your instinct, tells you to do than listen to the gremlin of logic, your intellect.

And what happens if your instinct is wrong, and it does not work? Congratulate yourself, for the next time in these circumstances your instinct will be all the better, having learned from this experience. If you rely only on your intellect, it could be wrong for you time after time.

Conversely, if you are an actor who cannot deliver a quality performance without detailed background knowledge and research, then be undaunted in striving for this. It is not really instinct or intellect—it is whatever is appropriate for you.

The Director Says:

Working at the Royal Shakespeare Company, I was able to observe the time they had two actors alternating in a major role. When it came to working on a new scene, one of the actors would leave the room whilst the other went in for an impressive analysis and discussion with the director. He would then act the scene. The other actor was summoned, who then acted the scene purely from instinct. Each was happy with his own individual approach, and each got equally good notices on his opening night.

SEE also: TEN-SECOND RULE

First Family Tree:	Homework
Branch:	**INSTINCT VERSUS INTELLECT**
Twigs:	Don't give up; Good and bad taste

Second Family Tree:	Rehearsing
Branch:	Thinking
Twig:	**INSTINCT VERSUS INTELLECT**

Interviews

How to give the right impression.

Remember that in these meetings, not only are your prospective employers interviewing you, they also are worrying about how you think **they** are coming across. The first rule then is to spend time and energy admiring and appreciating the performance that **they** are giving. It will also allow you to pick up why it is that they have called you in, and therefore you will know which bits of your image you can augment and make more effective.

Stage

Interviews for stage productions are not frequent events.

This refers to meetings that do not include either your reading of the script or your getting up and presenting a prepared piece, which probably means that the director already knows you, either personally or by reputation. It can occasionally happen in the theatre, and so you should be properly prepared.

Obviously, the way you come across is paramount in such a situation. Also, the way you look now is important, for the director might have worked with or seen you in the past and will want to know if you look like the same person he remembers. He might want to judge whether you will get on well with the rest of the cast or with the very awkward star that will be part of the production.

SEE also: KNOW YOUR IMAGE

Give them a hand and help them find out more about you. Tell an anecdote or a story; entertain them with a joke. Because the whole point of the meeting is for them to get to know how you come across, make sure that you come across well.

Screen

Often screen productions are cast by interview only.

Some actors, when they get very grand, will refuse to read for a part but will allow themselves to be interviewed. Sometimes the part you are up for will have very little dialogue, so the director will cast by the results of an interview, rather than have you read the odd word or two.

An interview, as opposed to an audition, will probably last longer, and you will be expected to talk about the work you have done. Maybe a few anecdotes will go down well, if they show your storytelling skills and comedic timing to an advantage. Try practicing your anecdotes in advance, remembering that overenthusiasm can be off-putting and boring, so just stick to what you do best.

SEE also: BE YOURSELF (PLUS!) and TYPECASTING

Try to do some of the work of the interviewer yourself—you see, they do not really want to know the intimate details of your life; they just want to get a sense of who and what you are. Instead of letting them do all the slog of asking questions, initiate some story of your own, take over the reins (if it seems appropriate), so that they can relax, and maybe grab a cup of coffee while you do your job of allowing them to get to know a bit more about you and the way you come across.

First Family Tree:	Getting work
Branch:	Auditions
Twig:	**INTERVIEWS**
Leaf:	Anecdotes and jokes

Second Family Tree:	Screen acting
Branch:	Auditions
Twig:	**INTERVIEWS**
Leaf:	Anecdotes and jokes

It's Not What It Used To Be

This is for those returning to the industry and finding it strange.

Many a time and oft, a gnarled actor has been heard bemoaning the changes in the industry with this familiar phrase: "It's not what it used to be." Well, of course it isn't—it never was. That is to say, the industry has always changed. Each generation of actors thinks it had a better time (whatever that means) when it was young and starting out. That is because the actors were optimistic and, dare one say, innocent in the face of overwhelming odds against making it (whatever **that** means).

Just think about what the changes have been since professional acting began. First acting was in open air and daylight, then indoors by candlelight, then brighter gas light, then electric light, which was so bright that the actors could no longer see the audience, who were then sitting in darkness. Imagine the difference **that** made to the actors. A long period of more stable acting during the first half of the twentieth century was interrupted by the introduction of silent pictures and then, even more worrying for a stage actor, talking pictures. The industry changed here quite dramatically, because actors had to adapt their techniques to the screen while still working in the theatre.

Then came **television!** The film industry went into something of a decline at this time, and the industry became much more split between those who mainly did television and those who stayed in the theatre. Television was blamed for the closure of theatres around the country as audiences stayed at home to watch their favorite, more well-known actors rather than support their regular ones at the local playhouse. With commercial television came new and lucrative work in TV commercials and voice-overs. This, in some measure, made up for the lack of theatre work for jobbing actors who did not need to be well-known at this time, and the subsequent commercials wanted for this new medium were a real boon to their lives and finances.

Before long, however, the stars of the theatre, film, and television realized that there was even more money to be made in commercials, and they abandoned their pride regarding being featured in advertising products and became stars through these very products. So, once again the jobbing actor found herself pushed out of another market.

Then animation took over, when producers realized that they could save even more money by not using actors at all! So the changes went on and continue today, with the use of electronic acting roles increasing all the time. Crowd scenes are mostly digitally created now; again even less work for actors working as extras.

If you look at the current Broadway listings, there is an enormous number of musicals being presented, which again means less work for the straight actor. With the star system and the demand for celebrity in theatre, there is now a situation where sports stars, weather announcers, and even ex-politicians appear in variety shows and extravaganzas of all kinds.

At each stage of every change, the older actors complain about the current conditions, referring back to some kind of golden age when it was better. Just remember, in fifty years time, someone will be calling today one such golden age. Assume therefore that you are living in the best of all possible worlds, and, like Dr. Pangloss, in Voltaire's *Candide* (musical by Leonard Bernstein), smile and look forward to each project and do not dwell in the misery of wanting to be back in the past.

SEE also: PERFORMING and STARTING OFF

First Family Tree:	Getting work
Branch:	**IT'S NOT WHAT IT USED TO BE**
Twigs:	Money is probably the answer; Never say no

Second Family Tree:	The Team
Branch:	Fellow actors
Twig:	**IT'S NOT WHAT IT USED TO BE**

Jobs Requiring Acting Skills

Well, at least you have an audience.

Other jobs, such as being a demonstrator, operating with market research, or being a tour guide, all require acting skills and can bring in a tidy income as well. They are a wonderful way of getting in touch with entertaining an audience, especially if you have not been able to do the training you wished you had.

Many of the skills required for acting a role, such as remembering lines, observing character, having attention to detail, and so forth, can be used to full effect in these other jobs. A tour guide particularly has to memorize many things: the names of places and people and so forth. In market research, you could be called on to do some mystery shopping or to play the part of an ordinary customer in a restaurant with a few special demands, making a mental note of all the details of the meal and service and not be seen writing anything down.

You need to have very good communication skills and be able to speak in public and show an interest in people, finding out their likes and dislikes, even adapting your accent and personality to put people at ease.

As a demonstrator, you need to learn about the product you are displaying and be able to sell it. Projection and eye-to-eye contact with customers are all part of the job. And particularly, being entertaining will make you more effective in the area you are working on, and you will enjoy it all the more too.

In other words, these other jobs will have you playing a part with guidelines but not a set script—all good elements of performing that can only enhance your next real acting role. If you are worried that you find yourself spending more time in these jobs than in paid professional work—stop right there! This **is** paid professional work, and you are doing it.

First Family Tree: Training
Branch: No training
Twig: **JOBS REQUIRING ACTING SKILLS**

Second Family Tree: The Team
Branch: You (your other life)
Twig: **JOBS REQUIRING ACTING SKILLS**
Leaves: Role-play; Teaching acting

Journey

Never stay in the same place.

Always finish at a different destination from where you began.

This seems like such trite advice, but we have found over the years that the performances that do not quite work, that leave us unmoved or unsatisfied, are always those where the actors left their characters at the same place as when we met them at the beginning of the play or film. Ultimately then we are left wondering why we bothered to invest our emotional intensity and time if the actors have not taken us anywhere. It is very seductive for an actor to come round in a full circle, to give symmetry to the performance, but to audience members it can be very unsatisfactory.

The Director Says:

When I was still a stage technician, I was working on a West End musical and was at the rehearsal when the villains of the piece asked the director how they should behave during the finale, the wedding of the hero and heroine. They were told to be their usual selves, and so they were, being villainous and devious as they walked down the church aisle. All the critics came down on the show and blamed it for going nowhere, and for being in the end a pointless evening. I claim that had the director guided those actors better and made them contrite and sorry for their sins at the end—if they had in fact gone on a journey in the show—the critics and the audience would have been much more satisfied, and the rather short run could well have been much longer.

Scour your part looking for differences, research the part until you not only can take the character (and so the audience) on a wonderful journey but also can make each act of the play, each scene of the movie, even each speech, an obvious progression from where you started.

162

There are exceptions to this, where the character you are playing is the one constant, and it is by the interplay between your character and the others you meet on the way that is interesting to the audience, and where either the other characters or the audience goes on a journey through the piece you are acting in. But beware—always make sure that someone has traveled. It is usually better if that someone is you.

First Family Tree:	Homework
Branch:	**JOURNEY**
Twigs:	Consistency; Less is more?; Step-by-step

Second Family Tree:	Performing
Branch:	Audience
Twig:	**JOURNEY**
Leaf:	Consistency

Know Your Image

How you come across—or choose to come across.

Stand in front of a full-length mirror. Really study your appearance and try to imagine what sort of character someone would **pay** you to portray. What you are looking at is what you were born with, and that is that, plastic surgery excepted. Oh, there is also your parentage, breeding, education, and current lifestyle to consider, but basically it is in your genes. There is not a great deal you can do about this. You can change your way of speaking, to a certain extent; you can choose certain clothes to fit an occasion or audition; men can choose variations of facial hair; women can choose different hairstyles and heights of heels, **but** the basic package will remain the same through thick and thin, and going under the knife can only change the edges. So why not develop the expertise to play the image you see looking back at you, until you can do it better than anyone else? You will stand a better chance of being employed and earning a living as an actor.

Every day the clothes you put on, the makeup you do or do not apply, and the hairstyle or facial hair you choose all sit within an image of yourself that is very carefully chosen. As an actor, you need to read that image carefully and make sure that it is what you wish to present in your chosen profession. This is also a good foretaste of what to do when playing a role, when creating the precise and accurate image that that character will have.

SEE also: COSTUMES, WIGS, AND SHOES

This also relates to the theory of accidental clothes, which when applied to image goes like this: if you do not like the picture you are presenting, why on earth were those particular clothes just so handy for you to grab first thing in the morning, rather than the other clothes hanging in your closet that get only occasional visits to the open air?

164

It is all very clear: either accept that the image you accidentally have is carefully chosen (at least by your subconscious) or change it. Notice how at the start of each day, you gaze into the mirror and adjust your face until **you** arrive. Notice also how different you (or your loved ones) look when asleep, when you or they have no control over the image presented to the world.

Going for auditions these days often means going with the correct image, and that means although you cannot change the central message, you can change the trimmings. Prepare yourself as if you are doing the job that day. There are so many more actors, with fewer jobs available, that presenting the correct image for a role can be the difference between getting the job and seeing it go to someone else.

SEE also: AUDITIONS

First Family Tree:	Getting work
Branch:	Typecasting
Twig:	**KNOW YOUR IMAGE**
Leaf:	Attitude

Second Family Tree:	Screen acting
Branch:	Typecasting
Twig:	**KNOW YOUR IMAGE**

Laughter

The joy and the pain.

A really good play, even a tragedy, should have some light relief somewhere. Real life has humor in the most serious situations, so do not be afraid of producing a ripple of laughter in a straight play. Apart from anything else, the audience needs moments during any play to relax, relieve the tension, or change their position slightly. Some of the best moments are when the audience has just experienced this and is jolted back into a really moving situation that could even produce tears. Wonderful.

Comedies can be quite tricky, when getting laughs is part of the contract. Comedy technique comes so naturally to some people that timing a laugh is second nature, but even the greatest clown can be thrown by an audience's reaction (or nonreaction). If you do not get a laugh you expected to get, ask yourself, "Did I do anything different?" Then ask, "Did the audience hear the feed line clearly? Was the business the same as usual?" Never blame the audience; it simply cannot be its fault. If the feed line or even punch line is drowned with a cough, or even laughter, from the audience then of course it must be repeated—and you must make it look as if your character wants to do precisely that.

The Director Says:

I was redirecting a famous veteran actor in a prestigious production, when I found myself saying, "You are losing the laugh because you are trying to get it on the feed line; wait for the punch line." She drew herself up, and told me she had won an award for that very performance some years before. I could hardly believe what I was hearing myself saying: "Nevertheless, leave the laugh for the punch line." Well, she did—and the laugh returned, and I breathed a deep sigh of relief.

You have rehearsed your comedy until the original reactions you got at the read through or blocking from members of the cast or crew have long since faded, and you have almost forgotten where the big laughs might be. In performance they can come as something of a surprise, but you should be ready at all times for the ripple, chuckle, or belter and plan to ride the laugh. This simply means that without dialogue you must fill the moment naturally, with either a little business or a freeze position, as if your character has been taken by surprise and is not quite sure what to do next. It is vital to time your next line so that there is no silence before you speak, unless the script demands it, so you need to judge exactly the right moment; it is usually an instinctive feeling. Sometimes it is necessary to sacrifice a smaller laugh for the audience to get the fulfillment of a huge one.

There are variations galore, but whatever you do, do not utter essential dialogue during a laugh. Sometimes the laugh will be prolonged and can even increase as the moments tick by. It might be that further action produces more hilarity to the point that you need to shut them up (or the play will never get finished!). There are ways of dealing with this situation: you can give a physical indication that there is more to come; you can use extra volume on your next line; or you can start to speak, then when the laughter starts to die down you repeat the line. The main intention is to move the audience on to the next sequence of the play.

A genuine audience is one made up of people who do not know you personally and might not even know your work, so you have to win them over and entertain them from scratch without being able to bring any prior knowledge of your personality or skill onstage with you.

Famous or well-known actors have an easier time, because the audience members have an expectation of what they might see and hear before they come on. Acting class and off-off Broadway (fringe) audiences, alas, are largely made up of fellow students, tutors, friends, and relations; not always a perfect combination for a genuine reaction to your work.

Everyone needs practice of varying degrees in front of an audience, so if you feel the lack of this, then find an audience in other ways: try your hand at being a stand-up comedian, become good at telling anecdotes at parties, be a wittier waiter; anything that helps you develop your actor–audience relationship.

SEE also: BREAKING UP (CORPSING) and COMEDY AND FARCE

Family Tree:	Performing
Branch:	Audience
Twig:	**LAUGHTER**

Learning Lines

How to do the most necessary thing for an actor.

There are some actors who cannot learn any lines until they have blocked the play and can associate words with moves and motivation, and so on. That is luxury rehearsal time.

More often, actors are expected to turn up to a much shorter rehearsal period knowing their lines or being extremely familiar with them. In the case of screen work, of course, rehearsals are almost nonexistent, and private study is essential. So, with no help from the director you must do a lot of homework.

There is no substitute for getting on with it. Start as soon as you get the script. Know the lines so thoroughly that you could change anything should the writer or director insist. Do not go along with the concept that it is impossible to unlearn something. A professional should be able to cope with these small matters. Learn your lines so well (in screen work particularly) that you could start in the middle of a scene, at any line in the scene, without being thrown, and be prepared to go back to a previous scene you thought was in the can and be word perfect all over again.

So, how do you learn lines? Practice everything like mad and do not leave anything to the inspiration of the moment. An old actor told us that saying all his lines out loud three times every day quickly put them into his failing memory—"Put it on the tongue!" he exhorted us. A good method is to start with the long speeches first, which means that when you memorize the whole part you will be glad to have these stepping-stones under your belt.

Look at the text for clues, noticing how short or long the sentences are; this will help you when you memorize, as you will know whether you are embarking on a long or a short thought. There might be some words you do not know the meaning of, or some pronunciations to sort out, and there can be some difficult words or phrases you need to get your tongue around.

Learn the cues as part of your own lines. The last few words of another character's speech prepare you for your next line. Write out these last few words on a card, and write your next speech on the other side. You can then see the card and try to remember what is on the other side, or have a friend or partner hold up the card to you, where you can see the cue and they can see and prompt you in what you ought to say.

There might be times when you have to cover for others' errors, if they cut an important sentence or phrase that you need to hear to make sense of the next thing you say. This is when a familiarity with their lines helps a great deal. This applies only to the theatre, of course, because any error when filming can be corrected in a retake.

When you say the words out loud, you might hear alliterations and assonances that the eye hasn't spotted. This helps you to learn the lines, as you now have connections between words and between thoughts.

Get someone to hear your lines when you are familiar with them—partners are good for this. If you can't remember a line, ask your partner to give you a hint rather than tell you the forgotten words. Word association is a very useful aide-mémoire. Find a connection between a word in the cue line and what you say in response, a word that begins with the same letter, for example, or a word with a similar meaning. If nothing obvious occurs immediately, you can always fall back on repetition.

Some actors find that writing out their lines in their own handwriting helps to get them into their brains; others find that reading the part into a tape recorder (or getting someone else to do this) and playing it in the car during regular journeys is a useful way to get better acquainted with their words.

Highlighting your lines is very popular because you can see, at a glance, how much you are involved in each scene. Highlight all your moves and business as well, maybe in a color different from the lines you speak, making sure you have covered every bit of the script where you are involved, because it can bring an episodic screen drama into some form of logic. Rather than highlighting each word, some people simply put a mark by the name of their character at the top of each speech. Make a note of your moves or business with a pencil, because these can change quite often during rehearsal and you'll need to erase these at times.

SEE also: FORGETTING LINES

Do not be misled by taking the situation of the scene as a starting point and imagining how you would react in those circumstances. You might then find that the lines do not necessarily fit, and you will wonder why you cannot learn them easily. You will start blaming the play, the writer, and even your lack of technique, but chances are you have started from the wrong end. Take the character from the lines, and learning the lines will then be so much easier.

Only when your lines are fully memorized can you have the true freedom to create and to act.

First Family Tree:	Homework
Branch:	Text
Twig:	**LEARNING LINES**
Second Family Tree:	Rehearsing
Branch:	Rehearsals (long, short, or none)
Twig:	**LEARNING LINES**

Less Is More?

This could not be more wrong!

This phrase has become something of a mantra, often recited at training establishments and in acting classes. What it means is that if you do gestures and expressions and words simultaneously, the audience will be confused and not quite get what you are trying to convey.

Unfortunately, it is taken to mean that you should be selective in your acting and cut it all down to only one thing. This will indeed be clearer to the audience than something muddled up with many other things, but there is an alternative.

When you study great acting, whether it is on the screen or on a stage, ask yourself if that performer is doing less or more for the audience than a less-esteemed actor does. If you watch closely, you will see that she is doing more; lots more. That is why she is so great, because she can communicate more to her audience than other performers can. In computer terms, you could say that she is sending out more bytes of information than they do.

So many actors are restricted by this saying, yet the real truth is that less is less, and more is more. Have a look at Al Pacino and Robert De Nero in their first face-to-face screen meeting in the movie *Heat*. Watch how much they do, and if you want a comparison, see the same scene done by two less well-known actors in *L.A. Takedown*, Michael Mann's first version of this movie (made for television). The difference between the two versions is astounding: with Michael Mann as the producer, director, and writer for both movies, the famous actors do a huge amount **more** than those who originated the scene. This is food for thought indeed.

Always remind yourself that there might be an opportunity at any moment to do more for your audience members, for they are (aren't they?) the ones you are acting for. Try to find a positive way of acting a negative thought. For example, don't act "not speaking" by simply not speaking but make as if to speak and then decide not to, so the audience understand that your silence is chosen.

SEE also: ACTING: WHAT IS IT? and OVER THE TOP

The reason "Less is more" has taken root is that in training situations there are, naturally, some performers who are not yet skilled at what they do, or even some performers who turn out not to be very talented, and some of their choices are not so good. It looks better to the teacher if they make these wrong acting choices smaller, or reduce the number of them, for that makes the scene work a little better, but it does not improve the acting. No, here is your life belt:

Less is less and more is more, so do more and do it well!

(The exception to this is speaking in a close-up for the screen where you must use less volume, but do a lot more with your expressions.)

First Family Tree:	Homework
Branch:	Journey
Twig:	**LESS IS MORE?**
Leaf:	Example: Anna Christie and her dad

Second Family Tree:	Performing
Branch:	Technique
Twig:	**LESS IS MORE?**
Leaf:	Example: Al and Bob's first meeting

Let the Words Do the Work

They are there to help you.

Writers spend hours agonizing over the use of a particular word or a particular form of punctuation. Respect their craft, and start off by rigorously trying to create your character from the words on the page. Remember, they are the only really true thing you know about your part, and excessive acting outside the lines you are given can often confuse the message of the script. It is your job to create the character that wants and needs to say those words.

Instead of trying to impose on the lines things you think should be there, dig into the words to see where **they** want to take you. One of the most exciting places to be is where the words act you, rather than your just saying the words. The text is after all the main spine of your performance, and everything else hangs from it and is controlled by it.

Because it is recommended that you study your lines very thoroughly, it helps if you can isolate your dialogue from the other characters. Just write down or type out your own lines. It is surprising how much clearer your character will seem when separated from what other people are saying.

Try to find clues within your lines to build up your character. Any little thing that could indicate your attitude, attributes, appearance, habits, or hobbies can be usefully used. Find props that indicate some of these things. If it comes from the words, then it will be believable. If there really is not a great deal there, then that could be the message: there is nothing there. Maybe your character is really boring (there is a lot you can do with that!). But the chances are that the deeper you look into the words the more you will find.

The Director Says:

I was lecturing in the Cooper Union Great Hall in New York, where Abraham Lincoln gave a memorable address, and made the point that if he was letting the words do the work, then the repetition of the word "people" would have made him

174

*say his famous quote thus: "of the **people**, by the __people__, for the **PEOPLE**" with
a nice build to the final "people." To my amazement, a woman in the audience
stood up and said one of her direct ancestors had heard the Gettysburg address at
firsthand, and the way I had just spoken was in fact the way Lincoln had said
it, as opposed to the modern way of building the stresses on the first word of each
phrase: "**of** the people, __by__ the people, **FOR** the people."*

The master craftsman of putting clues into the language and helping
the actor with characterization by the choice of words was Mr. Shakespeare
himself. Even though the examples we are using are from his plays, the
techniques can just as easily be applied to modern scripts, especially those
techniques that deal with the differences between complicated and simple
language, and all the wordplay. A modern play, a soap opera script, or the
words you have to say in a commercial will all be enhanced by applying the
principles that those actors at the Globe did all those years ago.

SEE also: OUTSIDE-IN VERSUS INSIDE-OUT and SHAKESPEARE: SIMPLE OR
COMPLICATED and TEXT

First Family Tree:	Homework
Branch:	Text
Twig:	**LET THE WORDS DO THE WORK**
Leaves:	Example: Brother and sister act; Example: Lady Bracknell's handbag; Example: Valuable verbals; Example: You, thee—and the gold
Second Family Tree:	Style
Branch:	Shakespeare acting
Twig:	Shakespeare: Wordplay
Leaf:	**LET THE WORDS DO THE WORK**

Medieval Acting

What is needed for this?

In those far off days, plays were performed on little stages, on pageant wagons out in the open, that had no room for scenery and that provided just a platform for the actors to talk to the audience. The whole play was therefore played out front, with the characters making a direct link between the simple religious and social points of the play and the lives of the audience members standing out front and to the sides of the performing area.

To play those texts this way today makes them come alive in a wonderful way, which works even better when the audience and actors share the same light, so that there is not a *them and us* situation that most modern theatres have but just *us and us*.

The reality onstage is not that Noah is talking to his wife, but that the audience members are watching two actors presenting aspects of a husband–wife scene, to be shared and commented on equally by the audience and actors.

In approaching such a play, then, by understanding how the characters were meant to be played and that the relationship between the actors and audience was a very personal one, you will be able to get a handle on how to play them today. Of course, the production style will be decided by the director, but within that, you will now know how to fit your acting choices into the director's framework as illuminated by the original intent and thoughts of all those years ago.

Family Tree:	Style
Branch:	**MEDIEVAL ACTING**
Twig:	Example: Mr. and Mrs. Noah fight

Melodrama Acting

Is it anything more than wearing a top hat, waving your arms, and talking out front?

At the time of the Industrial Revolution, thousands of farmworkers made their way from the countryside to the factories in town and provided a captive audience for the entrepreneurs of the day. They built huge theatres to accommodate this new audience and lit them at first with candlelight, then with gas. Even then, the interiors were very dim, and it was extremely difficult to see anything more than broad gestures, which is the truth that this style came up with.

To convey emotion and attitude to the far reaches of the auditorium, the actors had to make large gestures, as their faces were very difficult to see. Just as in ballet certain gestures and movements came to be acknowledged as meaning certain emotions, so in the theatre of melodrama particular gestures were associated with specific emotions, as you can see in the finale to *A Tale of Mystery*.

It is no accident that the plays of the time featured heroes who came from the country, and the villains (all those big twirling moustaches and black cloaks) were dressed in exactly the same way as the factory owners. The audience of factory workers could easily recognize whom to cheer for and whom to boo and hiss.

In Britain the traders and colonists were appropriating large parts of the globe, and to justify the belief that the British deserved to rule so much of the world, their natural poet Shakespeare was elevated to heroic heights, and the rest of the world was introduced to, and made to study and watch, his plays. In the melodrama theatres these productions attracted big sets, elaborate costumes, and large numbers of extras, and the theatrical spectaculars became more important than the words.

You can say that modern musicals are in the tradition of the old melodramas, as they are done in huge theatres, and the body language (in this case, in the choreography) is an important addition to the words. Naturally, all song and dance routines are done out front to the audience—no worry about the fourth wall here—and this too is very similar to the way *Murder in the Red Barn*, and other similar favorites of the nineteenth century, would have been performed. Our current theatre is related to, and can draw lessons from, even the most corny of those old productions.

SEE also: MOVEMENT AND GESTURES

Family Tree:	Style
Branch:	**MELODRAMA ACTING**
Twig:	Example: Signs of the times

Method Acting

Why is it so argued about?

A major change happened to the world of theatre and acting at the end of the nineteenth century. Up to that point, acting had either taken place in the open air or been in theatres where the lighting—candles at first, and then gas—meant that the actors could always see their audience. Even when the theatres greatly increased in size, it was still possible to see beyond the gas footlights to a large part of the auditorium, which had to be kept lit, as the gas houselights could be turned down but not out. The change was the introduction of electric light, which simultaneously allowed the actors to be lit much brighter and the houselights to be turned out to put the audience in the dark. The famous fourth wall was created.

With the fourth wall came naturalism, and the world of acting had entered a new phase. Instead of the actors speaking out front to the audience, they now would speak to each other, and there was a need for an outside observer to give advice as to what looked real. This was the beginning of the rise of the ever more powerful director.

Because the criterion was now realism, the old-fashioned bombastic style of acting was no longer appropriate to the new style of plays being written. The Russian director Stanislavski devised a whole set of ideas and exercises, based on personal experiences and sense memory. His system or method of acting applied to the then-current melodramatic style of acting and led to the great successes of his productions, especially of plays by Chekhov.

Unfortunately, his method of acting, when not applied to an already overblown form of acting, is a different thing altogether and became known as the Method when realized and practiced in the United States. The irony is that Stanislavski thought that his technique should not be exported, as he said to his friend when talking about his famous book *An Actor Prepares*. He suggested that his friend should not take the Method to the United

States, as the education, psychology, mentality—even the food—was different there. He told his friend that the book *An Actor Prepares* was needed to open up actors in Russia, but it was not applicable to the United States where the actors were already free. If they were to use such a method, they would unnecessarily spy on themselves.

Method acting is a wonderful technique to help nonactors get reasonable performances and to enrich talented actors' work. In the American university system, where it is essential to teach Acting 101 in a way that allows hard work to be rewarded with high grades (even though the talent might not be there), the Method comes to the fore. With its insistence on written biographies and copious research, with scripts needing to be broken down into units or beats, it is easy to see on the page who should get the better grade. On the stage, the talent is not subjected to such scrutiny, and indeed performances are not capable of being graded in a logical way.

SEE also: CONSERVATORIES AND DRAMA SCHOOLS

Method acting is a very, very useful technique that goes wrong when its proponents elevate its ideas into an almost religious belief, to claim that successful acting must or must not do certain things or be prepared in a particular way. It certainly gets its students to feel a lot more confident about themselves and the part they are playing, and such students will appear to be giving a better performance, but there are **many** different paths to excellence.

We are not going further into the techniques of Method acting here, as there are a lot of wonderful books out there already on the subject. The topics in this book are, perhaps, the answer to the *musts* of the Method with the quiet but firm reply of our own life belt:

Whatever works.

SEE also: ACTING: WHAT IS IT? and OUTSIDE-IN VERSUS INSIDE-OUT and WHATEVER WORKS

First Family Tree:	Rehearsing
Branch:	Rehearsals (long, short, or none)
Twig:	**METHOD ACTING**

Second Family Tree:	Style
Branch:	Modern contemporary acting
Twig:	**METHOD ACTING**
Leaves:	Blowing your nose; Improvisation

Mistakes

How an apparent error
can be a very positive thing.

Maybe there is no such thing as a mistake. Yes, you read it correctly: no such thing. What happened is what happened—and **that** is very interesting.

Words forgotten, or even mispronounced, are helpful tools for you to see where you need to rethink a moment or adjust a performance. If they do not come out right, it means the ideas being expressed are not sitting comfortably with the character you have created, or with yourself. It could be that your understanding of the character or situation is wrong, and that is useful to know. It could be that there is something wrong with your fellow actors' feed lines to you, and that is also useful to know.

There must be a reason why you screwed up, and instead of spending your energies splashing around begging forgiveness, spend a little time instead on wondering why it was that your brain came up with those differences or why you forgot those lines. You will be surprised just how often there is a good, not bad, reason why you did what you did. There could be a hidden idea that is submerged inside you struggling to get out, and it emerges as a mistake; this is very useful to know.

The Director Says:

*Sometimes actors complain that the director is not watching them—that he has his head stuck in the script. Yes—I admit it—we are making a careful comparison between what the actors **ought** to be saying, and what they actually are coming up with. This tells us a lot about them, about where their conflicts lie, and how to help them.*

*I started life as a physicist, and quickly learned that no experiment goes wrong: what happens is what happens, and if it is not what I expected—well **that** is interesting and worth exploring further.*

The Actor Says:

I was once rehearsing onstage, and we all thought the director was carefully following the script, when it became apparent he was fast asleep. The action ground to a halt, and we all tiptoed out for a coffee, so as not to disturb him.

If something is wrong, assume it is your fault (even if it is not). This forces you to examine your performance in detail, and it now means that you are the right person in the right place to do something about it (and it might even have been your fault anyway; for example, not feeding a line correctly to someone, who then forgets his).

Particularly notice if you come up with something weird or completely inappropriate, because even though it might be ridiculous, it might also be a major insight into presenting that scene. At the very least, keep a record of your major mistakes: you never know when you will detect a useful pattern that can unlock future problems.

SEE also: PROBLEMS

Family Tree:	Rehearsing
Branch:	**MISTAKES**
Twigs:	Don't give up; Forgetting lines; Illness; Punctuality

Modern Contemporary Acting

This is a style like any other form of acting.

You are so close to it that you probably see modern acting as a truthful reflection of real life. You have to look back only to the 1950s, when a brand-new form of reality acting (Method) burst on the world, which was declared to be the most truthful form of acting ever to be seen and everyone should emulate it. It is now known as a period form of acting, the 1950s mumble style, and modern actors have moved on from there—as they will one day from what at this moment is considered to be truthful but will one day be regarded as the early twenty-first-century style. Style is only a response to the type of theatre everyone goes to, the type of play that is popular, the type of theatre the audience sits in (or screen that the audience watches), and the political and social conditions of the society in which everyone lives at that time, whether it is early log cabin America or modern skyscraper life.

The performance the audience sees is always seen through the prism of current expectations, so because all audiences now watch more screen work than theatre work, theatre acting has adjusted itself to be closer to that of film. It is now almost standard to have microphones amplifying what the actors are saying, and certainly it is now standard to have microphones on all the performers in a musical.

As the demands of the contemporary world vary, with domestic television sets now having stereo sound and everyone soon having wide screens and surround sound, will the next innovation be a three-dimensional screen as standard? If this happens, it will change what the audiences see of actors, and in turn will adjust what they deem to be realistic.

The Actor Says:

I was working with an old actor, who as his party piece would deliver some of Romeo's speeches in the manner that he delivered them as a young actor in the 1930s. We all laughed at his old-fashioned, hammy acting—until he pulled out an old, yellowed review, which talked of his "modern approach and completely natural style of acting." Well it was—to a 1930s audience.

So you in your turn will find your precious natural acting deemed old-fashioned by the youngsters in the future.

To notice what is going on, and to be able to adjust constantly, is part of the skill of an actor who always wishes to be contemporary.

Family Tree:	Style
Branch:	**MODERN CONTEMPORARY ACTING**
Twigs:	Method acting; Outside-in versus inside-out; Radio acting; Screen acting

Money Is Probably
the Answer

The ultimate answer to the question "Why?"
(And a solution.)

When the question is "Why?"—"Why did I lose that job?" or "Why did they cancel my contract?" or even "Why don't they treat us better?"—the answer is usually the same: **money!**

Money can thwart you in all sorts of ways, from someone else's willingness to work for a smaller salary to one of the project's financier's decision that her protégé will be so much better in the role than you. Your part can be downgraded from a speaking role to that of an extra, as the production team struggles to save enough money from the existing budget to allow the director to use that extra-large crane that she has decided is so essential to a particular sequence.

The terrible conditions imposed on you, from inadequate catering to inappropriate costumes to shooting far too much in one day, can be laid at the door of money, for those on the production team will reluctantly admit to you that they have only two options: to accept what they know to be an awful budget or not to do the project at all.

The only weapon you have is this magic life belt:

The fairness technique: ask that it be fair.

Agree with what they propose, but make sure they know that you consider it unfair. People **hate** being considered unfair and will often change conditions, improving them for you, to avoid this label being put around their neck. Why should you pretend that a terrible decision for you is quite all right? Why should you happily accept what is blatantly unfair? Do not complain or make yourself a nuisance, but let them know in the nicest possible way that the decision is one-sided in their favor.

The Director Says:

*I once worked for an outfit where my job was very variable, and they were not sure what my fee should be. I suggested they pay me at the end of the contract, when they and I would know how much work had been done, how many days I had been asked to work—even though my friends and colleagues advised strongly against this. At the end, I presented three folders labeled "Nice," "Fair," and "Rock Bottom," each containing an invoice, and told them they could open only one of the folders—and of course (after some hesitation) they picked the one labeled "Fair." No—they did **not** all have the same sum of money written inside them!*

SEE also: PRODUCERS

First Family Tree:	Getting work
Branch:	It's not what it used to be
Twig:	**MONEY IS PROBABLY THE ANSWER**
Leaves:	Hierarchy; Producers
Second Family Tree:	The Team
Branch:	You (your other life)
Twig:	Rejection
Leaf:	**MONEY IS PROBABLY THE ANSWER**

Movement and Gestures

Suit the action to the word, the word to the action. —Hamlet

Moving from different centers is a good way to develop different characterizations. Walk around as if all movement flows from your chest—the chest comes first. Then try it again walking from your nose, and then your knees. See how walking from these (and other) different centers of attention can make you behave differently; this is a good way to create a unique character. You can extend this by following someone on the street (discreetly, of course!) and trying to move in the same manner. See if you can find the center of the walk you are studying, the point in the body where it starts; as you go along experience how it changes your attitudes, and try to work out why the walk has developed that way.

A famous actor tells us that she can decide if people will look at her in the street as she walks by, or not. By holding herself in a certain way as she moves, her front will jiggle up and down, and she will get gasps of recognition; walking another way, and no one will give her a glance as she slouches by—she is either using her chest as a center of attention, or not.

The Actor Says:
I once heard a well-known English character actress say: "Choosing the right shoes and wearing them in rehearsal is crucial, for shoes will make you move differently, and that will make you act differently." Likewise, whenever I am cast as an old person who would not have great freedom of movement, I simply scrunch up my toes, as if trying to grip a pencil, and it makes me walk with some difficulty and gives the immediate impression of "age." I also find that the trick for playing a "drunk" is to walk as if you were desperately trying to appear "sober." So you don't walk "drunkenly," you try to walk in a straight line, and fail every now and again.

Another way of developing different patterns of movement is to copy an animal. Go to your local zoo and study the inmates carefully. Pick one animal, and try to walk in the same manner, and see how this different way of moving can give you a whole new set of attitudes and feelings. This, and walking from centers, are good examples of acting from the outside in—where the exterior situation feeds an internal discovery.

The Director Says:

I was auditioning in America once and an actor was using a speech from Richard II, playing the introspective king. He stormed about the stage, hunch-backed, hopping like a kangaroo and speaking with a clipped English accent. After his final line, he did a lot of business before he bounced offstage. This end sequence diluted the overall effect of his last few words, and I remembered what my directing tutor had told me all those years ago in Boston: "An entrance is to establish—take all the time you like; but with an exit, nothing should happen after your final line but the exit itself—so say it just before you leave the stage." When I asked the actor how he had come up with his bizarre interpretation, it turned out he had been coached by his father, who had mistaken the handsome ineffectual Richard the Second for the crook-backed scheming Richard the Third, as played by Laurence Olivier in the film.

Acting with your back can be tremendously effective, and letting your shoulders slump at an appropriate time can be a wonderful moment for you and your audience, as a body can sometimes be even more expressive than a face, especially in a large theatre.

Never walk backward! (Unless specifically called upon to do so.) This takes you away from the audience, and makes them feel as if you are rejecting them. Instead, walk forward in a circle to get yourself upstage to the required spot. If you **have** to move backward, then gesturing forward at the same time can take the curse off this moment of rejection.

Gestures themselves are very powerful, and there is a whole school of acting that uses what is termed the "psychological gesture." This breaks down into different types—the punch, the push, the poke, and the wringing gesture. Each of these generates different characteristics in you, and you can develop a complex gesture that sums up the part you are playing in one physical bit of business. This can be used in the performance, or at the very least done in the wings, or off-camera, to get you instantly into your character.

The Actor Says Again:

I was playing in a long West End run, and after a year there was a cast change. Because the management felt they had chanced upon a winning formula and did not want to alter anything, the "take-overs" were required to copy the performances of the original actors. I felt sorry that someone else was having to repeat all my gestures, for they came from my own instincts and rehearsal process. An example of this was when I was playing a "pert" maid and told by the mistress that there would be "eight for dinner." I asked the other actor to indicate "eight" with her fingers, and when I repeated the "eight" a few lines later with the same gesture, it got a big laugh. This moment belonged to me, and any take-over repeating this business would not have my pride of ownership, and therefore not necessarily be able to do it to the same effect.

Actors are sometimes accused of "illustrating," as if that were in itself a crime. Actually, we believe that illustrating is fine, it just goes wrong when it is done badly in an unmotivated way, and so sticks out. So here is your life jacket (Hamlet said it first in his own words at the head of this topic):

Illustrate to your heart's content—but make sure it is always believable.

Study paintings or photographs of the type of person you are to play. Notice carefully how they are sitting, how they hold their bodies, and what sort of gestures they make. If it is a period piece, get expert help as to exactly how your character would have sat in a chair, walked, or given a curtsey or bow. These outside details will give you new insights into the part, help to build up a character for you, and lead to a deeper and more satisfying performance.

SEE also: COSTUMES, WIGS, AND SHOES and STYLE

First Family Tree:	Homework
Branch:	**MOVEMENT AND GESTURES**
Twig:	Example: Signs of the times

Second Family Tree:	Rehearsing
Branch:	Technique
Twig:	Outside-in versus inside-out
Leaf:	**MOVEMENT AND GESTURES**

Multicamera versus Single Camera

Or what you do differently with more than one camera.

The continuous dramas on television—the soaps—must produce a lot of airtime each day. To do this, they have a studio where there are a lot of cameras. The actors are rehearsed with their moves while the director also rehearses where the cameras will go and puts it all down in a camera script (if he has not prepared the whole thing in advance). When it comes to shooting, the actors do their stuff, the cameras go to where they are told, and the director (usually in a separate booth) gets the cutter to change from one camera to another. The whole thing is recorded in one go, so in effect the director is editing as he goes along.

This allows a lot of material to be done at one time, but it has the disadvantage that the actors will not always know which camera is on them at which time and be able to adjust their performances accordingly. It is hard to gauge what size shot it is and to match the acting to the size of shot.

There are some simple techniques to learn. To know which camera is on you, keep an eye out for the red light (such a light on top of or in front of the camera indicates that this is the camera whose output is currently being used). If you see the red light almost in front of you, then it is likely to be a close shot of you, so you can make your acting choices accordingly. If you see the red light out of the corner of your eye, then it is probably shooting a wide shot of the scene from the side, so you can use your body language to help convey the thoughts and emotions. If you cannot see a red light at all, then it is probably behind you shooting over your shoulder to get a close shot of your fellow actor, so do not sway into the shot and block the camera's view of him.

Often the boom operator will bring the microphone in for a close shot (to get more intimate sound) and take it away for a wide shot, again to get the correct sound perspective. Either way, this information about size of shot can influence whether you will be using your small facial movements or your large arm gestures—and, of course, the level of voice you will be using.

A single camera shoot (whether for the small or the large screen) means that for each shot everyone knows what is being done, what the edges of the shot will be, and what is required for the shot. The actors will know that everyone, especially themselves, will be able to pour all their energy and creativity into this one setup, and then move on to the next one. The lighting will be precise, not the generalized lighting that a multicamera studio demands, and it will be possible to do it more than once for all but the most rushed shows.

SEE also: DON'T GIVE UP

Family Tree:	Screen acting
Branch:	Shooting and acting
Twig:	**MULTICAMERA VERSUS SINGLE CAMERA**

Never Say No

Say maybe.

The Director Says:

If I could go back in time, and give myself one piece of advice when I was starting out in this great industry—it would be "Never say no." Whenever I have out of hand rejected a person, a job, or an opportunity, I have regretted it. You don't like being rejected, do you? Well, neither does anyone else.

An actor once begged to be auditioned for the role of Portia, but once I cast her she announced she did not want to go out on the tour. She obviously just wanted to be cast, not do the job, and it was her privilege to say no. It was my privilege never to consider her again in the future (despite several pleadings for auditions).

If you are suddenly asked to do a job, train yourself to answer that you have something penciled in your diary, but you would love to learn more about the project. If it turns out that you really do not want to do it, then the penciled clash can become an unmovable obstacle—but you really hope they will ask for you again in the future. Because you have not rejected them, they well might come back to you with a project that you **do** want to do.

If the job turns out to be something you really want to do, then you can tell them that you are canceling your previous possible engagement, and that will make them feel even better about you than before.

If you are asked for a job that you have moral objections to, such as advertising cigarettes, then do not tell them you have moral objections, tell them you have a penciled clashing date, but that you really want to come and meet them anyway. You then can meet up with a new group of people that can help you in the future, and you are not rejecting the idea of working with them (and perhaps being put down as a potential troublemaker)

194

but you will not be able to do the job if it comes your way because, yes, the penciled date has become an immovable ink engagement, and one that you cannot change. But you are really glad to have met them and hope they will think of you in the future.

This might all seem childish, but it is simply treating other people with respect and not letting them know that you feel the work they are involved with is beneath you. It is a way of keeping people's dignity (after all, they probably know if it is a dubious job). In the East it is known simply as saving face, and it works well for them, and it will work well for you.

The Actor Says:
*At the end of an extremely successful season at a provincial repertory theatre, and working with an up-and-coming young director, I was offered a further two parts to follow on immediately. Although I had no work to go to, I was persuaded by my new agent (who wanted to get me into television—more money for him!) to leave. The two parts offered were ones I had played before with great success—I always feel that repeating a part is rather like stepping back into a wet bathing costume—and I didn't give them a good face-saving excuse, instead I just said, "No, thanks, I should return to London." How stupid can you be? I would probably have had a ball, **and** he never asked for me again, as he climbed to the heights of the directing ladder.*

SEE also: DON'T GIVE UP

First Family Tree:	Getting work
Branch:	It's not what it used to be
Twig:	**NEVER SAY NO**

Second Family Tree:	The Team
Branch:	You (your other life)
Twig:	Rejection
Leaf:	**NEVER SAY NO**

No Training

Not the barrier others think it is.

It is quite difficult to have no training whatsoever, because anyone venturing into the world of professional acting will almost certainly have attended some kind of class or instructive tuition. However, it is not absolutely necessary to spend a colossal amount of money on training at a drama school or spend a long time at a university.

It is possible to enter the profession without any formal training, but it is unlikely that you would even wish to become an actor unless you had experience of performing somewhere. Experience of actually standing up in front of an audience is the only way you will learn what or what not to do, never mind whether you actually have fun doing it. There is no substitute for experience when it comes to developing the breadth of technique required to be good enough to be paid to entertain an audience!

The problem is, where does that experience come from? This is where a year or so in a recognized drama school or good university theatre department comes in handy. If nothing else, you will get the chance to perform. Amateur dramatics is another opportunity, and of course there is the world of summer stock, summer festivals, and community theatres to find out if this is what you want to do with the rest of your life.

SEE also: AMATEUR DRAMATICS and FURTHER TRAINING

The same rules will apply whether or not you have trained. You will be cast as much for what you look like and how you come across as for your immediate talent. You might be given a job because of your ability to ride a horse, fire a machine gun, embroider—elements such as these can be the edge that gives the job to you and not to someone else. These special skills needed for the part can be more important to the producers and director than where you learned your acting.

There are many examples of very successful actors who did not arrive by way of the training route, and as long as they wish to improve and develop, they will be fine. It is useful to have been with a group of fellow actors, so that you can see that disasters and disappointments happen to everyone and that fate has not particularly picked you out for special treatment but that common sense will solve most problems, as will a reminder of the actor's mantra:

No one promised you fair!

You can, of course, still ask for fairness and make sure they know when it is not being applied.

SEE also: MONEY IS PROBABLY THE ANSWER

Family Tree:	Training
Branch:	**NO TRAINING**
Twigs:	Be yourself (plus!); Fellow actors; Jobs requiring acting skills

Notes

Friend or foe?

Actors like to get notes, for it means that what they did was noticed. Directors love to give notes; it is the one time that **they** are ensured an audience. This means that note sessions can sometimes go on for quite a long time (three hours is not unknown). And when a note is given, it is usually accompanied by a solution. Even if you disagree with the solution, it does not mean that the note is wrong—something must have caught the director's attention at that moment.

The fact of a note is important, the detail is not always so, and the actor's job is to do something different, with or without discussion or explanation.

The Director Says:

I learned a lot about giving notes when directing in South Korea. Since I did not speak Korean—and my actors certainly did not speak English—all communication had to be through the interpreter, and it soon became apparent that the usual notes and solutions would take far too long. I realized that with the two words for "no" and "yes" ("annio" and "ne"), I could direct far faster than when directing in English.

An actor would come into a scene, and I did not quite like what he did. I would say, "Annio!" and the actor—knowing something was wrong—repeated the moment in a different way. "Ne," I said, and the rehearsal went rapidly along, with me relieved of having to give explanations as to why I rejected one moment, and accepted another, and the actors being relieved of having to justify what it was they had come up with.

How you should respond to notes is worth considering here. It is an open session with the entire cast. Don't argue back, and don't give detailed reasons as to why you did something. It is better to avoid long discussions at this stage.

198

Take any criticism with good grace; a witty remark can be acceptable. Grab a pen, spontaneously, to jot down a note or two, but don't sit there with a pen poised over a foolscap notepad as if you are expecting a large number. The rest of the cast will probably think you're an enthusiastic nerd.

The Actor Says:

*I once got **all** the notes and no one else got any. It was in the break between the final dress rehearsal and the opening night. I don't know why all the director's spleen was vented upon me, but it concentrated my mind for the duration of the evening, after which the director came to me and told me he had ticked off each note as I had put them into practice, and had the grace to praise me for my courage. That's directors' notes for you.*

Actors feel really sad if the director leaves them out completely in a notes session. They then don't know whether the director thinks they are wonderful (it would have been nice to be told) or dreadful (which could be the reason for being ignored). There is a useful lifeline here:

If you get no notes, assume you are wonderful.

As directors always think that they can cure any problem and help any actor, you must believe that if you are receiving no notes, everything is fine. Not only is this realistic but also it will lead to your having a happier life. Remember that a good note (or no note) means you are fine at that moment in rehearsal and can well be expected to change and improve as the days go by.

SEE also: STEP-BY-STEP

Of course, there are always the odd exceptions.

The Actor Says Again:

Once near the start of my career, when I was playing a leading character role in a farce, the director gave me no notes at all throughout the rehearsals. On the opening night I very much enjoyed Act One, but then the bombshell was dropped. At the interval the director came into the dressing room that I was sharing with two others, and after praising them to the skies, he turned to me and said, "And as for you, I simply don't know how the audience is going to stand you for the rest of the play."

Shocked, I ran out of the room, went onto the empty stage, sat down, and thought about what he had said. Maybe I had peaked too early? So I calmed myself and decided to take my performance down in order to build to the climax at the end of the play. The wonderful audience response at my solo curtain call made me feel a lot better, and I was later told that this particular director was renowned for having a whipping boy, as it were, which was perhaps why he had decided to treat me that way.

Don't feel bad, then, if you get to be the whipping boy—it can be the luck of the draw—and you must not let it affect you badly. Also, don't feel insulted if the director gives you a line reading (telling you how to say a line). Just treat it like any other note—that is, something must be wrong, and to solve it you have been given a solution that might or might not be accurate, but you must do **something** about it.

Notes to or from fellow actors can be tricky. Suppose, for example, that a fellow actor is doing something in rehearsal you feel is totally wrong; it could be the way he is saying a particular line, perhaps he is putting the wrong emphasis on it. You are dying to say something, but would it be the right thing to do? If the other actor is senior to you, he might not take too kindly to your interference. It would be worth having a private word with the director, if (and only if) the line he is misreading affects your part in some way. Further than that you cannot go.

If however it is a junior actor, and you feel your experience would be appreciated, take him to one side and ask him if he would mind your commenting on one of his lines. He can always ask to be left alone, or he can ask for the note.

SEE also: FELLOW ACTORS and HIERARCHY

Conversely, the tables could be turned, and someone in the cast has a strong feeling that you are doing something against his instincts. He gives you a note, and although you feel your way is right, try seeing his point of view, because if he feels strongly enough to say something, the chances are that something is wrong. It is a delicate balance either way, but the professional approach is to exchange opinions to achieve a better result.

Then finally there are the notes you give to yourself. It is a very good idea to keep a journal of your productions and note down things learned or things to do in the future. Nothing is more annoying than making a mistake and realizing that it is not the first time you have done that, but you had forgotten to remember it. Rereading the journal every now and again can show you patterns of behavior that perhaps need to be dealt with sooner rather than later.

First Family Tree:	Rehearsing
Branch:	Rehearsals (long, short, or none)
Twig:	Directors
Leaf:	**NOTES**

Second Family Tree:	The Team
Branch:	Directors
Twig:	**NOTES**

Open Auditions

Theatre cattle calls.

These are not so common now, thank goodness! What a terrifying prospect they can be: going into a room and facing a director, producer, and assorted others. Whomever they are, you can be gripped by the cold, empty feeling of naked terror, and you can lose the will to live at this moment. So, how can you face this prospect with anything like a calm and relaxed delivery? You have rehearsed your pieces over and over again. You have been tutored and coached, and you have deliberated over the choice of two contrasting pieces. You are well prepared but you still feel as nervous as anything.

As always, put yourself in the auditioners' shoes. Wherever you come in the order of those being auditioned, they will be grateful for an entertaining performance. Give them something different in the way you act, something they will really want to watch—unpredictability is the key. It does not have to be slapstick comedy (heaven forbid) or histrionics, just a few unexpected gear changes that will make it interesting. It does not even have to be an unusual choice; after all, it is the different way you are playing it that will be noticeable, not doing something different in itself.

If by chance you are asked to do your piece again, try not to repeat it exactly, move for move. Use different gestures and business, to keep it fresh. The spontaneity will be noted and admired.

To whom do you perform? Imagine the auditioners are part of a full house. If you are performing a soliloquy (a piece where you are the only character on the stage), you will be speaking directly to the audience, so spread it around and include them from time to time with eye contact (but check with her first; some people out front hate to be addressed directly, others demand it). If you are playing a character who is onstage with others, you will need to address them from time to time, so make sure that you cheat yourself round front (with business or props) so the auditioners get a good look at you full on and not in a constant profile to the audience. If there are three or more characters in the scene, then place them, imaginarily, downstage left and right and you in the center. Allow yourself to move toward one or each of them to give yourself a little movement, depending, of course, on the content of the dialogue. Make it interesting and varied at all costs.

Do not go in for a long pause at the beginning as you get into character and mood. Crash in there as soon as the start button is pressed. A pause before you begin is the kiss of death, because it gives them time to think. Be bold; go for it; and above all, pretend that you have been in once already, done the audition, gone out, and thought you **could** have done better, so now, **do better.** Be pleased with what you did, and leave them thinking that they would like to see more. Then go home and forget all about it (as if you can!).

SEE also: LESS IS MORE? and OVER THE TOP

Family Tree:	Getting work
Branch:	Auditions
Twig:	**OPEN AUDITIONS**

Opposites

Always a useful device.

Acting opposites is a vital technique for producing the element of surprise for the audience. If the audience knows what is coming, the effect of it is deadened and it loses the intended impact.

A simple example from a drama might be opening a letter. The letter has arrived, and you have picked it up and taken in into the kitchen, where you sit down to open it. Let us suppose that in the letter you have been left a legacy that you had no idea about. Your reaction to the good news will be that bit more pointed (and actually easier to play) if you had chosen to be in quite a low key mood, playing that this could be a bill or something you are not particularly looking forward to.

But if you had been playing in a really on-top-of-the-world state before opening the letter, you have given yourself nowhere to go. It might seem very obvious, but you need to have some point of view at the top of the scene. Having a contrast is a good idea. The reverse would apply, of course, if you know the letter contains bad news, such as you did not pass the test or you have a nasty medical condition and need an operation. Then you could start the scene by finding a reason to be cheerful, so the change for being miserable (using the opposite) will be clearer to the audience, and better for you to act.

The same rule of opposites applies in all manners of acting situations—the unexpected guest, the unwanted proposal, the surprise party, and so forth—but there is one situation that is particularly tricky, and you probably have seen it a million times (particularly on-screen): a character enters a room and finds something he did not expect. How often have you, the audience, known in advance that the character was going to be surprised, and how often has the actor really been able to convince you that he did not know? You need to practice this sort of thing over and over again, but using opposites will always make the moment clearer and better.

The use of opposites is particularly useful in screen acting and in the reactions that are on your face that change just before you speak.

SEE also: EXAMPLE: AL AND BOB'S FIRST MEETING and SCREEN REACTIONS

First Family Tree:	Homework
Branch:	Text
Twig:	**OPPOSITES**
Leaf:	Example: Noël Coward on the phone

Second Family Tree:	Rehearsing
Branch:	Technique
Twig:	**OPPOSITES**

Outside-in versus Inside-out

The real gulf between the United States and Europe.

Why do the Brits, and other foreigners, get an unnaturally high number of Oscar or Tony nominations almost every year? It is not as if they are born better actors, yet for their small population compared with that of the United States, they receive a high proportion of the nominations. It is because the basis they use for acting is different.

Being sincere and experiencing the emotion does not always communicate. The musician André Previn related how he conducted a symphony immediately after hearing that a close friend had died, and he dedicated that performance to his friend's memory. He was convinced at the time that this had led to a powerful interpretation by him, but afterward, looking at a video, he was shocked to see that his emotions had got in the way of the interpretation, not helped it. The pianist and conductor Daniel Barenboim put it well when he said to his fellow musicians, "Your task is to convey the emotion, not to experience it." Wise words from the world of music that also apply to the world of acting.

If you start your acting preparation from the inner truths and thoughts of your character, then there is no doubt that you will be well prepared mentally when it comes to performing the role. The problem is that it is not always shared with the audience out front. There are those, especially those trained in the United States, who somehow feel that if the actor is not going through the correct thought processes, then the performance must be in error—yet there are many examples of fine performances that arise not from a study of the thoughts and emotions but from other roots: the roots of technique and instinct.

If you have to cry, for example, it can be a great help to remember a very sad moment in your life and to use this to generate sufficient emotion to lead (you hope) to real tears running down your face. All very satisfactory—but

206

there is another way to look at it. If you get tears running down your face (and this can be artificially done with water), then the tears can make you feel very sad indeed.

The question is, Do you cry because you are sad, or does the act of crying make you sad? You have perhaps noticed in your real life that you do not really break down with misery until the tears actually roll. This can be done artificially, using a tear stick, which stimulates the eyes into producing tears. Running water down your face to help generate the emotion is a very acceptable way to proceed (and a lot quicker as well). The outside factor (the tears) produces the inside emotion (the sadness).

This can well apply to other areas of acting, where we are sure you have come across the technique of finding a walk for your character, or a series of gestures, or even an animal image, and from that flows the characterization. Again, there is no shame or blame in starting work from the outside.

The Actor Says:

A friend was explaining to me that when some young members of the cast asked him what preparation he went through to be able to cry each night at a specific point, he told them he didn't do any. He just let the words work upon him—and in this case it was a Shakespearean father saying good-bye to his daughter: "For your sake (jewel)." Brabantio had just been using the intimate "thee" talking to Othello, but turned to his daughter and changed to the impersonal "your" followed by the tenderest compliment "jewel." These changes generated the emotion, and as he spoke to me and said the line, more tears immediately flowed down his face. Yet again the outside had spurred on a wonderful inside.

SEE also: LET THE WORDS DO THE WORK and SHAKESPEARE: WHAT YOU CALL PEOPLE

Really good acting flourishes when it has freedom within a framework, which can be that of an emotional inner reality that is wonderful for the performer but unfortunately is sometimes not always wonderful for the audience. Another framework is that of the text, the technical aspects of an appropriate accent, the period styles of movement, and the effects clothes have on a performance. This is more the basis of acting training outside the United States, and the reason why young actors cross the Atlantic in both ways in search of other pathways to good performances.

First Family Tree:	Rehearsing
Branch:	Technique
Twig:	**OUTSIDE-IN VERSUS INSIDE-OUT**
Leaves:	Blowing your nose: Movement and gestures

Second Family Tree:	Style
Branch:	Modern contemporary acting
Twig:	**OUTSIDE-IN VERSUS INSIDE-OUT**
Leaves:	Example: Plunging in the deep end; Ten-second rule

Over the Top

Your biggest fear does not exist.

There is no such thing. You heard right: there is no such thing—and before you shout us down, listen to this. Something that is good acting is good, and the bigger it is, the easier it is for the audience to see, understand, and enjoy. The smaller it is, the more risk there is of its not being seen or appreciated.

Something that is bad acting is always bad—but you only really notice it when it is big. Big good acting is admired—but big bad acting is immediately labeled as *over the top* (OTT) and condemned for its size and scale, when in fact the fault lies not in its size but in the fact that it was just bad acting.

The Director Says:

*I tried an experiment over a number of years with graduate acting students, when I gave them a simple melodramatic speech (something from a murder-mystery play usually), and made them do it as well as possible. I then asked them to do it "bigger"—and again, and again. Each time they did it bigger, I would ask for the next time to be bigger still. And here is the point—as long as they kept the truth and honesty in it—no one, I repeat **no one** in all those years, was ever able to go over the top. I would beg them, "Please, just this once, go over the top." And they would try, and they would fail, because OTT does not exist as a unit all by itself.*

So, in rehearsal in particular, there can be no such thing as going too far. Your scale might be inappropriate, but if you keep it all motivated and believable, all the director needs to ask you to do is take it down a little. Diving into the deep end is exhilarating for you and your director.

SEE also: BELIEVABILITY

A really great actor will always do those things that at first seem startling, but when she does them you realize that they come across as completely justified, completely truthful—and wildly interesting (never over the top). The less than great actor does those things that are expected of her, and although she can be wonderfully truthful and motivated, the audience members' eyes can start drifting off to the other performers or to the other sections of the screen to see if there is something even more interesting there than what is going on with the actor currently under the spotlight.

First Family Tree:	Getting work
Branch:	Auditions
Twig:	**OVER THE TOP**

Second Family Tree:	Performing
Branch:	Technique
Twig:	**OVER THE TOP**
Leaves:	Commitment; Example: Plunging in the deep end

Pauses

Use them sparingly.

Pauses are like money or gold: use them too much and they become devalued and lose their effect. Good actors will plan their pauses to be used at the most effective times, not just to bring attention to themselves. Why you do not speak is just as important and interesting as why you do, but it must be done for a very good acting reason.

Try to see where a pause could be replaced with a piece of business that can run together with the dialogue, for the audience will think the pause is the end of a speech and will start to look to see who is to speak next. Worst of all, they might think you have forgotten your lines. And if you are going to pause, make sure that something is happening in it, that it is an active pause, and not just a time when everything stops.

The Director Says:

When rehearsing a stage play, I will always do a run at which I ask the actors to cut out every pause, so that all we will hear out front is continuous talking. Even if it makes a nonsense of the script (someone has to exit before a line is spoken), they must do it for this rehearsal. Once launched into this, an extraordinary thing happens. A lot of the pauses that we all thought were necessary are not. At the end, I tell the actors that they can only get back a pause if they can make a good case for it—and many moments happen where, with business combined with text, the whole thing takes off wonderfully.

The Actor Says:

I find that these "cut the pauses rehearsals" are treated as "speed runs," and everyone talks faster than usual, with no thoughts behind the lines—which does not help at all.

Always check with your fellow actors about what you are doing, for what to you is a nice pause can be the very thing that kills your fellow actor's moment. If everyone pauses, the play as a whole can fail to hang together. At the very least, warn your fellow actors where you will be pausing, so they can plan for it. Good writers (such as Shakespeare and Pinter) tell you exactly where the pauses are, so you will have no need to add any more.

A good pause, well earned, should be full of audience expectation—not just an actor's internal indulgence.

First Family Tree:	Homework
Branch:	Text
Twig:	**PAUSES**

Second Family Tree:	Performing
Branch:	Audience
Twig:	**PAUSES**
Leaf:	Example: Princely business

Performing

The reason why you are an actor.

This is the main thing, the reason you became an actor—giving a performance on-screen or onstage. It was not to shine in classes, at workshops and seminars, or even at auditions. You became an actor to perform. Never forget that.

Professional acting is not about your enjoying yourself, although we hope you do so on most occasions. It is not about going through a significant emotional experience and coming out of it a better person (whatever that means). It simply is **being paid** to entertain an audience. Entertainment comes in many different forms, including of course serious events when you move the audience members to tears or make them think about profound issues. Strangely enough, the hardest forms to achieve are in comedy and farce, which is why they are covered in a separate topic.

SEE also: COMEDY AND FARCE

Anything that detracts from your performance must be a bad thing, and that means that to give too much of your concern to problems (for things are never as wonderful as you thought they were going to be), to uncooperative people, or to an inadequate script is to spend your energies unwisely. Do not allow the work you have done in preparation or rehearsal to be undone by any annoyance, however justified it might be.

There is another phenomenon to be countered, and that is the wish to use this performance as a stepping-stone to another one. You can sometimes spot the actor who is radiating that he is not really interested in this job, and he is only doing it while waiting for a better offer to come along. But he has accepted **this** part, and he should be putting all his energies and abilities into it (and that is of course the best way to be invited to do more work).

To consider a job as a stepping-stone to something else means that you will never really be there, as you hop from one stone to the next. Another way to look at it is to consider each job as an island that can be explored and lived in to the fullest. You might well be able to jump to another island, which again you can (and should) explore extensively and maybe stay a long while. In the case of certain soap operas, you might stay there for the rest of your working life. Live where you are; don't spend your precious acting time dreaming of being somewhere else.

However arduous the circumstances, find the ways of enjoying each experience. After all, you **are** acting, and acting has been your passion and ambition for years, hasn't it?

Family Tree: **PERFORMING**
Branches: Audience; Problems; Technique; Truth

Problems

How to deal with . . . whatever.

always be problems; in fact, there will never **be** a trouble-free
. Problems are the name of the game, so to get upset and let that
acting is completely unproductive.

e a particular problem too much prominence and drown in an
nisery will be to deny the very process of being an actor, which
ve and to create something that never existed before. For this to
is completely natural for there to be problems, and your job is to
in a positive and creative way, not to indulge in them, and let
np you.

irse it can be rather wonderful to have a tremendous problem, and
one know how horrible that problem is, but make sure you are not
e worry to appear more of a hero when you finally solve it.

tor Says:

nile when given a problem—partly to annoy those who rush so anx-
ve me the bad news, and want to see my explosion or collapse, but also
ving problems is what I do most of the day. When a new, really juicy
up—well, I will need to use more of my talents and abilities to solve
nile.

e well-known saying goes,

worry too much about today's problem—tomorrow's is already in
ail.

allow aggravations to affect you, otherwise all the wonderful
did in rehearsals will be destroyed and wasted.

Photographs

An essential for every actor's self advertisement.

A photographic session can be a hazardous, sometimes terrifying, experience. Some people approach it with dread; some with relish. The main
thing is to prepare for it so that you look and feel your best on the day. Not
easy, but there are a few essential things that need attending to. First of all
make absolutely sure you have the correct quote from your photographer
and you know exactly how much you are paying, including all finished
prints. Does it include touching up? Is it extra for matte or gloss? With or
without a border? Try to cover everything, so that you do not get that nasty
shock of extra expense. Let's face it, they cost enough as it is.

Especially for female actors, whatever you think you want your image
to be, you will be glad that you got your hair done! Seriously, try to arrange
an appointment with your favorite hairdresser in the morning and have
your session in the afternoon. Apply a light makeup base and mascara (no
heavy eye lines), and no dark lipstick. It all depends whether you want a
glamorous or natural look. Get expert advice, especially from your agent.
Take with you several tops and an assortment of earrings and so on, according to your taste and desired result.

Remember that the photographer is your employee. Do not let her make
all the decisions. Before you go, have some opinions about the effect you
want to achieve and the type you wish to portray, and do not be diverted.
Of course, her experiences of positioning will be useful, and whether you
are working outdoors or in a studio will alter many things. Lighting is her
province, but in our experience there are two things of paramount importance that you must insist on.

First is height: however tall you are, your photograph should reflect
it, not try to hide it or tell a different story. After all, when you walk
into the interview, the director will want to see an image as close to the

photograph as possible. Everyone accepts that hairstyles and color can change, men's facial hair can vary, and clothes tell their own story, but height will never change.

If the photographer shoots from below to take your picture, then the result gives the impression that you have a big, heavy frame. If you are sent for a job, and it turns out you are five-foot eight (or shorter), then the interview will not go well, for the impression would have been misleading to say the least. Please, do not cheat on your photograph, or you can find yourself in an unsuitable casting session. It will be a great disappointment, not to say annoyance, to your interviewer.

The Actor Says:

For example, I am four-foot eleven, and every character I play will be—well—short. So I arrange for my photographer to take at least 50 percent of my pictures with the camera above my eye line. Since I tend to have to look up to most people, that impression comes through in the picture, which gives the correct message that I am not very tall.

Second, do have some photographs taken with some teeth showing, even if you are not particularly proud of them. To have a set of photographs where 99 percent of them show a determinedly closed mouth is to have a set of photographs that does not allow you the full choice for different possibilities in the future, as well as makes it appear that you might have something to hide.

The Director Says:

I was looking for an actor to play a dying man, and the gaunt photograph led me to send for a particular actor. When he turned up, he also had a magnificent scar across his face—hidden in his picture, but a great addition to the image he was presenting, and I wished it had been in the photo. Another time I wanted a teenager with acne and had a tricky time trying to guess which photograph was hiding this blemish, so I could get someone with the right look.

When we look through an actor's directory, it is very noticeable that photographs have been glamorized and touched up or that the actors have used photos that are from a long time ago. This causes them to look much

younger than they now are, without the
parent in the interview.

If a director or casting director sends
photograph, then she will expect that look
up. If in real life your looks and persona
photograph, then the directors will be ann
time. On the other hand, if the very pers
world is you—the way you look, the way yo
question to ask is, Will they find you from
won't, have **you** chosen the right one to se

SEE also: RESUMES

First Family Tree:	Getting work
Branch:	Agents
Twig:	**PHOTOGRAPHS**

Second Family Tree:	Screen acting
Branch:	Auditions
Twig:	Casting directors
Leaf:	**PHOTOGRAPHS**

There wil
productio
affect you

To gi
agony of
is to impr
happen, i
solve the
them swa

Of cc
to let ever
inflating

The Dire

I always
iously to g
because so
one comes
it, so—I s

As t

Don'
the n

Don
work you

There is no magic wand waved over you when you leave a particular job, place, or training establishment. The same old problems will be waiting for you at your next stop—so solve them straight away, and take your solutions with you.

SEE also: MISTAKES

First Family Tree:	Performing
Branch:	**PROBLEMS**
Twigs:	Battle of the sexes; Breaking up (corpsing); Forgetting lines

Second Family Tree:	The Team
Branch:	You (your other life)
Twig:	Rejection
Leaf:	**PROBLEMS**

Producers

Their part in your career.

Producers control the purse strings, and because everyone lives in a money-based society, it means they have the power: the power to choose, to insist on, to cast, and to sack actors. This explains why everyone is very nice to them.

In an ideal world, the producer will pass on any of her thoughts to the director, who in turn will find ways of reinterpreting them to give to you, if they fit in with the overall structure and thought of the production. In an ideal world, that is.

In reality, producers have been known to take actors aside to give them their own private instructions, with or without the knowledge of the director. Because money is influence, producers feel that their opinions must be not only listened to but immediately obeyed as well. This often puts the actor into a difficult position, with two paymasters demanding different things.

The Actor Says:
I have known theatre producers on a first night sitting in the wings so they can give their notes to the actors the moment they come offstage—whilst the director is sitting out front waiting for the end of the performance before she gives her own notes.

In the world of screen, where the sums involved are so much larger, the influence and input of the producers are so much greater. It is quite common for anyone on the creative team, including the director, to be sacked on the spot if the producer's ideas are not put into action, and although this can seem draconian, many of the great successes in the film world have been as much the work of the producer as the director. Never forget that David Selznick, the producer of *Gone with the Wind,* had worked on, and approved, a color storyboard of every shot in the film **before** a director was

220

even contracted, and the one who started directing this fabulous epic was not the one who finished it (the one who got the Oscar!).

It is easy to make them into the villains, but without them, there would be no show, no film, and no one to employ us. They have to take the risks, endure all the aggravation, and then watch others take most of the glory and praise. It is only at celebrations such as the Oscars that you see and hear from a producer.

The Director Says:

I have worked with some wonderful producers, and some really horrible ones. The advantage of being in this industry as long as I have is that when you come across one of the unpleasant ones, it does not upset you. I was working with a truly awful specimen, and the rest of the crew wondered why I was not getting upset about it. I truthfully told them, "I have known worse."

SEE also: HIERARCHY

First Family Tree:	Getting work
Branch:	It's not what it used to be
Twig:	Money is probably the answer
Leaf:	**PRODUCERS**

Second Family Tree:	The Team
Branch:	**PRODUCERS**

Projection

How to make yourself heard.

Projection has nothing to do with being loud. There are actors who bellow their lines, and yet are hard to understand. There are other actors who barely raise their voice above a whisper, and yet everyone hears them, regardless of the size of theatre they are working in. So what is going on?

Projection is a technical term, which means you speak differently onstage than you do when speaking to a person in real life. The **real** difference is that you **want** the audience to share your thoughts, and so projection is really about sharing, not shouting.

Obviously, if you want to share your thoughts with someone sitting sixty feet away, without the benefit of a microphone, you will speak louder than if he were only five feet away. The point is that you concentrate on the wish to share, not on a technical raising of the voice.

Audiences also understand what you say by observing your lip shapes, and it can often be that a problem with hearing the actors is solved by increasing the lighting a little—if you cannot be seen, you often cannot be heard. At the very least, be aware of this, so that any really soft lines are accompanied by the audience's being able to see your mouth.

This can be a major solution to those difficult monologues, such as Firs' death speech, in Chekhov's *The Cherry Orchard*, where the character is dying and so should be speaking softly but the people at the back of the theatre want to hear what he is saying. By delivering the speech as a soliloquy directly to the audience members, you can ensure that they can see your lip shapes, and by directly addressing the audience they no longer wonder about how they can hear an ill man so clearly. This is what the author intended anyway, and it addresses the one truth of the whole evening, that there is an audience out there, that the actor knows it is there, and so talking to it is quite natural. (This practice has been used in all forms and ages of theatre.)

You very rarely have to project your voice for screen work—in fact, the opposite is usually true. Switch on your television right now and listen to the low level of speaking on all major performances in film and television dramas.

SEE also: SCREEN VOCAL LEVELS

First Family Tree:	Homework
Branch:	Voice
Twig:	**PROJECTION**
Second Family Tree:	Performing
Branch:	Technique
Twig:	**PROJECTION**

Properties (Props)

Your effective friends.

Some actors love props, and so should you, because you can reveal a lot about your character by the way you handle a particular prop and by the choice of which prop you have at hand. They also can be used to cheat your face or body round to give the audience the full benefit of what you are thinking.

Small props such as cigarettes, lighters, and ashtrays can seem like simple things on the surface, but a slightly shaky hand on the first night as you strike up can make you look like an amateur smoker. Make sure that the lighter works, and always have matches handy near the lighter, just in case. Check your personal props before the show and ensure that there is a drop of water in the ashtray so that your cigarette is properly extinguished when placed there. How often have you seen one start to smoulder again when the actor is in no position to put it out properly, for she might even have left the stage?

Books are wonderful props. Make sure that the page you have to refer to is clearly marked and the words that you must read have been inserted into the book, rather than relying on memorizing them. (It is advisable to learn them anyway, just in case the passage **is** missing or the lights fail.) Personal props such as notebooks, pens, pencils, spectacles, watches, hand-kerchiefs, and handbags are useful and are normal accessories, but always practice business with even the simplest of props and **always** check that they are there.

The Actor Says:

I was once onstage with some dozen characters when one of them had to produce a letter that solved the mystery and brought the play to a close. To his horror, when he reached into his pocket for the said letter it wasn't there. Another actor came to his rescue and made up the story with reasonable conviction, but after curtain down approached the offender with, "That'll teach you to check your personals."

I am sure from then on he always did, and the lesson learned went into my own memory banks.

Experienced actors will get their props, or close copies of them, into the rehearsal room as soon as possible, so that the intricate planning needed to use them can start at once. Things such as putting water into the teapot so you get used to how long it will take you to pour out four cups of tea will save agonies later on, when the reality of the play needs to be addressed.

In the film world, of course, the use of props is paramount in the endless problem of cheating your face round to camera, when either you or the director demands it. Whereas in the theatre you tend to hold a prop in the hand furthest away from the audience (so that there is no danger of it obscuring your face), for the screen you tend to hold it in the hand nearest the camera, so that by looking at your prop, you are bringing your face round to the camera.

Props on-screen need also to be cheated, that is, brought up into shot, much more than in real life or onstage. What might feel most uncomfortable with a cup or cigarette that is held within inches of your face will look natural and real when framed in a tight close-up.

Props also have to be very carefully used, so that the same prop is held in the same hand on the same syllable of a line, making sure that continuity will be maintained. Some actors try not to use props, so that they will not be bothered with lots of continuity notes; they stick their hands in their pockets and just stand there. This also leads to very boring and dull acting. A far better solution is to use props and use them well, both to bring your face round so that the camera can see and relish your expressions and to reveal some of your inner thoughts and attitudes.

Make screen props your friends!

SEE also: BUSINESS (BIZ)

First Family Tree:	Performing
Branch:	Technique
Twig:	**PROPERTIES (PROPS)**

Second Family Tree:	Screen acting
Branch:	Screen cheating
Twig:	**PROPERTIES (PROPS)**

Pulling Focus

Make sure you have their attention.

Have you ever been in the theatre and heard a voice but not immediately known which actor was speaking? This is the fault of the actor involved, whose job was to make sure that the audience is looking in the right direction at the right time.

Watching a scene like this, you sometimes miss, or only half hear, a line of dialogue, because you could not see who was speaking. This means that the speaker of the line did not pull focus beforehand. So, the golden lifesaving rule is as follows:

Look, move, speak.

Your cue is coming up; wait until the previous speaker is delivering the last word, look toward the area you want to address, and move a part of your body—a hand gesture might be enough or, if your line is particularly important, stand up or move toward someone (there are many options). It is your job to make sure the audience members know whose voice they are hearing, unless, of course, the author intends otherwise. The "look, move, speak" guideline should not be labored but done in one quick movement.

Of course, pulling focus when it is not the right time for the audience to look at you is called upstaging and is punished in the usual ways (in normal circumstances, that is).

The Actor Says:
I was watching a friend of mine in a play when I noticed that during what should have been his laugh line, an older actor had produced a green silk hand-kerchief from his pocket and was vigorously mopping his brow. When I asked my friend about the missed laugh he told me that because he had got a good laugh on

226

an earlier line, which he hadn't got before, the other actor felt that was one laugh too many and had purposely pulled the focus to himself to kill it. I could almost have understood the jealousy here, except that the handkerchief-waving actor had actually **written** *the play!*

Other actors onstage can and should help to pull focus to the speaker by aligning their bodies, giving them their eye line and making sure that the audience is looking in the right place.

SEE also: MOVEMENT AND GESTURES

You might hear the expression "pulling focus" when you are acting on-screen, but this time it means that the camera is going to change focus from one character to another.

Family Tree:	Performing
Branch:	Technique
Twig:	**PULLING FOCUS**

Punctuality

Commonsense courtesy.

There cannot be an actor in the world who has never been late on a single occasion, but in most cases it is usually a one-off, under extremely exceptional circumstances. Make sure that your apology for your lateness includes a really good excuse—and it does not actually have to be the truth. The more acceptable the reason, the quicker you will be forgiven.

The Actor Says:

*Thinking he had a free day during his film schedule, an actor friend of mine was out on the golf course and well on his way in the match, when he got an urgent message via his wife: "They're calling for you on the set!" Dropping everything and deserting his golf partner, he made a dash for the train, couldn't get a taxi and found himself panting by the roadside thumbing a lift. The driver of a passing ambulance recognized him from a long-running soap (in which he had played a **doctor**), and took him to the location. The crew, seeing the state of him, assumed that he had been involved in some sort of accident, rather than misreading his call sheet, so he decided to play along with the fiction, getting sympathy all day, instead of being castigated for his terrible unpunctuality.*

People will not praise you for being punctual, but reliability in this area will enhance your reputation. Those actors who turn up late with monotonous regularity will soon find job offers dwindling. There is nothing more annoying than lateness in others, when **you** have managed to be there on time. This discipline should be part of your job and be applied from training days onward.

On a shoot, of course, punctuality is even more important. When filming, you are at the mercy of many outside factors, not the least being the weather. Suppose the director is doing a two-handed scene outdoors and has just completed an over-the-shoulder shot of one person, with sun-shine-dappled scenery behind. As the camera is moved to do the opposite shot, the team notices that the sun is about to go behind a big black cloud that will last until the end of the day. Everyone rushes to their places, but halfway through the scene the sun goes in, and now the director has the problem that for one shot the person will have sunshine behind her head as she speaks and for the other shot there will be sun followed by shade.

And then the director remembers that the actor was thirty seconds late onto the set, and if she had been there on time, the team would just have got the shot in the can. If **only** the actor had been punctual, even down to a few seconds.

Because of experiences like these, most actors are good timekeepers, and this leads to their being in demand by employers in nonacting casual jobs, because they are punctual and honest about the hours worked. They certainly have a good reputation for turning up when they should.

First Family Tree:	Rehearsing
Branch:	Mistakes
Twig:	**PUNCTUALITY**

Second Family Tree:	Screen acting
Branch:	Shooting and acting
Twig:	**PUNCTUALITY**

Qualifications

Necessary—whatever they are.

Get as many of them as you can, particularly if they have nothing to do with acting. Study acting of course, but be aware that related courses, such as media studies, being rather generalized, will not help you in your career and will only take time away from when you might have been getting to grips with something like paralegal training (and so be able to pick up those nicely paid alternative jobs that actors must do).

There is a feeling out there (mistaken as it so happens) that if you devote yourself only to acting, the world will recognize this as a mark of determination. It turns out that you are only blinkered as to what really happens in this life.

First of all, the job of acting is one that many people wish to do, and so there are and always will be many more potential actors than there could ever be jobs. This means that when it comes down to choosing one actor over another, it is very rare that the decision is based on talent alone; the other factors come into play. An actor auditioning for a truck driver has a better chance if he has some slight experience driving heavy vehicles; an actor having to perform with kids will have a better chance if he has worked with or taught children in the past (or has lots of his own!).

Any qualification that can point you out as a slight specialist in a certain field can put you ahead of all the others who look like you and act like you but do not have your experiences and do not have your qualifications.

You will need to earn money as you walk the path of performing, and qualifications help to put you in line for jobs related to one of your interests, rather than your eating your artistic heart out doing some job stacking shelves that gives you no fulfillment at all, just a paycheck at the end of the week. It is not an accident that so many actors work as waiters; after all, is not presenting the menu and taking and giving the order some kind of performance? Waiting on tables can be a good way of supporting yourself when you are young, but beware—it does not seem such a good idea to a middle-aged actor.

The Actor Says:

Between leaving school (with no qualifications) and going to RADA, I spent five years doing office work for the Automobile Association, taking part in amateur dramatics in the evenings. I have always had a passion for maps and working out routes for people, but the AA insisted on my taking evening classes in shorthand and typing. Guess which skill had the greatest earning power? During a very lean period between acting jobs early in my career, I was able to take a fill-in job typing scripts for a big film company, which was absolutely fascinating and highly enjoyable.

Sort out something that you still enjoy doing and find fulfilling, so when you reach that age when the calls of family and security grow louder, and in fact you end up spending more time doing this than working as an actor (which nearly all the actors we know do), then at least you have the satisfaction of keeping your creative self alive and kicking, and ready for the big break when it comes.

These types of jobs are much sought after, so you need to train for them. At an early stage in your career, it is a very good plan to get the qualifications that will allow you this lifeline. If nothing else, it will please your parents, and encourage them to continue to support you as an actor!

First Family Tree:	Training
Branch:	University courses
Twig:	**QUALIFICATIONS**

Second Family Tree:	The Team
Branch:	You (your other life)
Twig:	**QUALIFICATIONS**

Radio Acting

And voice-overs and audio books.

Microphone technique requires a unique skill because it almost completely excludes physical business and facial expression. In other words, it is all in the voice.

The main advantage of radio is that you do not have to completely memorize your lines, but you do need to know them thoroughly. Without the advantage of facial expression, the vocal range of emotion needs to be fully explored. Accents and dialects are less convincing on radio if they are not authentic, and this will undoubtedly be reflected in the casting. Foreign accents are particularly noticeable if they are not the native tongue of the actor.

In radio drama you will usually get your script in good time, and you can mark it up as you like, bearing in mind that if you do have some dialogue at the bottom of the page, it might continue on the top of the next page. This means practicing turning the page as silently as possible, keeping it away from the microphone without your voice disappearing. Turning pages is difficult, so there is no discredit in asking for a music stand if you want one; it will hold three pages without overlapping. Some actors hold all their pages loose and some turn over pages that are stapled together, but now that cheaper paper is being used it is noisier.

People rarely go through their scenes with their fellow actors in the green room while waiting to record, or even talk about the script or their part in it, so be prepared to do all the homework yourself. Do not overprepare, as the line that you decide is the key to your character can well be cut. Beware of the midmorning tummy rumbles, and eat something at about 11:00 a.m. to ward them off.

You have a read through, and then you do what is known as rehearse–record in the studio. This will be done chronologically in relation to acoustics—whether indoors or outdoors. Because microphones have become more and more sensitive, you can have about five to six actors in a semicircle: everyone is on mike. If the director (or the producer in some U.K. radio) says you are slightly *off mike*, she means that your voice is not being picked up properly and you need to direct it more toward the microphone. You will always have a studio manager who will tell you the range of the mike. If there are crowd scenes in the drama, then all the cast members ("Omnes" in some scripts) will take part regardless of their main role, whether it is being massacred on the battlefield or being part of an angry mob screaming, "Burn the witch!" and so on.

Now that radio plays are recorded in stereophonic or quadraphonic sound, the actors will be given distinct moves and directions to place the characters according to the microphone geography. Sound levels, voice levels, and business with or without props will be worked out in rehearsal. It is always advisable to take some heavy-soled shoes with you—the director will probably suggest that in the covering letter—so that you can be heard walking. There will be a spot effects person, so you don't pour your own drink, although you might have to sip or gulp it on cue, so the assistant will hand you the cup or glass.

How do you appear to be eating and drinking when someone else is clinking knives and forks and wine glasses? It is all done with the voice, although some actors use bananas to help simulating eating, and some others prefer a very small piece of bread or cake. Kissing (alas) is done with the back of your own hand, but with modern stereophonic equipment, directors and actors are starting to make it the real thing; apparently they can tell the difference! Practice at home, so that you can act from a script while giving a convincing impression of stuffing yourself with a heavy meal or having a strenuous romantic encounter.

When talking to the director in the studio, don't fall into the novice habit of talking toward the booth where the director is actually sitting, but send all your messages into the mike. Paint the scene for the audience with your words, and remember that a silence can well help them imagine it. If you find a scene is a bit dead, see if doing some business (tidying a desk, plumping a cushion) will bring it alive.

Naturally, the voice is very important, and so is your breath. Practice breathing all over the microphone—cover the mike in breath. When entering a scene you approach the microphone normally, but when exiting you back away still facing the mike. If you have to walk on the spot, don't be surprised if you seem to have forgotten how to walk!

The running time is often very important. Obviously the production team will be responsible for the overall timing of the program, and each scene will be recorded separately. You can, however, suddenly be asked to cut a few seconds off this speech or that sentence (maybe for timing or for artistic reasons), and you will need to be able to feel exactly how to do that.

Do not stop if you make a mistake, as mistakes are dealt with very differently than in other mediums. There are advancements in equipment these days that positively blow the mind. Consonants can be added or removed by the sound engineer, for instance, and various technical tricks have been devised to make life easier for the actor. So concentrate on the performance, and let them deal with the minor errors.

If you really like the idea of acting for the microphone, whether on radio, for voice-overs, or for audiobooks, then persist with all the usual channels. Make a good audiotape (seek advice on local requirements) and plug away at getting an audition. If nothing comes of it the first time, improve your approach by making a new tape. Do not keep trying to flog the same one if it did not work out. Keep trying, because if you do get a foot in the door early on in your career, you will have a wonderful standby in years to come. Although the voice gradually ages over the years, you will never be physically too old for a part! Look at current cast lists, listen to narrations and voice-overs, and notice how many famous and familiar names and voices you recognize from the past—it speaks volumes.

First Family Tree:	Training
Branch:	Further training
Twig:	**RADIO ACTING**

Second Family Tree:	Style
Branch:	Modern contemporary acting
Twig:	**RADIO ACTING**
Leaf:	Voice

Readings

How to impress at this most vital time.

There is a major division between readings for the stage and readings for the screen.

Stage

The auditioners are interested in potential.

For the stage, in your reading you are doing two things: letting them know about your acting and the way you come across, and letting them know your potential. The longer the proposed rehearsal time, the more they are going to wonder if you will fit in with the rest of the cast and, more important, how you will respond in the rehearsals.

At this stage you do not know how the director intends to proceed, and so you must let him know what type of actor you are, especially anything about you that will bring honor and triumph to the director. A clever piece of business always goes down well, as does a specialty that you can do, whether it is making a funny voice or face, whistling loudly, or being a happy risk taker.

Even if you are completely suitable for the role, and your reading has gone really well, you will often be asked to do it a different way. This is not necessarily what the director will want from you, but it is a way of testing out how well you take direction. Asking intelligent questions of the director before the reading, including queries about whether a particular accent or class is required for the role, shows that you understand the importance of these questions, and shows that you are a versatile and cooperative artiste.

Screen

The auditioners need a result.

For screen work, all is very different. Because rehearsal time has all but disappeared, and directors now come into the industry with no experience of directing actors or of acting, the whole process is much more one of directors' seeing performances and choosing the one that fits their requirements. The reading will be very much what the director wants you to act on the set, so this major difference is that for a stage reading you are displaying potential, but for screen readings you are required to give results.

You must come up with a completely committed performance, even if you are not sure what is required of you, although you will know that because they sent for you, there must be a good underlying reason for their calling you up.

SEE also: TYPECASTING

Make sure that your face is seen, and is not hidden behind the script. It is more important for your face to be seen and you risk misreading a few words than for you to be completely accurate but obscured. Always remember to react not just in your lines but also in the lines that the other person is reading. If you have had time to prepare the reading, then plan to do some relevant business during your own lines **and** when the other person is speaking—this is always impressive.

A good tip to remember as you are delivering a line is to put your thumb on your **next** speech. This will allow you to look **up** as the other person speaks, with your thumb telling you where to find your next line. Too many actors try to read ahead when the other person is speaking—to spot any difficult words and so on—forgetting that their reactions during the other person's speeches are just as important as their acting when they are speaking.

However, the main reason why people do not get work on-screen from readings is that their vocal projection is too loud. Never forget, in theatre you are pushing out to the audience, but on-screen you are pulling them in, so for a screen reading you can **never** be too soft. You can be too loud (and many, many others before you have been). They will not tell you to lower your vocal level; they will simply think that this person is too theatrical and the camera does not love your face.

SEE also: SCREEN VOCAL LEVELS

First Family Tree:	Getting work
Branch:	Auditions
Twig:	**READINGS**

Second Family Tree:	Screen acting
Branch:	Auditions
Twig:	**READINGS**
Leaf:	Text

Rehearsals (Long, Short, or None)

Is longer always best?

Long Rehearsals:

How to Get the Best from a Long Rehearsal Period

There is no doubt that with established companies rehearsal times for standard productions are getting longer. Why should this be?

Actors are like athletes or musicians. They need to keep up to scratch by constantly practicing their craft. A professional golfer acknowledges that she will be below par if she has not played for a while, as will a solo violinist. Why should acting be any different?

The famous old actors usually went from job to job—and their work was all in the theatre. The Barrymores, Lunts, and Oliviers could bring their highly polished acting instincts, their experience, and the acting tempo of their recent success to each new project.

Actors today often come to a theatre production not having acted **onstage** for a long time; unemployment and screen acting work now take the lion's share of an actor's life. There will need to be a time for them to bed down and get back to being match fit, and this is reflected in the longer settling down time at the start, and why rehearsals need to be longer now perhaps than they were in the old days. Design and costume people also now need a longer lead-up time for their work and so need to meet the actors sooner.

The problem of a long rehearsal period is of not peaking too soon, for there comes a time when a performance needs its audience. The danger then is of spending so much time on the outer edges of rehearsal, improvisations and all, that the detailed work is left too late, and you end up with a performance that does not reflect the long time available to make things excellent. It is part of your job to pace yourself toward the first meeting with an audience and let the production team know if the arrangements they have made do not fit in with what you know works best for you.

Short Rehearsals:

How to Get the Best from a Few Days' Rehearsal

In the old days (the good old days?), actors did not rehearse for very long; in fact in Shakespeare's time they did not really rehearse at all. In Restoration times, an individual actor would rehearse one-on-one with another actor by getting them to repeat a certain way of delivering the lines. Later, during the period of Melodrama, actors went on with a very short preparation time.

With the arrival of naturalism, longer rehearsal periods became necessary—or at least fashionable. Stanislavski famously spent a long period getting his actors to a high level of achievement, whereas Broadway and other centers of world theatre were spending about three weeks in preparing those great productions that have become classics.

Film, of course, that upstart art, had begun to get actors to act straight away—after all, rehearsals were time paid for with no results on the screen.

In theatre things started to change in the 1970s, with the number of actors in work diminishing—and the number of weeks spent rehearsing the plays increasing. Now it is quite usual for a main company to spend many, many weeks discussing and rehearsing a play—and yet when the time comes for an actor to take over a role, because of another actor's unavailability or illness, why, that new actor often has to perform in these great productions with little or no rehearsal at all! Talk to understudies or to those who have taken over a role on Broadway or London's West End and you will hear tales of horror—of the takeover actor never even meeting her fellow actors until her opening night or of principal actors being reluctant even to go through the production once before the new actor has to face an audience under the lights. All very like the good old days, in fact.

Short rehearsal times have always been a feature in the history of the theatre, and so they should be relished and taken advantage of. The actor should not feel done down by the lack of many weeks of rehearsal; it can make you the better actor and your performance more fulfilled. We overheard the following at a major theatre in England: "I am sorry my production was not better—I only had six pitifully short weeks to rehearse it." Tell that to the Barrymores, the Oliviers, and all the host of renowned actors in the great green room in the sky, and they would snort with derision. To be able to perform quickly, from one's instincts and nerve, is the very essence of being an actor.

For the stage, tighter and tighter budgets are forcing some theatres to ask that their actors turn up with the lines already learned, with a minimum of time spent on staging the play. They are behaving just like the original theatre managers in the Elizabethan days, in fact.

SEE also: TEN-SECOND RULE

No Rehearsal:

Alas, It Is Here to Stay

This is becoming standard for most screen work. It is so expensive to make screen dramas that the budget gets swallowed up by all those big earners, with little left over to pay for preparing the actors. Also, the star system is so dominant that a major star can give only a very limited time to a project, and so the amount she does have with the production is often spent on shooting as much as possible, and not on preparation. The fact that the star is expected to give the usual performance also helps in this arrangement of priorities.

SEE also: TYPECASTING

If you find yourself with no rehearsal, use the necessary speed of coming up with a performance to your advantage. Just jump in the deep end, and the quicker you are, the more you'll be using your instinct rather than using your intellect, and the better you can be. Quick can be best (and it takes as much energy to act slowly as act quickly).

SEE also: INSTINCT VERSUS INTELLECT

Family Tree:	Rehearsing
Branch:	**REHEARSALS (LONG, SHORT, OR NONE)**
Twigs:	Directors; Discussions; Learning lines; Method acting; Step-by-step

Rehearsing

Enjoy preparing for performance— don't make it therapy.

Arriving at rehearsal with a blank slate, waiting for the director and company to inspire you with the creative process, means that you will start the race with all the other competitors already halfway around the track. Arrive at rehearsals with all sorts of ideas, opinions, and suggestions, so that you have material to feed you from the start. The more experienced actors do this as a matter of course, and it is uplifting and surprising how much they can bring to the very first meeting.

Nearly all rehearsals start with a read through, and the actors sit around a table with their scripts on their laps trying to make sure that they do not make a mistake. As it continues, they slyly peek ahead to their next speeches, making sure there is no word there to trip them up. Most do not enjoy the process, and directors often admit that that is the worst bit of the rehearsal process, but they often need to get a timing on the whole thing.

There is a better way to approach the read through, and that is to use it as a platform to influence those listening into considering your performance in different ways. For a stage production, this is the time experienced actors introduce bits of business, even indicate moves, so that the director can be receiving some input at this early stage of rehearsals. For the screen, the read through is where experienced actors let the director know that at any time, if they should so wish, the actor is available for a close-up—and they do this by not reading loud enough to impress everyone sitting round the table, not even loud enough for others in the scene to hear, but soft enough to suit a big close-up.

SEE also: SCREEN VOCAL LEVELS

241

The Actor Says:

I was playing the part of a Tea Bag in a children's show and was horrified when the director used the first of only three weeks of rehearsal for improvisations. He would have us change roles to find out all about the other characters in the play: Gingerbread Man, Mr. Salt, Mrs. Pepper, etc., and other diverse exercises. I was anxious to rehearse the songs, dances, and dialogue, which we eventually did, of course, but far too late for my liking. When I discovered that the ten-foot high platform on which I was to perform had been built two feet narrower than the design I was, frankly, terrified as well as severely underrehearsed. I blame myself for not enjoying this job at all, because I had allowed the inadequate rehearsals to annoy me, whilst I should have done my own homework, practiced by myself, and come up with a more pleasing performance despite the problems (although there was nothing that I could have done about that wretched platform, except take a hammer to it!).

Rehearsal is not just a process of finding out what is right but also a time and place to discover all the ways that are **not** right.

The Director Says:

I was completely taken aback by the way the British actor Ian Richardson was treated in rehearsal. Time and time again, he would come up with good ideas, wonderful suggestions—and was constantly knocked back, being slapped down by the director with, "Woolly thinking!" I was aching with sympathy for the actor, but then noticed that he did not mind at all; in fact a lot of his ideas were mutually contradictory. When I talked to him about it, he simply said that his job was to come up with ideas; whether they were accepted or not was up to the director. By opening night, the performance was full of brilliant invention, and a large number of the best ideas were his, chosen from a host of others that did not make it to first night.

SEE also: OVER THE TOP and STEP-BY-STEP

Do not apologize for getting something wrong in rehearsal or for not quite doing what was wanted or required. An apology lets you off the hook and allows the moment to pass by, but not apologizing means that the error stays in the arena, which allows you to deal with it and not brush it under the "Oh that's all right" carpet.

Take risks in rehearsal. A good way of working is to find out all the other ways of making a moment work and not just sticking with the first thing that you came up with.

Take a small pencil case to rehearsals for such things as a spare pen and pencil, colored marker pens, a small pair of scissors, a tiny stapler, an eraser, a tape measure (somebody always wants your measurements!), a few paper clips and safety pins, sticky tape, and correction fluid. A book of puzzles can be helpful if you have the sort of director who wants everyone in the room all the time, even if they are never used that day; he will often object to your reading in rehearsal but not to your doing a crossword or knitting a jumper.

Family Tree:	**REHEARSING**
Branches:	Commitment; Improvisation; Mistakes; Rehearsals (long, short, or none); Technical and dress rehearsals; Technique; Thinking; Whatever works

Rejection

How to deal with the inevitable.

Actors have egos—of course they do. Some are bigger than others, but it is very easy for an actor to think only in terms of herself and how each potential contract affects her.

It is always difficult, in any walk of life, to put yourself in the shoes of those people on the other side of the equation. Really skillful politicians will do this: they imagine how the opposition will react to certain proposals, what they will say, and how they will criticize, and then they adjust their words accordingly.

As an actor, try to imagine what goes on in the private discussions between producers, directors, casting departments, and backers, all of whom will be putting their own interests before that of the actor, or each other for that matter. Keep hold of the actor's lifesaver against drowning in a sea of depression if not all goes well:

Never assume it is in the bag until you sign the contract.

In fact, keep this advice in mind until you start the job, or until you have finished it, and even then you can face the agony of having your entire part cut out of the film. Aurore Clément in *Apocalypse Now* had to wait twenty-two years before audiences got to see her performance in *Apocalypse Now Redux*—rather too late for the performance to gather her any awards or advance her Hollywood film career.

The Actor Says:
I recently auditioned for a featured role in a commercial, where a man and wife (me) were in bed, being kept awake by a noisy party going on next door. She is

trying to pacify him but he is getting really annoyed. Finally he has a great tag line: "Why can't they just have sex like everybody else?" A nice opportunity for a comic reaction from the wife, I thought. The powers that be, however, decided that it would be funnier if the woman was asleep throughout the scene. Although I had been penciled for the job, and told that I could be sure I'd be doing it, the part was then cut to a walk-on role, the pencil was taken off, and I lost what would have been a nice, lucrative job. Disappointed? Yes, I think you could say that! When I watched the commercial, they had even changed the husband's tag line to something nondescript.

So, be warned: this can, and probably will, happen to **you** at some point in your career. Luck, disappointment, opportunity; it is all relative. It will affect you differently, depending on where you are on the ladder of life. Those in the limelight, whose careers have really taken off, consider a few days of uncertainty as to what they were doing next an intolerable situation. Imagine that: having jobs lined up, jobs clashing, having to choose between two or maybe three jobs at one time.

Finally, if you have been rejected, end it all by sending them a thank-you note. You will, perhaps, not want to, but if you were in their shoes, how would **you** like to be treated? If you felt guilty about some casting decision and felt that the actor involved might hate you, would you ask for her again unless you **knew** that she bore no grudge?

Never assume that a bad experience with someone will mark you or the other person for life. Always start off as if there had been no bad history between you, and often you will find that what was once rejection is now acceptance; the change in circumstances can change everything.

The Director Says:

I once had to replace someone for not knowing her lines, and we parted on bad terms. I found a few years later that I was to direct her again in a show that had been precast. I wrote to her suggesting that we both start again from scratch, and I discovered she was a delightful actress, and that our previous trouble was due to her complicated private life at the time, and she should be credited for not letting my previous rejection of her get in the way of the job in hand.

SEE also: DON'T GIVE UP

First Family Tree:	Getting work
Branch:	Auditions
Twig:	**REJECTION**

Second Family Tree:	The Team
Branch:	You (your other life)
Twig:	**REJECTION**
Leaves:	Attitude; Illness; Money is probably the answer; Never say no; Problems

Restoration Acting

Is it anything more than waving your arms about?

In England in the seventeenth century, when the theatres were restored after being shut down by the puritans, only two theatres were allowed to open at first, and the audience was a very specialized one. It consisted of people with time on their hands and enough money in their purses to be able to spend their afternoons in the theatre, not earning a living. The theatres were lit by candlelight, and this changed the acting, for to act in such a restricted light meant that the actors' faces were hard to see, and only when the actors crossed downstage to get the full blast of the footlights could the audience see their facial expressions at all clearly.

Before the shutdown there had been a direct link between the ruling classes and God, which was destroyed when the king's head was cut off and the ruling classes lost all their power. When it was suddenly restored, together with a new king Charles II, there was no longer a direct link between the divinity and power, and this led to an enormous amount of cynicism about responsibility and duty, and love and honor, and public morality was at such a low level that even today they would be judged unfavorably.

The plays at that time often dealt with sexual questions, uncovering what society kept under wraps—in fact, the use of beauty spots was initially not to bring attention to a pretty face but to cover up the results of syphilitic sores that so many of them had. To share such provocative thoughts out front, with an audience who would have looked and sounded like those performers on the stage, was to make them real in the sense that everything done and said was a direct comment on those sitting out front.

Just as today the audience of a David Mamet play would look (and be dressed) in a similar manner to those people onstage and expect a critique on their current morals and behavior, so it was then, and the plays then had the same topical impact as our modern playwrights have now.

The tight-fitting shirts (they had not yet invented gussets) made it very difficult to raise an arm; the large amount of lace around the wrist made it difficult to disentangle one's fingers; and the sexual allure of a man's calf meant that men would show it off at all times (and even went to the extremes of wearing falsies; that is, boosting the size of a calf the way modern bras boost the size of a breast). To walk about with restricted arms, lacy fingers, and flaunting one's calves leads to—yes—the specific Restoration walk, which is, yet again, a simple truth of trying to walk in those costumes and in those conditions. Style has again been shown to be at heart a truthful response to the world and theatre at that time.

The Director Says:

When I was at Boston University studying for my masters in theatre arts (directing) I had to attend all sorts of classes—and when it came to the Restoration section of the history of theatre classes, my professor insisted that I read out all the main speeches.

Why was that? There were some fine actors in that class—certainly better than me. Although the rest of the class (and the professor) assumed I would know of the Restoration style because I came from England, to be truthful I had never read, seen, or ever thought about such a play before—yet not only did I read it well but I probably read it better than anyone else in that class (which is why I got to do all those speeches). It took me quite a few years—and some experience of directing Restoration plays—for me to understand what had been going on.

You see, my colleagues had been trying to make the lines sincere, truthful, and real—and I had been trying to get laughs and make the lines entertaining. The lines were written to be entertaining, not to be a slice of life of the 1700s—so the approach based on a sincere delivery just did not match the language and demands of the original author.

The modern actor then needs to take in the knowledge of how the original plays were presented, and with the production team find the way of sharing it with the audience now. Is it to find the modern equivalents in the story? Is it to give a nice reconstruction of an old-fashioned event? Different productions will come up with different solutions, but the core of it is an understanding of what was originally required of the performers.

Family Tree:	Style
Branch:	**RESTORATION ACTING**
Twig:	Example: Mr. Horner is exactly that

Resumes

**The words that tell us all about you
(sometimes called a curriculum vitae—or CV for short).**

We are not going to suggest how you should lay out a resume because styles change so often in this department, and different things are needed by different employers and different regions in the world. We, however, recommend that it looks neat and be typed or printed and brief.

Give as much information as possible regarding your skills. Include any specialties, expertise, or unusual physical features. It is good to include any extraordinary abilities, such as operating farm machinery (for example). The fewer actors there are who have that particular skill increases your chances of being considered for a part that requires that very thing. Always think in terms of those things that **you** can offer that are outside most other actors' abilities.

Be careful not to exaggerate too much. If you can sit on a horse comfortably, ride gently, and speak dialogue at the same time, that is one thing, but if it were assumed that you could ride to hounds, jump fences, or play a winning jockey, you would be in serious trouble. There is unlikely to be time to train up to the standard required, but, more than that, misleading information could lead to major insurance problems in the case of an accident, especially if you lie about your driving status or ability to swim.

Help the casting department of the industry as much as you can, and do not say you can do something that you cannot do, but do make sure that any particular talent is noted, from being able to whistle through your fingers to being an expert windsurfer. Most directors or casting directors subtract about 10 percent from what actors say they can do; you in your turn should therefore **add** 10 percent to make sure that your real abilities are noted.

What is looked for on a resume is a familiar credit, anything that the viewer recognizes as a well-known title (film or play) in a prominent venue with a recognized director. Maybe not all in one credit, but if you have only one outstanding name to flash around, be proud to flash it!

Please do not exaggerate credits or claim fictitious ones. In this modern age of Internet access, you can and probably will be trapped in a lie. Avoid too many obvious drama school and training credits; you weren't being paid, but **you** paid to do them, and so they attract very little interest. Whatever you do, do not mix your training credits with your professional ones—the resume readers are quite adept at sorting them out, and they find it irritating to have to do so.

Always make sure that there are plenty of contact numbers and addresses on your resume. Always type the covering letter, because illegible handwriting is most irritating, and try never to go over to two pages.

If you are in an actor's directory, quote the current page number or say that you can be found on their Internet service. This will save you the expense of having to send a photograph with the resume.

SEE also: PHOTOGRAPHS

First Family Tree:	Getting work
Branch:	Agents
Twig:	**RESUMES**

Second Family Tree:	Screen acting
Branch:	Auditions
Twig:	Casting directors
Leaf:	**RESUMES**

Role-Play

A growing area of work.

Role-play is similar to working as a tour guide or demonstrator, and it is a very good area of alternative employment. Many actors take these jobs as an extension of the acting profession, and they can be geared to your convenience and free you up for auditions and interviews for the real stuff, when they come your way.

In role-playing jobs you are required to study a form of script, which might be a background to your character and the situation that is being explored that day. These are usually attached to a particular job. You then improvise all your so-called scenes.

The main reason professions such as medicine, law, or even car selling use actors in role-playing is for training their staff and new recruits, so the actor is required to be an ordinary member of the public, but with a specific problem directly connected to that particular profession.

Medical training requires people to be pretend patients, for example, and you might be asked to memorize a whole series of illnesses and symptoms and talk them over with a trainee doctor. The trainee will, of course, be judged on his medical and psychological reactions, and the actor will get a brief as to how to deal with the situation and how far to go. Role-players have been asked, for example, to break down when the doctor tells them they have only a short while to live, and the doctor then has to cope with the subsequent hysterics or whatever. You have to be the real thing for as long as it lasts. A friend of ours had to have a heart problem for thirty-two doctors a day for three days. After all that prodding and poking, he felt rather ill.

The same routine is required for training lawyers, where you will be required to be comfortable with some simple legal terms and be prepared to discuss quite complicated cases. Your job, always, is to stay in character

251

within the brief but to use your personality to convey a real problem or dilemma and improvise the required situation.

There are two-day or weekend jobs where you might be required to travel to a strange place and stay in a hotel overnight, playing the part of someone (whomever) for the whole time, except, of course, in the privacy of your own room. Treat the whole job as if a camera is trained on you to catch your secret acting performance, and relish starring in such a long movie.

In some role-play situations, a stationary video camera is turned on the scene so that trainees can later see how they handled the scenario they were asked to act out. This is also useful to you the actor, because watching the video gives you an opportunity to spot any mannerisms or bad habits that might be creeping into your acting. You are able to honestly appraise what your playing age range is and to judge the degree of truth and reality you played in the scene.

The Actor Says:

*I suppose the nearest I have been to role-playing was in a television reality show in which I was given a character to act but would have to make up the dialogue according to the situation as I found it. There were other actors in the scene, but the two central people were members of the public: a woman, suspecting her boyfriend of being a flirt, tries to trap him by setting him up to flirt with another woman. The main seducer was a very pretty young girl, and my job was to pretend that he had glanced at **me** in a certain way, too. Since my comedy technique was not required, and one of the members of the public recognized me, I felt that this was not a field I should continue to explore.*

Apart from taking part in training programs, you can play historical characters in museum displays and school real-life experience programs. We know of actors who, given a basic outline of authentic dialogue in historical situations such as playing a Victorian schoolmaster, footman, or lord of the manor, take on a museum full of children for up to two hours.

Whatever the situation, actors can, while performing a character, make a real contribution to the national education program for young and old, which makes it a worthwhile earner in more ways than one.

First Family Tree:	Rehearsing
Branch:	Improvisation
Twig:	**ROLE-PLAY**

Second Family Tree:	The Team
Branch:	You (your other life)
Twig:	Jobs requiring acting skills
Leaf:	**ROLE-PLAY**

Screen Acting

How it is part of modern acting and a style all of its own.

This section is about what you do differently when acting on screen, as opposed to acting class or the theatre.

First of all, imagine that when you are on a proscenium stage, there is a triangle that starts with you and spreads out to the far sides of the auditorium. You will be required to fill that huge triangle with your performance. If, however, you are in front of a camera, the triangle is reversed. The viewers are at the sharp end of the triangle and it spreads out toward you. In other words, onstage you send out your performance, whereas on-screen you draw the audience to you.

For some reason, acting teachers around the world will chant at a student that something is "too televisual" when it is too small, as if screen acting were a more true, sincere, and smaller version of stage acting.

In fact, it is not true at all, as the screen demands far more cheating and untrue physical relationships than life or theatre ever demanded. You just have to see how very close actors have to stand in relationship to each other, occupying the personal space that only close friends are allowed to occupy, to see how it is not like real life. Listening to a marvelous screen actor speak her lines so softly that only the audience at home can hear her, and the person she is speaking to on the other side of the table would never hear her at all, again shows how this truth is the truth of the screen: it is a style like any other.

What you have to do for screen acting therefore is totally different from what you do in real life. For a start, the screen defines the reality, so if it is not there on-screen, it is not happening as far as the audience is concerned. Actors are frequently asked to cheat their own positions and the positions of the props they handle, and that makes them feel extremely awkward.

These feelings are the first difference between acting for the stage or for the screen.

The next big difference for the newcomer is in the vocal level used. In a theatre your voice will vary according to the emotion and situation, but it will also vary according to the size of the building you are playing in and if any microphones are amplifying your speech.

On-screen, the variations are much more, and for different reasons. The actors will vary their projection level (how loudly they speak to each other) according to the size of shot: the tighter the shot, the softer they will speak.

SEE also: SCREEN VOCAL LEVELS

Onstage the audience tends to look at the person who is speaking, and the other actors had better not do any large moves or bits of business during this or they will be accused of upstaging. None of this happens in screen acting, where the director–editor combination will decide who is on-screen when, and the audience might watch you as you listen as much as watch you when you are speaking, and **this** means that your listening has to be much more active than it is either onstage or in real life.

Your relationship with the script for screen acting is different from that in the theatre. For the screen you might well find that you are encouraged or even required to alter the script to suit your own particular qualities. Actors new to the screen are often startled to discover this, because they have been taught that the script is sacrosanct. Listen to what Anthony Perkins said about working with Alfred Hitchcock on the film *Psycho*, from the book *Alfred Hitchcock and the Making of Psycho* by Stephen Robello (HarperPerennial, 1991):

> *About four weeks in we were getting along very well but I was still hesitant about bringing him a page of dialogue which was as blackly worked over as this one was. He was in his dressing room . . . and I said, "Mr. Hitchcock, about my speech in tomorrow's scene." He said, "Uh, huh," . . . and I said, "I've had a few ideas that I thought maybe you might like to listen to." . . . He said, "All right." And I started telling him what they were. He said, "Oh, they're all right." And I said, "But, but, but, you might not like them." . . . He said, "Have you*

given it a lot of thought? I mean have you really thought it out? Do you really like these changes you've made?" I said, "Yes, I think they're right." He said, "All right, that's the way we'll do it." (p. 88)

The other main note for screen acting is that, in the main, typecasting is the name of the game, where actors are cast by the way they look. However much you may want to change this, the silver screen has been doing this since they started importing European starlets to be in the Hollywood movies in the silent days, and nothing has changed since.

If an error occurs, whatever you do, don't stop acting. Many a good moment has been ruined because a chance mistake that worked wonderfully well fizzled out when the actor stopped acting because she thought something had gone wrong.

Although you will have a director, the best directions you will ever have are, first, that **you** got the job and, second, the choice of shots. A long shot implies that you should come up with a more theatrical performance, but a close-up needs a much more intimate one.

This whole topic is dealt with in much greater depth in *Secrets of Screen Acting* (2nd ed.), published by Routledge.

First Family Tree:	Training
Branch:	Further training
Twig:	**SCREEN ACTING**
Second Family Tree:	Style
Branch:	Modern contemporary acting
Twig:	**SCREEN ACTING**
Leaf:	Example: Broadway versus Hollywood
Third Family Tree:	**SCREEN ACTING**
Branches:	Auditions; Screen cheating; Shooting and acting; Truth; Typecasting

Screen Cheating

What is really happening in front of the camera.

Doing stage work, you can trust your feelings, and if what you are asked to do feels odd you can work on it, or ask your director to change or guide you so you can feel good about it. Working for the camera, the actors will often say they feel terrible about a certain thing they are being asked to do, but the director will announce happily that it looks good to him, and that is that.

Objects have to be cheated up into shot, so the audience can see what it is that the actor is doing, whether drinking a cup of tea or writing a report on a clipboard. You can be asked to type on a keyboard that is only inches from your chin or read a book so close to your eyes that you cannot focus on the page.

Actors have to stand really close to one another, far closer than they would allow themselves in any normal or theatrical situation, so the camera can see a nice two-shot. The actors have to pretend they cannot tell what each other had for lunch. Your nose can be only an inch away from another actor—you must have seen such confrontational scenes—yet would you **really** be that close to an adversary?

Actors have to look in a certain direction for the camera to see them, even though they should look in a different one if they were really talking to the other person.

Picture the scene: a wife is washing the dishes at the sink, and her husband comes up behind her to talk. You see her face big on-screen, with his face just over her shoulder, as they discuss the kids, their marriage, their divorce—and you realize that in no way would real people have a real scene in that situation. They would be facing each other, so that they could see each other's expressions. But, no, working on screen she can see nothing, and all he can see is an out-of-focus back of head, as our two actors successfully **cheat** the scene so that the camera can see both of their expressions all of the time.

All this cheating will make you feel uncomfortable and unreal (until you get used to screen acting), but it will look good, and you will have to reconcile yourself to the screen actor's lifesaving mantra:

You may feel lousy, but still look great.

The American actress Marie Windsor told of the cheating she had to do as a tall actress, quoted in her January 23, 2001, obituary by Ronald Bergan in *The Guardian:*

At five foot nine, I was too tall for most leading men. There were only two stars who didn't mind that I was taller than them—George Raft and John Garfield. Raft told me how to walk with him in a scene: we'd start off in a long shot normal, and about the time we got together in a close-up, I'd be bending my knees so I'd be shorter. I had to do a tango with Raft and I learned to dance in ballet shoes with my knees bent.

You cannot always show your loved ones how you really feel at certain moments or show the traffic cop who has pulled you over for speeding how you feel about being stopped. You put on a polite look to mask your true feelings, and this works well for real life. For the camera, the audience needs to know what you are **really** feeling, and this means that for screen work you must put onto your face those very thoughts and feelings that in real life you hide. Do not worry, a wonderful thing happens when they shoot you in a close-up: the audience members think that they are the only ones who can see your face, so although you are surrounded by other characters, in a close-up it is as if you are alone and can show on your face what you really feel.

The Actor Says:
I have often had to act a scene for the screen to an empty space, with just a mark for my eye line. I have had to act a meal scene where my chair was precariously balanced on tall blocks, and play a scene in a car sitting on the brake handle in order to get the correct two-shot for the camera. Of course I felt stupid and

uncomfortable, but the satisfaction of knowing that if I could see the camera meant the camera was seeing me in the right position drowned all doubts.

All these thoughts on screen cheating have the huge advantage that you can switch on the television right now and check out whether this is what happens. Watch carefully, and you will see that people are far more revealing than they would be in real life, but, of course, this is not reality, this is screen truth.

Family Tree:	Screen acting
Branch:	**SCREEN CHEATING**
Twigs:	Eye-to-eye contact; Properties (props); Screen reactions; Screen vocal levels

Screen Reactions

Different from normal—or stage—reactions.

When someone else is speaking, you do not put reactions onto your face because socially it is rude to do so, and onstage it is called upstaging (pulling attention to your face when the audience should be looking at the other actor). So onstage you wait until the other person has spoken, and then you launch into your acting: speaking and then letting others know how you feel by putting expressions on your face. Actually, there would be no point in doing this earlier as no one would be looking or noticing anyway.

On-screen, there is a reversal of this process, and there is a magic formula that will save your performance from being lost at sea:

React before you speak.

Watch a major star in a role, and suddenly you will notice that she always puts expressions and thoughts onto her face and **then** speaks. There are good technical reasons for this—the editor has to have something to cut to, and if she and the director don't like what the actor does they can always cut it out, but they cannot put it in if the actor has launched into a speech with no reactions to introduce it.

SEE also GEAR CHANGES

You have no idea when (or if) the director or editor will want to cut to your face while you are listening to others, so you must keep your face alive all the time: keep it moving like a candle in the wind. If the shot is a close-up, then a strange thing happens: the audience members watching it feel somehow that they are the only ones who can see the expression there, and so you can act the subtext clearly, even though in real life, or in stage life, such a thing would not be shown at that time.

The Actor Says:

On several occasions, because I have a very expressive face and do good reactions, I have been filmed in a single shot just listening to a dialogue sound track, in order for the director to be able to pick some suitable expressions to edit into the scene. The other actors were not there—just me and the cameraman. I expect that is why I got the job in the first place, since I always do a lot of reactions at the reading.

As the great American (Method) director Elia Kazan said:

The art of motion pictures is one of photographing looks, not photographing dialogue.

(As he showed in his classic movies *A Streetcar Named Desire*, *East of Eden*, and *On the Waterfront*.)

Family Tree:	Screen acting
Branch:	Screen cheating
Twig:	**SCREEN REACTIONS**
Leaves:	Example: Al and Bob's first meeting; Example: Noël Coward on the phone

Screen Vocal Levels

The *most* important aspect of screen acting.

When you are on-screen, if you are seen as a full figure (a long shot: LS), the audience sort of expects you to be speaking as if you were in a large theatre. If you are seen down to your waist (a mid shot: MS), you will be expected to be speaking as if you were in a small theatre. Just your head and shoulders (a medium close-up: MCU), and the audience expects realistic speech from you, as if you were just speaking naturally; and if your face fills the screen (a big close-up: BCU), then you will be expected to speak as if you were on a pillow next to each member of the audience, or your lips were just two inches from their ears.

Applying this to the way you speak means that you should vary the level of projection **not** according to the usual criteria of how far away you are from the person you are speaking to or how big the theatre is but according to the size of shot you are in. And the best way of establishing that is to notice where the boom is (the microphone picking up the sound levels) and to project **not** according to where the person is that you are speaking to but according to where the microphone is.

This is an odd feeling (remember, on-screen your feelings are no longer the clear guide that they can be onstage), but it **is** how major stars work. Watch some movie clips with such stars as Harrison Ford or Scarlett Johansson and you will realize that they practically **never** project to the person they are speaking to but project to the **size of shot**.

Be particularly careful when using an accent not your own. There will be a tendency to overproject when using such a voice.

It is interesting to see those really experienced film actors, such as Gregory Peck in *The Guns of Navarone*, who, when needing to raise their voice in anger, actually keep the same low vocal level but wave their arms about angrily instead.

The golden rule then is to keep your vocal levels intimate, so try to keep what you are doing in the range of what all the other performers in your cast are doing, and remember this life belt:

Never act louder than the star!

We use the word *act* deliberately, because you might have to shout at the star (in character, of course), but in general your average vocal levels should not be higher than those who command the highest salaries or be greater than those whose names have the greatest pulling power.

The Director Says:

*I had just finished typing this, turned on the television, and was watching a well-made drama and, as usual, the biggest star of the show consistently spoke at a lower level than the others. Now I **know** that directors don't tell them to do this, nor do sound operators (I check this with all the sound people I work with), so I realized that the stars must be telling themselves—and we in turn are telling you.*

Family Tree:	Screen acting
Branch:	Screen cheating
Twig:	**SCREEN VOCAL LEVELS**
Leaf:	Dialects and accents

Sex and Violence

How to deal with these evergreen requirements.

When it comes to these hot items, there seems to be an absolute division between the world of the stage and that of the screen. On-screen, all is allowed, given the local censorship or guidelines in force, as the audience happily watches the knife slide into the body or, er, something else sliding in. All is allowed, as the audience members know that it is not actually happening at that moment, and that with all sorts of camera tricks available, and the use of stand-ins, they are not actually seeing what they are watching up on the screen but seeing a facsimile of it. At least, they think so until the film's publicity department starts spreading dark rumors about how the stars were perhaps **really** doing it.

Frankly, a lot of films these days rely on plenty of gore and titillation for their youthful audience to scream and giggle at. It will be acceptable for them, because deep down they know that somehow it has been faked. The same is not true of a theatre audience.

If one actor onstage really slaps the other actor, and the audience hears a loud noise and sees a large red mark appear on the other actor's cheek, then the whole play will stop for a lot of the audience members. They will start to think, "I bet **that** hurt," and then they will wonder if the same thing happens every night or whether the actors tonight are just doing it for real because they are upset with each other. The audience will then drift off to thoughts such as "Do they do it every night? Did they do it all through rehearsals or just leave it to the first night?" All this time, the play will be continuing without the full attention of those in the audience distracted by the reality of the violence.

No production team would dream of allowing actors to experience actual pain night after night in the theatre (although those working for the screen are not so squeamish, and actors are expected to put up with quite a lot of real discomfort for certain shots), and no matter how incredibly real it might look, the audience knows that it is not so. They know that it is a trick knife that cuts a throat, that the gun is firing blanks, and that the blood is fake, and so on. This illusion and trickery should also be applied to the sex scenes.

This seems strange at first, but the more real violence, or of course sex, there is onstage, the more the theatre audience members get distracted by it. If they see a passionate, all-encompassing kiss, they start to wonder if the actors **really** fancy each other. Maybe they like each other too much—how do their partners feel about that? Would it not be strange if they really hated one another and had to do this passionate kiss every night? All these are true reflections, but they stop the audience from following the play. Nudity has the same effect, where the reality of the bodies on view can quite upstage the erotic intention, whereas partially unclothed bodies are very exciting indeed (as the world of striptease has always known).

Onstage the weird conclusion is that for the audience to follow, believe, and not be distracted by the sex and violence on display, the actions have to be hidden or cheated. A slap then that does **not** lead to a reddening cheek but is done in a technical way allows the audience to know there was no real pain involved and will let the play continue happily. And a passionate embrace that does not involve tongues allows the audience to keep inside the reality of the situation and to follow the actors' journey, unimpeded by distractions of truth.

SEE also: BELIEVABILITY

First Family Tree:	Rehearsing
Branch:	Technique
Twig:	**SEX AND VIOLENCE**

Second Family Tree:	Performing
Branch:	Truth
Twig:	**SEX AND VIOLENCE**

Shakespeare Acting

How to do it with happiness.

Modern actors seem to have a worry about doing Shakespeare, forgetting perhaps that the plays were written for uneducated actors, with very ordinary backgrounds. If they could do it with ease, well, so can you.

The actors in the days when Shakespeare was writing his plays performed a different play every day of the week, sometimes not repeating plays for up to a year, and they worked from cue scripts or sides. The result was that the actors took all their instructions from the text, **not** from the context, as modern actors do. With no time for rehearsal, no director, and no complete script, each actor prepared all character and acting notes from the actual text they spoke, just as a modern orchestral musician gets everything from his own given notes and not from the complete score that only the conductor has.

To work from such a basis—from your own text, with no outside influence or instruction and with no rehearsal—sounds so impossible that we decided to try it out, and that is what we did with the Original Shakespeare Company in the 1990s, where we presented full-length plays. We can report back with confidence that it works wonderfully well, whether it is a comedy, tragedy, romance, or history.

The actor working on a Shakespeare text, then, is like a musician working from a score—the musician gets instructions from the notes, timings, and notations, and the actor can get similar instructions from the use of prose or poetry, such as the way the language varies from simple to complicated, the verse and subsequent line endings that are so useful, the wordplay, and the simplest note of all: what you call people is Shakespeare's way of telling you how your character **feels** about them.

Some actors find that working from the original text before the editors have got at it, the First Folio of 1623, helps them so much they will use

266

no other. If you find yourself in this category, be happy by all means, but our advice is not to tell anyone else. Experience has shown us that the use of the First Folio receives an extraordinarily negative response from those who prefer that **they** are the supreme arbiters of what Shakespeare meant and how to play him.

In the Shakespeare examples we have quoted in this book, the original First Folio punctuation and line lengths are used, but we have modernized the spelling and reluctantly taken away the capitalization of so-called random words (so it will look like the Shakespeare you are used to).

The lifeline is as follows:

Trust Shakespeare—he has done most of the work for you already.

Family Tree:	Style
Branch:	**SHAKESPEARE ACTING**
Twigs:	Shakespeare: First Folio; Shakespeare: Prose or poetry; Shakespeare: Simple or complicated; Shakespeare: Verse; Shakespeare: What you call people; Shakespeare: Wordplay

Shakespeare: First Folio

Isn't this too old and antique to be of use?

When you read any piece of Shakespeare's work, you are not reading the original, and you are not reading what he wrote.

Some of Shakespeare's plays were published during his lifetime, but half of them were published for the first time in the First Folio seven years after his death. Two fellow shareholders, the actors John Heminge and Henry Condell, presented the edition. Because the words there are not identical to those in the earlier published single copies of some of the plays, and because of perceived errors in the text, all subsequent editors have felt free to change words, punctuation, and line lengths to present a version of the text that they feel is more accurate and is edited to be literature. They do not, of course, agree with each other, and so there are now many, many variations offered for each piece of Shakespeare, and interestingly, the more famous the piece, the more changes the editors feel called upon to make. They tend never to look at the text with an actor's eyes or from an actor's point of view.

The Director Says:

I have found that playing the text from the First Folio has huge advantages. I have used it since 1980, and have always found that this original script offers more help and guidance for the actors than modern edited texts; not sometimes, not mostly— ***always.*** *When I get actors to redo any piece they have done from the past, but this time using the Folio, their performance always gets better.* ***Always.***

The First Folio is not always grammatical or logical, but it is fundamentally theatrical. The text was written to be acted, not to be read, and First Folio text is packed full of instructions to actors who had to present plays at such a rate that there was no time for rehearsals in the way it is understood today. In fact there was not even the complete script to study, only their own lines. Given this, the actual words to be spoken were the only things the actor could base his performance on, and so the original text is important and fascinating.

In the Folio, a lot of words that would not normally be capitalized are, and when text is modernized, the editors as a matter of course remove them from all but the proper names, deciding to regularize the situation. The original capitalization turns out to be a guide to the acting of the piece, not just a piece of irrelevant Elizabethan printing practice; they seem to be stepping-stones to help the actor get through a wonderful speech, when they have had little time to prepare it.

The Actor Says:

*When we first began using the Folio text, we too decided **not** to keep what appeared to be a random choice of capitalized words, and it was only when I was working on Portia's "Quality of mercy" speech with an actor that I noticed something interesting about which words were capitalized.*

Those "random" words that started with a capital seemed to be largely Christian images: Monarch, Crown, Scepter, Majesty, Kings. *I had always been told that this was the great "plea for mercy" speech, but although the word* mercy *appeared five times it was never capitalized. When looking at the Folio capitals, the speech seemed to be more tongue-in-cheek, almost mocking Shylock. Why does she call him the derogatory "Jew," when she has already established his name?*

Since I knew that Portia has a trump card up her sleeve in the trial scene (drawing no blood with the pound of flesh), I saw the scene quite differently and encouraged the actor to use the capitalized words to inform the speech with a different attitude.

As far as the line length is concerned, a half line of text followed by another half line means **come in on cue**, whereas an unfulfilled half line means **take a pause**. However, when you look at the original text, you find many **more** half lines there than in modern editions to help you work out when to do some stage business.

Shakespeare wrote as people spoke, by punctuating the text with natural speech patterns. Unlike literature that is carefully punctuated so as to be grammatically correct, Shakespeare punctuated the way people actually spoke, so the original punctuation is crucial, for it defines where the individual thoughts end. It is plain to see that editors give themselves total permission to change the Folio punctuation; what is not so clear at first (unless you are a performer) are the changes that this makes to the intention and meaning of a speech.

The original spelling in the Folio often helps you to understand what accent to use or what emphasis to make, as in one speech your character might change from a long drawn out *mee* to a simple *me* and back again.

The First Folio—a set of directorial instructions from four hundred years ago—and a lot more about this whole subject is in *Secrets of Acting Shakespeare—The Original Approach*, published by Routledge.

Family Tree:	Style
Branch:	Shakespeare acting
Twig:	**SHAKESPEARE: FIRST FOLIO**

Shakespeare: Prose or Poetry

How to spot—and deal with—the difference.

In prose text each line uses up all the space available and just runs on to the next line continuously until the end of the speech. Capital letters are in the usual places: at the start of a sentence and for proper names or titles. Here is an example by Olivia from *Twelfth Night:*

OLIVIA:

> O sir, I will not be so hardhearted: I will give out divers sched-
> ules of my beauty. It shall be inventoried and every particle
> and utensil labell'd to my will: as, item two lips indifferent
> red, item two gray eyes, with lids to them: item, one neck, one
> chin, and so forth. Were you sent hither to praise me?

In poetry each line begins with a capital letter, and the length of the line is determined by the type of poetry being used (in Shakespeare's case, the vast majority of it is in iambic pentameters—five *di-dums*). The following is by Viola, again from *Twelfth Night:*

VIOLA:

> I see you what you are, you are too proud:
> But if you were the devil, you are fair:
> My Lord, and master loves you: O such love
> Could be but recompenc'd, though you were crown'd
> The nonpareil of beauty.

This is the interaction where one character, Olivia, is speaking in prose and the other, Viola, is speaking in poetry. Shakespeare was using these two

271

forms of speaking to show the difference between the attitudes of the two characters, and he went on to give more clues about Olivia when she suddenly starts speaking in poetry (the first time in the play that she does so). The change from prose to poetry shows the change in the inner attitude of the character.

In a similar way, but in reverse, the Duke in *Measure for Measure* speaks in poetry at the start of the play, but when he overhears the fraught conversation between Isabella and her brother Claudio, he speaks in prose for the first time. This shows perhaps that he is becoming more in touch with the real world and less in touch with the airy-fairy world of the court.

The instruction to the actors when speaking in poetry is that their character is a heightened person, or is in a heightened state. This is something everyone knows about, when writing poetry to their loved ones or commemorating a valuable life with a poem.

When a character is speaking in prose, the instruction to the actor is that these lines are not heightened, and so the character either is incapable of speaking poetry (being a low-life person perhaps) or is choosing at this time not to speak in poetry. The term *prosaic*, meaning dull and ordinary, sums up what prose can mean to a performer. The character is then very much what the actor brings to it, and a personality-based performance is what Shakespeare intended when he wrote in prose. The following famous riff by the porter in *Macbeth* was based on what the actor had brought to the part—Elizabethan stand-up comedy, in fact.

> *Knocking within.*

PORTER:

> Here's a knocking indeed: if a man were porter of hell gate, he should have old turning the key. *[Knock.]* Knock, knock, knock. Who's there i'th'name of *Beelzebub*? Here's a farmer, that hang'd himself on th'expectation of plenty: come in time, have napkins enow about you, here you'll sweat for't. *[Knock.]* Knock, knock. Who's there in th'other devil's name? Faith here's an equivocator, that could swear in both the scales against either scale, who committed treason enough for God's sake, yet could not equivocate to heaven: oh come in, equivocator. *[Knock.]* Knock, knock, knock. Who's there? 'Faith here's

an English tailor come hither, for stealing out of a French hose: come in tailor, here you may roast your goose. *[Knock.]* Knock, knock. Never at quiet: what are you? but this place is too cold for hell. I'll devil-porter it no further: I had thought to have let in some of all professions, that go the primrose way to th'everlasting bonfire. *[Knock.]* Anon, anon, I pray you remember the porter.

Is this last line a hint to those entering to give him a tip, or one to the audience to give him a round of applause? Whichever; Macduff then enters and speaks in poetry.

SEE also: GEAR CHANGES

Family Tree:	Style
Branch:	Shakespeare acting
Twig:	**SHAKESPEARE: PROSE OR POETRY**
Leaf:	Example: The silence of the lads

Shakespeare:
Simple or Complicated

Good choices for the Bard—good for other texts.

Shakespeare knew how to be straightforward, as shown when Anthony says to his followers in *Anthony, and Cleopatra*:

ANTHONY:

>Be gone, my treasure's in the harbor. Take it:

or as Macbeth is addressed by his Lady:

LADY MACBETH:

>Give me the daggers:

All pretty straightforward, so you see that if you have a simple speech, then you can speak it directly. If, however, you have a complicated speech, then perhaps something else is going on. Here is Hamlet in his famous speech, which starts off very simply, then gets very complicated:

HAMLET:

>To be, or not to be, that is the question:
>Whether 'tis nobler in the mind to suffer
>The slings and arrows of outrageous fortune,
>Or to take arms against a sea of troubles,
>And by opposing end them: to die, to sleep
>No more; and by a sleep, to say we end

The heartache, and the thousand natural shocks
That flesh is heir to?
Etc.

It happens so often that modern actors will take their attitude from the situation rather than the words, and here the words tell the actor when the character starts with simple sincerity and when he changes to a darker more complicated mood.

Here is Lysander speaking to his love Hermia:

LYSANDER:

How now my love? Why is your cheek so pale?
How chance the roses there do fade so fast?

So there is a change between the first, factual bit of the speech and the second, overblown line (using a metaphor!), and this tells the actor to start off simply and then get very romantic or very distraught, whatever the actor's response to those lines is—but there **must** be a change.

Think about a romantic encounter, maybe your own, that starts with two strangers meeting then goes through the embarrassments of their getting to know each other, going out on dates, finding accommodations with each other, and ending up with the blissful union of two like souls in a wonderful marriage. How do they speak to each other at each stage?

At first the language would be simple and friendly: "Would you like to go to the movies?" As the relationship progresses, the language will get altogether more complicated: "I am awfully afraid I am getting rather fond of you." How strange to couple the word *awful* with *fond*, but the couple is not really sure where it is all going, and the actual emotion between the two people is probably somewhere on the line between *awful* and *fond*. Only when the individuals are sure of each other, and of themselves, can they come up with the simplicity of "I love you."

Shakespeare used exactly the same techniques, giving simple statements when it is warranted and complicated statements when the person is struggling to express a complicated feeling or message.

Some time back in the United Kingdom there was a train crash, and the railway official was being interviewed on television as to why the accident had happened, because the trains were equipped with radios. He replied, "Although our systems are terrestrial, the topography was against us." (Translation: the trains were in a valley and could not pick up the radio signal.) Now here the individual was concentrating **not** on giving information but on appearing important, or of not compromising his employers. In other words, this is an example of a truly Shakespearean reply in which the **structure** of the language gives valuable **acting** notes as to what is called the subtext.

This is in fact your first lifesaver, a wonderful acting note for approaching Shakespeare:

The subtext is in the structure of the language.

Someone struggling to express himself with wit and humor, with metaphors and clever language, is someone struggling to express a complicated feeling. You go wrong if you take a complicated speech and say it simply, just as you go wrong if you take a very simple speech and give it all sorts of complicated interpretations and emotions.

Never forget this other life belt regarding Shakespeare:

Articulate speech is emotion in recollection, not the moment of emotion itself.

At the time of very bad news, or of a serious accident, you will find it difficult to speak; some while later, they cannot shut you up. Take this thought into a complicated speech of Shakespeare's: it is **not** the moment of experiencing a great emotion; it is the moment you are remembering it and able now to speak about it.

The worlds of Shakespeare's words and our own are not so very far apart or alien to each other after all, and acting the difference between the structure of your speeches in any script will bring you good acting dividends.

SEE also: GEAR CHANGES

Family Tree:	Style
Branch:	Shakespeare acting
Twig:	**SHAKESPEARE: SIMPLE OR COMPLICATED**
Leaf:	Example: Brother and sister act

Shakespeare: Verse

Mostly Shakespearean
(but Arthur Miller used verse too).

Shakespeare wrote his verse mostly in iambic pentameters. They sound difficult and academic, but all it means is five lots of *di-dum*, so that a standard line will go as follows:

Di-dum, di-dum, di-dum, di-dum, di-dum.
(If music be the food of love, play on,)

The last word gets a little extra choice by being the last stressed *dum*. There are ten bits, and five feet, in the line. If there are more than ten bits, and the last bit is a *di* making it eleven bits, then that means it has a feminine ending:

Di-dum, di-dum, di-dum, di-dum, di-dum, di.
(I left no ring with her: what means this lady?)

The last word is a bit weakened by ending with the unstressed *di*.

However, whatever you call them—iambic pentameters or five *di-dums*—they are there to help you. To run lines on and ignore the poetry is to ignore one of the clearest clues given to an actor, for in poetry, the **line endings** make sure you choose the end words, and so gain extra information. The **use** of the verse has the remarkable effect of making the whole more natural and believable. It is not a question of making the verse naturalistic by avoiding it and jumbling all your lines together but a question of using the verse to become more natural to your audience.

The French language needs more letters than English does to express the same idea as these famous lines from *Twelfth Night* show.

English

> If music be the food of love, play on, (28 letters)
> I left no ring with her: what means this lady? (35 letters)

French

> Si la musique est la pâture de l'amour, (30 letters)
> Je n'ai point laissé de bague; qu'a-t-elle en tête? (37 letters)

(So it will come as no surprise to find that the basic verse line in a French play is twelve *di-dums*, or an Alexandrine.)

When Shakespeare wrote in poetry, he made each line more or less the same length. If a speech ends with a half line, and the next character starts his speech with a half line, that was Shakespeare's way of saying, **Pick up your cue,** or **Do not leave a pause.**

If he put a half line in the middle of a speech, then he was instructing the actor to take a pause for some stage business. So in the middle of his speech, Macbeth has a half line:

MACBETH:

> Is this a dagger, which I see before me,
> The handle toward my hand? Come, let me clutch thee:
> I have thee not, and yet I see thee still.
> Art thou not fatal vision, sensible
> To feeling, as to sight? or art thou but
> A dagger of the mind, a false creation,
> Proceeding from the heat-oppressed brain?
> I see thee yet, in form as palpable,
> As this which now I draw.
> Thou marshall'st me the way that I was going,

This pause after the half-line "*As this which now I draw*" is necessary, as it will take him some time to get his sword out.

And how did Arthur Miller get in here? Well, in the original One Act version of *A View from the Bridge,* quite a lot of the speeches for different characters were written in verse. In particular, Alfieri the lawyer has many speeches written in modern blank verse. In the Two Act version of the play, there is some minor rewriting of the script, but the main difference is that the many bits of poetry are printed—word for word—as prose. Was this so the modern actor or reader would not be put off by the poetry? The layout is still there to help with those speeches for those willing enough to look up the first version and see what Arthur Miller originally intended as his instructions to his actors.

SEE also: TEXT

Family Tree:	Style
Branch:	Shakespeare acting
Twig:	**SHAKESPEARE: VERSE**
Leaves:	Example: Olivia's ends; Example: Princely business

Shakespeare:
What You Call People

Thee or you? My Lord or my Liege?
(And Chrissie or Christine?)

In French and in German, there is a difference between the first person intimate—*tu, du*—and the first person formal—*vous, Sie*. Spoken English used to have such a distinction in the use of *thee* and *you*. It is no longer in general use today, but in the Elizabethan times it was, and when we find these differences in Shakespeare's work, we should use them as guides and help as to the situation and how the actor should respond.

This change in how you address others is important when you are studying what name each character calls the other characters. In a modern world, you know if someone is being familiar with you (using your first name) or being distant (using your last name), and this can certainly be applied to any script you study. All through the plays of Shakespeare, the title or style of address used can minutely graph the changing relationships in a scene, such as when the Duke is banishing his niece Rosalind from the court in *As You Like It:*

DUKE:

    Mistress, dispatch you with your safest haste,
    And get you from our court.

ROSALIND:

    Me uncle.

DUKE:

    You cousin,

Within these ten days if that thou be'est found
So near our public court as twenty miles,
Thou diest for it.

ROSALIND:

          I do beseech your grace
Let me the knowledge of my fault bear with me:
If with myself I hold intelligence,
Or have acquaintance with mine own desires,
If that I do not dream, or be not frantic,
(As I do trust I am not) then dear uncle,
Never so much as in a thought unborn,
Did I offend your highness.

First of all, the Duke addresses her as *you*, indicating that this speech is to be heard by all the court, but then he switches to the more intimate *thou*, indicating that this part of the speech is for her ears only (a fascinating interpretation, and one that most actors ignore by just playing the entire scene angrily).

Rosalind then starts by calling him *uncle*, but she quickly reverts to the more formal *your grace*, follows swiftly with another attempt at being friendly with *dear uncle*, and ends up with the most formal of all, *your highness*. This shows how she is changing in her relationship with him, as she tries to prevent her banishment. These are good clear instructions to the actor from Shakespeare as to when he intended her to change and try new arguments.

The Actor Says:

A regular actor with the Royal Shakespeare Company is a great exponent of the Shakespeare guidelines Patrick and I have set out in this book. In a July 23, 2004 review of Hamlet *by* The Guardian's *Michael Billington, I read this:*

> *Significantly, Richard Cordery's nervily bonhomous Polonius avoids eye contact with Meg Fraser's Ophelia while advising her to sever her ties with Hamlet.*

I emitted a squeal of delight because I knew exactly what he was doing. Polonius has just had a scene with his son Laertes in which he addresses him as "thee" throughout, then he is alone with his daughter Ophelia and addresses her only as "you." So Richard was being intimate with Laertes, and having observed the note from Shakespeare, being distant and formal with Ophelia and acted accordingly. Easy eh? And the critic thought it "significant."

The change between the different things you call people was chosen by the author then and are chosen by authors now, as they help to indicate what the relationship changes are between characters by using such things as a nickname or a full title. Noting what to call people is a good device to use when you are studying modern and classic scripts.

SEE also: OUTSIDE-IN VERSUS INSIDE-OUT

Family Tree:	Style
Branch:	Shakespeare acting
Twig:	**SHAKESPEARE: WHAT YOU CALL PEOPLE**
Leaf:	Example: You, thee—and the gold

Shakespeare: Wordplay

Very useful for the stage, films, and commercials.

Musicians have been known to play in the orchestra of a stage musical, having never before read or heard the music to be performed. They look at the notes carefully, because with no rehearsal this is the only information they will get as to how to play for such shows as *The Producers* or *The Phantom of the Opera*. This process is known as putting in a deputy (or dep) and is the closest modern equivalent we can find to how the Elizabethan actors approached a script. Just as those musicians have to rely on their notes, so did the actors have to rely on their words and the connections between them.

The fact that the words alliterate or assonate with others, or have rhymes at the end of a line (which should be played as rhymes), shows that the character being played wants to indulge some particular wordplay at this moment.

The Elizabethan actors were playing many different parts over a short period of time, maybe even with the same sort of plot, and they needed obvious and quick instructions from the author as to how they should play them and as to what was going on. Wordplay is a vital part of this communication.

Here is a list of the main wordplay headings:

Alliteration: This is when words that are close together have the same initial consonant, and they serve as little arrows pointing out the final word, to give it extra choice.

Assonance: This is when the vowel sounds of words close together are the same, and it also serves as a little arrow pointing toward the words.

Clever words: This is when the character is actively choosing the ingenious use of words.

Double entendres: This is when the character uses a word or phrase that has a perfectly clean meaning but also a sexual or bawdy one. The word die, for example, meant not only expiring but also the "little death" of sexual ecstasy; and Hamlet's use of "country matters" has always got a snigger from those in the know (and the word cunning, come to think of it).

SEE also: EXAMPLE: MR. HORNER IS EXACTLY THAT

Metaphor: This is when words or ideas are said to be the other things, and it is evidence of the character being even more clever.

Midline endings: This is when Shakespeare ended a thought in the middle of a line, and it is a deliberate message that the ideas of the next thought should crash into the end of the previous one and that there should be no pause but a change in the tempo at this point.

Repeated words: This is when a word or sequence of words is repeated immediately, and it serves to draw attention to them and to make the actor really choose to say those words again.

Rhyme: This is when the end words of two lines rhyme with each other, and the effect is to bring attention to the last word.

Separations: This is when the end consonant of one word is the same as the starting consonant of the next, and this forces the actor to separate the words (not run them together). This choice is in itself the acting note.

Simile: This is when words or ideas are said to be like other things, and it shows that the speaker is choosing to be a bit clever.

SEE also: GOOD AND BAD TASTE

Wordplay is your key to unlocking so many speeches and scenes—and we don't just mean those written by Shakespeare.

Family Tree:	Style
Branch:	Shakespeare acting
Twig:	**SHAKESPEARE: WORDPLAY**
Leaves:	Example: Valuable verbals; Let the words do the work

Shooting and Acting

What happens on the set.

One of the main issues when acting for a camera is how casual it can seem. You sit around in a trailer (if you are lucky), in a green room, or on a catering bus, waiting for hours while the crew is away doing some other scene not involving you. When the crew is finally ready for your scene, you wander onto a set. There is none of the stage-acting buildup of rehearsal, dress rehearsal, preview, and first night with presents and cards: no, you arrive at your mark, and start acting.

It is even worse when it is over, and you get a perfunctory "Thank you" before the production team rushes on to the next scene, and you wander off to get changed and get a cab home. There are no curtain calls, and no people coming to your dressing room telling you how marvelous you were.

Everything is planned and done with an eye to saving time (and so saving money), and scenes will be shot in the incorrect order if it means they can save time, even though it is harder for the actors because they are not acting the scenes in the emotional order they occur in the script.

Marks are set for the actors to come to and hit. If you give the most wonderful performance but miss your mark, then you could be out of focus, so the whole thing counts for nothing. If you give a rather dull performance but hit all your marks, your performance at least will be usable. Moral? It is often more important to hit your marks than give a good performance (although they would prefer you to do both, naturally).

There will be a dress rehearsal of the shot, where the camera and actors work happily together, the sound operator gets the sound, and everything is as it will be during the take. When the take happens, if you do anything differently, if you get an inspiration to do a line a little louder than you had in rehearsal, or if you decide to lean your head forward to emphasize a particular line, you will ruin the take. It is ruined because the sound operator had adjusted her equipment for the levels you were using during a rehearsal, and you might have overloaded it with your sudden outburst. The camera might have shot you out of focus, for the sudden unexpected movement of your head would have caught the operator unaware, as she must adjust the focus every time the distance between the actor and the camera changes.

If you want to do something differently, then ask the director. Tell the First (First Assistant or AD), and let the sound operator and the camera operator know, so that they can adjust for any changes and make sure that your inspirational performance can get to the camera without being affected by technical mistakes.

Often the person you are talking to in a film is not in the same room with you, as a star will often go back to her trailer when the reverses are being done, and you might have to act with a stand-in or assistant reading the lines. Interestingly, your acting often improves when you have a stand-in rather than the real thing there, so do not get upset if it happens but relish the thought that you are now able to act freely, without worrying that you will be upstaging your fellow actor or wasting her time.

In a multicamera studio production, you might have had some rehearsal in a marked up rehearsal room or just be called onto the set to rehearse or record, or both. You will have a better idea of the complete script, as it will be done scene by scene, but the order can still be illogical as far as emotional builds are concerned. You will have to adjust to the many cameras as they swoop and move about your performance.

If you really don't understand what is going on, stick to being relentlessly obedient. Often in the rush to complete a shot the actors are given only the barest of instructions, with no accompanying comforting explanation. You need to trust instructions (unless they might lead to personal injury) and just do exactly as you are told.

SEE also: DIRECTORS

Family Tree:	Screen acting
Branch:	**SHOOTING AND ACTING**
Twigs:	Editing and acting; Film versus television; Multicamera versus single camera; Punctuality; Stars

Stars

Are you sure you want to be one?

You read a lot about stars, their private lives—usually disastrous—and their exotic lifestyle, and you decide that the gains are worth the pain. You want to be a star.

There is something else to consider, and that is what it takes to become a star. No, we are not talking about talent, although that does seem to be quite a necessary ingredient. We are talking about what type of personality you need to fight your way through the undergrowth to finally end up at the top of the tree.

There are so many obstacles in the way of reaching the heights that those who finally make it, those who finally fight their way through, might also be those who are inadequate in some other way. Hidden demons drive them so hard that they overcome all the setbacks and rejections. It might be that you actually need a character defect to climb up to the top of the ladder of success.

Many, many of those who get to the top (whatever is meant by that term) are unhappy individuals with a manic need to be loved and to succeed, and that is at a huge cost to themselves and to their loved ones, if they have managed to hang on to any.

There are many wonderful actors who have not achieved the heights of Hollywood fame, and that was because they considered that the Faustian bargain was not worth it (Dr. Faustus sold his soul to the devil in return for worldly success). Do not get us wrong; if you do achieve the heights, well done! But please do not tell the rest of us that if someone is really talented, they will succeed; this is simply a way of justifying your own success. There are many talented people who have not made it, and that might be because they have observed the way of life necessary to become **and stay** a star, and they judged it to be not worth the human and personal cost.

Everyone feels a bit of a failure, everyone thinks they can do better, and everyone is jealous of the person on the next rung up the ladder, whether they are a beginner in a small production in a small town or one of Hollywood's greats, grumbling that he earned only $15 million for his last role and his rival is getting $20 million.

If going higher in the industry gets you to do the work you care about and play the roles you feel strongly about, then success is, of course, to be welcomed and embraced. If, however, it makes you paranoid and lose all your old friends as you scramble to get even higher, then you must gently wonder if, in fact, it was worth it.

The Actor Says:

Two of the stars I have appeared with in British situation comedies had very different ways of dealing with supporting actors. In one sketch I was asleep and had practically no dialogue, but on waking, became the butt of the joke and had the tag line. After the read through I was sent home and told to wait for my call. When we resumed rehearsals, the parts had been exchanged—I now had the lines and the star had the pay off.

In the other sitcom, the star was so generous to me (a mere unknown) that he placed me where the camera could pick up my reactions, and made sure my lack of height was noted, since he could see how that would add comedy to the scene.

Acting with stars has its own pitfalls to be aware of. Remember that they are the ones bringing in the audience (you hope), so anything that will make them more effective even at your expense will be considered (by them) to be quite acceptable. Be prepared to be allowed only a limited number of moments or laughs and for the play to be twisted to suit the perceived character of the star, even if this changes the play and your contribution to it.

The main problem when acting with a star in a film is that your natural excitement and wish to be noticed might make you overproject. Never forget that you are acting for the apparent shot size, for the camera, and that the main thing is to impress with your low vocal levels. Film stars can be very insecure, so you should do with great happiness whatever it takes to help them give a luminous performance—and they can be quite extraordinary in what they produce for the camera. After all, at the end of the shoot, you can pop into the local supermarket or bar to meet and talk with your friends, and they cannot.

Don't forget—fame is what others give you; success is what you give yourself.

SEE also: HIERARCHY

First Family Tree:	Screen acting
Branch:	Shooting and acting
Twig:	**STARS**

Second Family Tree:	The Team
Branch:	Fellow actors
Twig:	**STARS**

Starting Off

Your first steps.

Actors usually start with some theatre acting under their belt, if only at school, so the various types of theatre acting need to be considered.

There is amateur dramatics, a good and popular place to begin. You join a local community theatre group, while earning a living in some other capacity. This way you can play a big variety of parts and, after some years of loyalty, might even get to choose specific plays and roles you always wanted to do. This first step can also be the only step you make, but if it keeps you happy, so be it.

Then there is fringe theatre or showcases, often called off-off Broadway. This is usually unpaid work, or profit share, and is stuffed with actors keen to gain experience in anything or simply to tread the boards and keep the brain cells working. There will always be unpaid projects you can apply for, so you need to consider what the payoff is going to be. Many casting directors will use such productions to get to know actors and their work, but beware! They will cast you only in a role that they have seen you do, so if the unpaid part you are offered is not the type you are likely to be up for as far as screen work is concerned, then doing this role will not help. Remember: casting directors are looking for results, not for potential.

The Actor Says:

I find a dichotomy in fringe theatre between those who feel it is an opportunity to work and be seen (although they are not being paid) and those such as myself, who strongly object to paying to see a fringe show knowing that none of my money is going to the very people I have gone to see. Why should the producer, stage management, crew, and front-of-house people be paid, and actors exploited because of their (often) strong desire to be seen to be acting?

At the very least, make efforts to ensure that some of the monies end up in the actors' pockets. If anyone connected with the show is to receive any money, then make sure you at least get your bus fare. Actors' putting up with terrible financial conditions leads to future actors being similarly exploited. Your silence gives consent, and we don't want to go back to the days when actors paid to be in shows, do we?

Then there is the professional theatre, where somebody pays you to act. This is all very lovely, but what are they paying for? Probably not so much for your versatility as for your speciality. This can be anything from authenticity in a certain accent or dialect, a sporting capability, a musical or physical skill of some sort, or simply the way you look.

When you get into the profession, there will be many things that seem stupid and old-fashioned. Instead of telling everyone how your ideas can work better, assume that everything is in fact done for a good reason, and spend your energies working out why it is done that way. As the years go by, you will be embarrassed to realize that what seemed stupid and inefficient at first is in fact the best way to do it, or the best way to behave.

The Actor Says:

*After asking her permission, I recently gave a young fellow actor a note, so that she could get a laugh she was missing. Her dressing room companion jumped in very aggressively with, "Is this what people do? I know this is only my second job, but we were taught in acting school never to give notes to other actors." Actually, it **is** what actors do, for they want the play to be as good as possible, and **will** talk to each other to work out how to make each moment work. She'll learn—and learn better manners too, I hope.*

The Director Says:

I must say I don't like actors giving each other notes when I am not there, as it makes it impossible to know exactly what is going on, and so I have to give my notes in ignorance of the full background.

Family Tree:	Training
Branch:	**STARTING OFF**
Twig:	Acting: What is it?

Step-by-Step

Where to be each day of rehearsal.

Acting can be a very annoying business, and you can spend a lot of your time being angry: angry with other people maybe, but most of all being annoyed with yourself—annoyed that you are not better. Relax: take it one step at a time.

It is a conceit to imagine that you will come up with a complete finished performance the very first time you go through a role. The whole thing will come bit by bit, and so your job is to be where you should be, bit by bit. Do not try to be at first-night level at the first rehearsal; be where you should be at the end of that day.

Use your anger at not being perfect, but temper it with the reality that your job is to be ready for when the cameras roll or for the opening night. Trying to be beyond where you should be at each rehearsal often means stopping the very process that **will** get you there. This is not to say that you should grow slowly from rehearsal to rehearsal, as it is imperative to do your basic work as quickly as possible and to give yourself time to polish things up at the end.

The most common reaction of actors new to the industry is great surprise at how fast professional experienced actors work; they seem to get there so quickly. This is because they have discovered that comprehensive preparation gives them a good platform to work from, and they might already know their lines, even though this was not asked for. The first step must then be to do your homework and dig out stuff prior to rehearsals, even though in acting classes it has always been the rehearsal period when you did these things.

Be aware that once you get into run-throughs, and then the inevitable technical and dress rehearsals, there will be no time to adjust a performance or explore a new avenue. All your major discoveries and decisions must be made in homework or in a rehearsal, and done early in the process so when you move on to run-throughs of the play, you already have the foundations laid. Leaving problems or tricky moments to late in the day often means they are never really dealt with, as the actors must attend ever more complicated technical rehearsals to make sure the impressive scenery is working properly and the director's concept is coming across clearly.

First Family Tree:	Homework
Branch:	Journey
Twig:	**STEP-BY-STEP**

Second Family Tree:	Rehearsing
Branch:	Rehearsals (long, short, or none)
Twig:	**STEP-BY-STEP**

Style

What does it mean?

The Director Says:

When I was a theatre student at Boston University, it was the practice to invite the star of any touring play to address the students, and answer questions. Whenever it was a British actor (such as Paul Schofield or Richard Burton) the first question was always the same—"How do you act style?"

After a lifetime in the theatre and screen work, I feel I now know the answer: it is to be faithful to the original author's intention, not only to the character and sense of the play but also to the author's understanding of what the actor–audience relationship was when the play was written.

This relationship has varied during the centuries, and we have written specific articles about each period, including our own modern contemporary acting. The difference in acting a style from a play written way back in time is the overall fact that if the original audience expectation was for it to participate, then to repeat that relationship is to address a fundamental truth. We see this today at the circus, when the modern audience members are happy to shout at the clowns in a way they would not at a comedy. So for a period style production, a lot more talking to the audience can be required.

If the original actors at a Restoration play knew that the audience was waiting for specific comments from them about particular members of that audience, then dealing with that and speaking out front making those connections is to be truthful to that play and to that style, and therefore is truthful within that context. So, rude comments about people from the country would be addressed to those in the audience who were not dressed fashionably, and so on.

This change in approach continues to this day, where audience members' expectations of a performance on Broadway are very different from their expectations, even with the same actors, of a Hollywood blockbuster. You have only to compare the passionate and loud stage work of Kevin Kline on Broadway to the way he murmurs his parts on-screen. Be truthful to the audience–actor relationship where you are performing, and all else will fall into place.

The thing to worry about in playing a period stylistic piece is how to maintain your body language. Normally this is easy to read, with changes in your thoughts and attitudes being clear and obvious to the audience by the way your body moves. However, in a style piece the different movements needed for that period, or associated with those costumes, can drown the actor's body language and make it appear that the customary thought changes are not there. Be particularly aware of this problem and work hard from the start of rehearsals to solve it, to allow your body to sing with your thoughts even when it is encased in a doublet and hose.

SEE also: MOVEMENT AND GESTURES

First Family Tree:	Homework
Branch:	**STYLE**
Twig:	Comedy and farce

Second Family Tree:	**STYLE**
Branches:	Medieval acting; Melodrama acting;
	Modern contemporary acting; Restoration acting;
	Shakespeare acting

Teaching Acting

Perhaps your teachers were once where you are now.

Teaching can do many things for you, from paying the rent to getting better contacts for more professional work, but it has one wonderful result if you do it the right way: it makes you better at your craft. The moment you start to tell someone else how to do it, you refine in your heart and mind how it is you practice your craft, and perhaps how you can do it even better. You will be in an environment where the very thing you want to be involved with is the meat and drink of the department—and that must be better than certain offices you might end up working in.

The Director Says:

I always used to despise Restoration comedy, thinking it was not for me—but then I realized that I was cutting myself off from one important aspect of dramatic history. I made myself available to direct and then teach it at a drama school. After four or five productions I found I enjoyed it and (at least to my eyes) I was good at it—and it made me a better theatre practitioner.

Things go wrong when the teacher resents any success the pupils have or tries to outshine them in any exercise. But they go right when, as a group, they explore and advance their knowledge of the craft of acting.

Very often the establishment you teach for will have a policy of following one form of theatre rules or another, and that can be interesting. Applying principles that you are not quite convinced about can sharpen and refine the work you do.

The good thing is that you are still working in the business of acting, still studying texts, and working on acting solutions, and as you identify and cure problems in others, you will find these efforts have the same effect on you.

First Family Tree:	Training
Branch:	Conservatories and drama schools
Twig:	**TEACHING ACTING**

Second Family Tree:	The Team
Branch:	You (your other life)
Twig:	Jobs requiring acting skills
Leaf:	**TEACHING ACTING**

Technical and Dress Rehearsals

How to use them constructively.

The play has been blocked, rehearsed, and whipped into some kind of shape. All you need now is an audience! But before that can happen, you will come to the technical and dress rehearsals. Your patience and concentration will be required a great deal.

Before the full dress rehearsal can take place, of course, you need to go through the technical process whereby all entrances, exits, and sound or lighting cues are individually worked through. You might be required to say some of the lines in the middle of a scene, so be prepared to pick up cues quickly. You are not required to act these moments; they are simply for the crew to know when to ring door and telephone bells and bring up the correct lights at the moment you touch a switch or light a fire, and so on. Because it is the technical rehearsal, concentrate on those moments, as there is no one out front to watch your acting. All attention is going to lights and cues and sound levels.

Be prepared for some very long days, especially if your production is a lavish extravaganza with a full orchestra, scenery flying in and out, furniture being trucked on and off, and chandeliers falling, to say nothing of children and animals with chaperones and handlers, all needing their moment in the sun. You can well have time enough to complete a crossword or puzzle book. Bring in something to rest on, food, and water; anything to help you keep up your spirits and energies for the real job of helping put the whole thing together.

It is a very good idea, by the way, to have a dressing room hobby (useful for all the hanging around on film sets as well). Many actors have made the most wonderful things in the spare time given to them in offstage situations, from needlepoint to model airplanes. Some actors have been known to run poker schools in the green room or, at the very least, to play a Scrabble game to fill in the time. However, anything too involved with other people is a danger. Concentration on the game can be a great distraction, with the strong possibility of being off, because there will inevitably be varying entrance times for each actor. So, watch it!

Be prepared mentally for any eventuality, and keep calm, especially in the costume department. The designer and director are more responsible for what you look like than you are, so do not worry if you think you look dreadful; it was not your choice. Quarreling with them now will have only one loser—you.

Because the actual dress rehearsal is the first time you run through the play in full costume, with all effects, but without an audience, you should give it the full works, bearing in mind that it is as much a rehearsal for the crew as for you. Make sure that there are no little problems unsolved—this is the time to sort them out, so that the only new thing to deal with on the first night is the audience. Jotting things down in a notebook to remind yourself or others of problems encountered is a smart idea, because the day can be so confusing that there is danger of your remembering what it was you wanted to fix too late—the audience is already out there.

At the end of the process, when the play has opened and bedded down, go back over this time and your notes to see what you could have done earlier in the rehearsal process to deal with the problems that inevitably cropped up in the technical and dress rehearsals. **Now** you will understand why the more experienced actors did all that preparation so early. It was necessary.

Family Tree:	Rehearsing
Branch:	**TECHNICAL AND DRESS REHEARSALS**
Twigs:	Costumes, wigs, and shoes; Crew

Technique

The craft behind acting.

Technique is a dirty word in some people's book. But technique is a wonderful and necessary thing and is used by everyone, whether they acknowledge it or not. Of course it is, because you cannot possibly act without it. For example, imagine having to do a dozen or more takes of the same scene on a film set without using technique. Imagine trying to recreate the same feelings and bits of business over and over again, just relying on your own raw emotions to get you through.

So in film and television, where everyone relies on your being on your mark, cheating your face round to camera, and placing props in exactly the right position, technique is imperative. It is there to structure the scene, and it is the actor's job to make all that phony-feeling stuff appear absolutely real and believable. That is what you are paid to do, to make it look good. Nobody watching your performance cares two pins how you actually feel. A lot of acting feels phony, because it **is** phony. It is pretending, and it is not easy to make it look comfortable and natural. So practice technique and learn to love it, and eventually you will enjoy feeling phony!

So what is technique? Well, it is all the tricks of how to make things look real. For example, if an actor needs to do several things at the same time, for screen or stage, the modern actor tends to do them all simultaneously and hopes that the audience will get it. Alas, this is not always effective, as the audience can have trouble picking out what it is you are actually conveying. Instead, use the one-by-one technique.

The trick is to do one thing, then another, and then another. Work out the order to do them so that the audience members can clearly understand what each piece is telling them without their getting confused, and then they will understand what you are doing, put everything together, and think that you **were** doing them simultaneously.

Suppose you have to present a character who is cold, tired, hungry, and ill—to present these feelings all together would lead to a generalized moment, leading the audience to think that you were just ill, because that is the strongest one. If you did them one-by-one but started with being ill, then the audience would think that all subsequent messages were part of the being ill moment, and would miss them. You should carefully choose the order for one-by-one, and do the hardest one first.

Start by being hungry: search for any old piece of food on the ground. The audience sees that you have not had something to eat for ages.

Then be tired: yawn and stretch. The audience perceives that you want to go to sleep.

Then be cold: shiver. The audience understands that you want more clothing.

Then be ill: be convulsed with gut ache. The audience realizes that you are cold, tired, hungry, and ill.

Technique such as one-by-one is simply a way of getting results that look natural, believable, and spontaneous.

The plan is to decide what you want the result to be, then work out how to achieve this result in the easiest possible way. If the complaint then is that this seems to be working from the outside-in, so be it. Working back from a finished result to the reason why it arose is a great technique for getting excellent performance values.

First Family Tree:	Rehearsing
Branch:	**TECHNIQUE**
Twigs:	Believability; Business (biz); Gear changes; Opposites; Outside-in versus inside-out; Sex and violence

Second Family Tree:	Performing
Branch:	**TECHNIQUE**
Twigs:	Business (biz); Comedy and farce; Eye-to-eye contact; Less is more?; Over the top; Projection; Properties (props); Pulling focus

Ten-Second Rule

A rough and ready guide.

The following life belt is very simple to remember:

If you have to think about something for longer than ten seconds, it is wrong.

Acting is as much an instinctive process as any other process, and the curse of modern acting is the endless analysis and talking that goes on in rehearsals. Well, stage rehearsals really, as the world of screen acting is far too busy to get bogged down in philosophic showings off.

It is very nice indeed to sit around and discuss a play, and it can throw up revelations for everyone. All those sitting round the table joining in the discussions (or just listening in, hoping they will not be asked for their own opinions) will be much better equipped to give a lecture on the play or to lead a workshop on the inner workings and meanings of the play. But does it make them act the play better?

Some actors act better when they know all that is going on, when they can identify and observe the arc of the play, **and some do not.** There is no absolute link between understanding and being able to perform, and your life belt is as follows:

It all depends.

Directors love leading discussions—it is what some of them do best— but the actors have to get up and actually do the work. There are many actors even now as we write who would rather be rehearsing a piece, than sitting round the table talking about it.

The ten-second rule is to clarify what is important and what happens when things are tried out rather than talked about. It can be better to do something in three different ways, and then see which is best, rather than spending ages discussing it, so there is time to do it only once. Try to manipulate things so that you get to try things, so come into rehearsal prepared and willing to do a scene in several different ways, and ask to do so—you might be allowed to show the results.

Often, the most talented people are required to act at lighting speed—think of the demands on a regular in a television comedy, on a chat-show host, or on a stand-up comedian. They must come up with solutions really fast, and sometimes the faster they work, the better it is. They are forced to apply the ten-second rule, so try it yourself—you will be amazed what your subconscious will come up with when it is challenged to work in this way.

SEE also: INSTINCT VERSUS INTELLECT

First Family Tree:	Rehearsing
Branch:	Thinking
Twig:	**TEN-SECOND RULE**

Second Family Tree:	Style
Branch:	Modern contemporary acting
Twig:	Outside-in versus inside-out
Leaf:	**TEN-SECOND RULE**

Text

What to do with your main body of information.

There is only one thing you really know about a character you are to act—and that is what you say. All the rest is flummery and guesswork (including sometimes what the author says about the part).

The audience will hear what you say, so if the character is rooted elsewhere than in the text, the audience will see and appreciate one character, while hearing a different one in the words. If you create your character from the text, then by definition when you say those words, you will be believable!

Authors spend a lot of time creating their characters, and they have learned that not all actors will read stage instructions or even be guided by them—so they agonize over each word, making sure it drives the character on and creates the part that they have conjured out of their imagination. For the actor and director then to spend hours (days even) working on anything but that text does seem to be a little perverse, when the beautiful words and ideas are already there on the page, just waiting to be lifted off and used.

Authors do not always know the best way for their work to be performed. There is a famous tale of Arthur Miller, after a rehearsal, congratulating one of the actors in his play *All My Sons* for completely capturing the character and thoughts of the part he had written. When Mr. Miller then discovered that the actor was, in fact, **not** having the thoughts the writer had assumed he was having, they had an argument that led to the performance's never being so good again. Now, which was correct: the performance that the author enjoyed or the presumed thoughts that the author had written? An author's craft is different from that of an actor, and each should be respected for the contribution that it brings.

The Actor Says:

*I was lucky enough to be in an original Tom Stoppard play that began life in a fringe venue and transferred to the West End (so it can pay off to do this sort of work sometimes). Tom attended rehearsals every day and showed surprise from time to time when an actor would give a certain line reading that produced a laugh that even **he** was not expecting.*

Some teachers and directors recommend that you go through the play and write down everything anyone says about your character. This is to help you build up a fuller picture, but it does have some drawbacks. Suppose the other characters are lying, exaggerating, or imagining what they see in you. In real life, people talk about you behind your back, but if you were to find out exactly what they say, would you change your personality to fit that description? We are sure your answer is "definitely not."

No, the only safe guide to your character in a play is what **you** say and do. Therefore, you should look very carefully at your own lines, not just to learn them but also to wonder what sort of character would choose those particular words and phrases. Your job is to create the kind of person who wants and needs to say those lines. Do not try to imagine what **you** would do in a given situation but try to portray the **person** who would say those lines at that time. In other words, if you **start** with the lines, then **that** character in **that** situation will be totally believable.

There are, of course, good plays and bad plays, good writers and bad writers (everyone has suffered the perils of bad dialogue). You might feel very strongly that your character simply would not say that line or phrase. Tell the director how you feel, to get his help in either adjusting your performance or adjusting the line. This particularly applies to screen work, where the speed of production often means that the actors have to adjust their lines to suit their already established characters.

The Actor Says Again:

I once read in an acting book that the way to success was to work only on good scripts, and to say no to all the others. My career has been full of many different jobs, but only once did I actually have to choose between two conflicting ones. All the other times, my choice was not between a good or a bad script—even if one could always identify which was which—but between acting or being out of work.

If the script seems rather serious, read it again, looking for the jokes. If it seems a bit bland, read it again, looking for the gear changes. If you think there is nothing much there, challenge yourself to find why this script or play is still being done or why the producer is so keen to present it now.

It is always a good idea to look at another copy of the text—very often, the version of a play published by the author can vary in interesting ways from that published as a record of what the Broadway show consisted of. There is the famous case of the extra scene in Arthur Miller's *The Crucible*, which does not appear in all versions of the play but can give you added information and insight even if your production is not using it. Also, in many cases the stage instructions in your script are those added by the stage manager of the Broadway or West End run that were then printed as the acting edition and are not necessarily those of the author. Check up and see—it can be a great help.

The Director Says:

I was directing an Agatha Christie play and wondered why the comic gardener made only one appearance, and why the doctor went upstairs to see his patient, only to return almost immediately with a diagnosis. Research and finding another version of the play revealed all—the original actor playing the doctor had also invested money in the play, and on its pre-London tour resented all the laughs the gardener was getting. He used his influence to get the gardener's second comic entrance cut, even though it made his own visit upstairs impossibly quick. I restored the missing scene to great effect (and appreciation from the actor playing the gardener!).

I also found out that the published version of Bell, Book, and Candle *from the West End production had the action changed to London and the characters to English, even though the play works so much better in its original Manhattan setting, with American accents, as published originally in New York.*

Be particularly careful to see an alternative version if you are doing a script that has been translated from another language. Translators often give themselves huge leeway to change the play, in addition to just putting the words into English, and a different translation can help you understand your character better.

First Family Tree:	Homework
Branch:	**TEXT**
Twigs:	Example: Broadway versus Hollywood; Gear changes; Learning lines; Let the words do the work; Opposites; Pauses

Second Family Tree:	Screen acting
Branch:	Auditions
Twig:	Readings
Leaf:	**TEXT**

The Team

You never act alone—you need others.

When a project is a huge success, the author knows that it was entirely due to what she put on the page. The director naturally is certain that without her contribution the whole thing would have been a disaster, and the designer is equally certain that her vision was the thing that made the whole project special. All the actors will boast that they are the pivotal part of the project—remember the character actor in *Shakespeare in Love* (the film about the creation of *Romeo and Juliet*) who when asked by his cronies what the play was about, replied: "Well, there's this nurse . . ."—and the technicians don't need anyone to tell them they are key to the whole thing.

Put yourself into their respective shoes, and then see how you should relate to them. Screen work is of course extremely technical, where each shot requires a whole group of differently skilled people to work in unison. The theatre is now getting equally complicated, with plays requiring film inserts, video screens, and all the excitements of a modern techno production.

Very often when it comes to the first night or to the shoot, you will not have so much contact with the director. You will be dealing with the range of stage and floor management people, who all have to deal with actors frequently and know the difference between a cooperative actor and one who is a pain.

Which will you be? Here is a hint: many of the future directors, casting directors, and agents will start off at the bottom of the ladder and might come across you when you are both at this stage of your careers. Do you want them to employ you in the future? Or are you happy to be able to boss someone around, the way you have been by the world recently, and so get your revenge?

The Actor Says:

I was booked to play a maid (yet again) in a television costume drama, but without first being interviewed by the director. I was required to have a Scottish accent, learn the lines, and turn up on location to shoot the exterior scenes. All went very well; I was in four out of the five episodes and made some good friends. At the cast party afterwards I asked the director how he had come to cast me sight unseen—wasn't it a bit of a risk? "Oh, I know your work," he said. "I saw you in Gaslight *at Watford Rep." I said, "I can't believe you remember a performance from at least thirteen years ago," and he replied, "I remember you very well, I was on the book." Yes, he was the assistant stage manager in his first job, and I had been playing a Scottish servant, and I had not remembered the prompter, though I must have treated him well. The moral being: Always be nice to those on the way up—you never know when you may meet them again! (It may even be on the way down.)*

It is amazing how often actors, meek and mild when they are working in an office or a store, become raging tyrants when given an acting job. It is understandable but not recommended. After all, how do you know which one of these so-called underlings has the ear of the director—or an even closer relationship?

These people close to you are your first line of defense when things go wrong—people to get things for you, maybe even cover up a mistake of yours—so work from the very beginning to make them your friends and colleagues, not your enemies and adversaries. In the theatre, your dresser helps you with your costume and can make your life pleasant by the little extras she does for you; on a film set your First (First Assistant or AD) is the link with the floor, with the director, and to cut across them is not wise at all.

The Actor Says Again:

I was acting a barmaid in a commercial in which I had to recite a list of food items at top speed. The words were almost indistinguishable, so the fun of the advert was seeing the reactions on the customers' faces. They started shooting the customers first, and after forty takes not fluffing once, they moved the camera round for my close-up. Suddenly my lips just wouldn't form the words, and the director called for a thirty-minute break. The First (the AD) wandered over to me quite casually and said, "Don't worry, just think of the overtime!" He then continued to chat about everyday things, and the diversion must have worked. We resumed the shoot and I was word perfect again. Thanks to the thoughtfulness of the First (who probably suggested the half-hour break), I was able to successfully complete the shoot.

SEE also: ATTITUDE

Family Tree:	**THE TEAM**
Branches:	Crew; Designers; Directors; Fellow actors; Producers; You (your other life)

Thinking

Beware of acting only inside your head.

There is bad news. Audiences are not mind readers. To think something—to think wonderful things—can often come out of intense and meticulous rehearsals. That is good, but unfortunately many actors stop there and feel that they have done their bit, and the rest is up to the audience.

This leads to the actors' having a better time in performance (because of all the wonderful thoughts and feelings they are having) than the audience has in watching them (because the audience does not always know what is going on or why). The solution is to do something, anything, rather than just to think.

In real-life conversations, when you change the subject you usually also change your mannerisms. For example, the neighbor will exchange pleasantries about the weather, before hitching up his trousers and getting to the real reason he stopped to talk—to complain about the noisy music last night; the supermarket manager will button up his jacket before telling us our suggestion has been rejected; and the doctor will start shuffling his papers when he is about to give us the results of the tests.

Your putting this into practice on the stage or screen cheers up the audience members immediately, as they now **know** when something has happened and can get on with working on why—rather than coming out of the film or play muttering, "I have no idea what was going on in there."

The more inventive the piece of business is in revealing the change of inner thoughts, the better the audience likes it. Your life-support machines are as follows:

If the audience doesn't get it—forget it.
Don't just put it in your mind, put it in your body as well.

SEE also: BUSINESS (BIZ) and MOVEMENT AND GESTURES

First Family Tree: Rehearsing
Branch: **THINKING**
Twigs: Instinct versus intellect; Ten-second rule

Second Family Tree: Performing
Branch: Audience
Twig: **THINKING**

Training

Different routes to becoming an actor.

There is no one recognized way of becoming an actor, and there are always actors who seem to be exceptions to whatever rules are suggested. There does, however, seem to be one constant in all those who successfully come through the different routes—such as training programs, rock bands, television presenting, stand-up comedy, and so forth—and that is a wish to entertain and to have a good connection with the audience that is either at home watching the small screen or in an auditorium watching the big screen or the stage.

The Director Says:

I directed the British rock star Cliff Richard in the first stage play he had ever appeared in. Although he was new to acting, his great experience in the world of entertaining meant that he was able to adjust to the demands of acting on a stage very quickly. The only new thing for the rest of us, having a rock star in the cast, was the huge crowd of fans gathered outside the stage door at all times, strumming their guitars every time the door opened—and the look of disappointment on their faces when they saw it was only me.

Those teachers who specialize in subjects such as voice production, fights, mime, and so on usually need to have appropriate qualifications, and they know exactly what it is they need to tell their students. For teachers of acting, it is often not quite the same.

This does not mean that there are not excellent teachers of acting—or some wonderful actors working as teachers—but that the craft of acting is not so easily measured as the crafts of voice and movement. Fashions in acting also change during the years, and it is important to make sure that you are not being trained for a theatre or screen that no longer exists. For example,

313

although it is good in principle to be trained to be versatile in the range of parts you can portray, in practice this skill is now very rarely needed.

You are much more likely to begin your career (should you be so lucky) by playing very small parts on-screen. At the moment there seems to be little opportunity to learn screen-acting skills at most training establishments, even though this is probably going to be the main income for the actor. Further classes and training will be useful, and may well be necessary.

Family Tree:	**TRAINING**
Branches:	Amateur dramatics; Conservatories and drama schools; Further training; No training; Starting off; University courses

Truth

What is it? A fundamental question.

In real life you sometimes do not let your face show what you are really thinking. It would be impossible to work with or talk to people if they could always see exactly how you felt about them, whether it was mad passion, disgust, or extreme indifference.

Acting on the stage or in front of the camera, of course, the audience wants to know what the characters are really feeling about each other, and so a good actor will add these feelings to her performance. Onstage this means the actor reveals more in the body language, as that is what the audience can read most easily. On-screen it means the actor puts on her face all the hidden emotions, so the audience members can share the thoughts and gather the subtext, as the close-up is the best way for them to get that extra information. It is the opposite of what you do in real life, but it is the most truthful thing an actor can do, for she is letting the audience into her emotions and secret thoughts. The way you do this is one of the main differences between stage and screen acting.

Welcome to the shady world of acting truth versus the real thing. To limit yourself on camera or onstage to what you would do in real life is to hide from the audience the truth of your thoughts, so you show the apparent truth. All artists adjust or change reality to give the appearance of truth: painters alter landscapes, sculptors change bodily shapes, and actors are untruthful to convey the subtext to their beloved audience.

A better word than *truth* is *believability*. Convincing liars in real life can be extremely good actors, for they are believable even though they are not telling the truth. In other words, so long as the character and situation are believable, **actual** truth might not come into the equation.

How many times have you heard drama teachers and directors say "Make it truthful"? What is truth to one person might not be to another.

315

Actual truth is not only impossible to define but also a matter of opinion. **"Make it believable"** is easier to understand and perform. In other words, **you** might feel you are being truthful, but if the audience members do not believe what they are seeing and hearing, you have failed to convince them. Frankly, what **you** feel is irrelevant.

Some acting teachers recommend that you try to experience the things that your character has to go through. It is easier to research and **observe** what other people do in certain circumstances rather than actually experience them. For example, you might be asked to play a death scene. How many of us have experienced that? Your character might be mentally ill or disabled (when you are not). Research and observe by all means, but you cannot literally experience what it is like to be so afflicted. You do not have to **be** a brain surgeon or a mathematical genius to play one. In the film *A Beautiful Mind*, did Russell Crowe, playing the mastermind John Nash, really understand those mathematical equations? No, of course he did not. You can act only as much as is given to you on the page, so, if in doubt, trust the author.

The skill of the actor, therefore, must be in so completely affecting the audience members that they are carried away by a situation created by the production team: the writer, director, actors, designer, cameraman, and so on. This process of creating an illusion requires a great deal of technique before the final spontaneity, which makes everything appear to be happening just at that moment.

The Actor Says:

In a television drama about Hitler (I was playing "Second Whore/Rape Victim"), I was quite brutally handled by the actor playing the officer, despite my request for him to go a little easy (after all we were right at the back of the shot and barely visible). He was unable to do this as he felt he had to be truthful, which only led to some truly heavy bruising on my arms!

Quite simply, the truth is not always your friend.

The Director Says:

As an assistant director to a production at Stratford-upon-Avon near the beginning of my career, I was aghast to see an actor smiling in performance when he should have been sad. I was even more surprised when he responded angrily to my note, so I decided to investigate further. Watching from the wings I could see that he was, in fact, producing real tears at this mournful moment—but unfortunately from the back of the auditorium it just looked as if he was smiling. His real emotion was not conveying itself to the audience, and if he had just wiped an imaginary tear from his cheek, that technical business would have been more effective than his real tears. I thought then—a strange thing, this truth business.

Every time actors pause when the audience laughs, every time they repeat a line because the audience has drowned out the words, they are not being truthful. They are, of course, being theatrically truthful, and it is useful to consider these two aspects of it all. The word is bandied around, as if it was all agreed that the ultimate achievement is to be completely truthful, but that all depends on what the audience is believing.

Stage actors already cheat; that is, they do untruthful things when performing, by not standing directly behind each other or even by waiting until they are on the stage before doing their acting, but this is overlooked as something so necessary, it is not worth debating. But in fact all aspects of acting have to be filtered through the prism of audience truth.

Frankly, the audience members want to know what is going on, and they also want to know how you think about it. This is why delivering a soliloquy directly to the audience and not to the invisible man works so well: it is addressing the only fundamental truth of the evening, which is that the audience knows that there are actors up there and the actors know that there is an audience out there.

Screen actors do more cheating than stage actors do, as the demands of the camera make them stand in unnatural ways or handle props in an untruthful manner. The director's monitor is the arbiter of screen truth—if it looks fine, then it **is** fine.

A really expensive fur coat (the real thing) looks false onstage under the lights, whereas a cheap nylon facsimile looks real. It is the same idea with emotions. Trickery—all is trickery.

SEE also: ACTING: WHAT IS IT?

First Family Tree:	Rehearsing
Branch:	Whatever works
Twig:	**TRUTH**

Second Family Tree:	Performing
Branch:	**TRUTH**
Twigs:	Believability; Sex and violence
Third Family Tree:	Screen acting
Branch:	**TRUTH**

Typecasting

How to use it to your advantage.

By all means be varied and versatile, and all those good things that are dealt with in classes and training schools, but do not ignore the real reason why you get the roles: the way you look and the way you come across. The first reason comes from the packet of genes you got from your parents, and the other reason is a result of all the experiences you have gone through from conception to now, which leave you with a certain background, philosophy, language or accent, or even religion. And these two major factors (apart from extensive surgery) are beyond your control, so make them your friends.

Those roles you thought you came into the industry to do, and did so successfully in acting classes, are immaterial; it is the roles you get in the profession that count. These roles will mostly be based on your typecasting. Before you complain too much, listen to the following.

There is a play from the seventeenth century in which a character called Richard Burbadge (who was Shakespeare's main actor back then) has a scene deciding what type a new actor should play, judging by his looks and voice:

BURBADGE:

> I like your face, and the proportion of your body for Richard the Third. I pray, Master Philomasus, let me see you act a little of it.

So if typecasting was in use four hundred years ago, how can you avoid it today?

If you go into any art gallery, you can probably at a distance recognize some of the artists—**there** is a Picasso, **that** is an Edward Hopper. Painters do not get paranoid that their particular style is the same from painting to painting; they embrace their strength and find the varieties in **that.** The same should be true of actors and typecasting.

Do you want to know what your typecasting might be? Well, in which of your most successful performances would it have been really difficult to recast you had you fallen ill? That's the one; that's what the world wants you to play, and that's what you probably do better than anyone else.

The best acting note that you are ever given is that **you got the part.** Just think of the competition, of the large number of actors who would prefer that they were doing it, not you. There must have been a good reason why the part came your way, and do not fool yourself that it was because you were the **best** actor they saw or considered for the role. It was because you were the most **suitable,** and, in particular, you **looked** right. Yes, type-casting can be (and **should** be) your friend.

You want to be cast against type? Remember, this works only when the audience already knows the original and can appreciate the difference between the usual typecasting and the character the actor is portraying today. Would you have admired his performance in *Guys and Dolls* so much if you had never seen, or heard the name of, Marlon Brando?

So instead of working out how you can be different with each role, tell yourself, "Out of all the people possible, they chose **me.**" And then act the reason why you got the role. Ring the changes by finding the variations within your type for that particular piece.

Once you have succeeded in establishing yourself as a known actor, once they start to ask for you by name, then you can consider going for the variety of parts that you always wanted to do. You can use typecasting then as the key to unlock the door of versatility—once you have made yourself employable and wanted.

SEE also: AUDITIONS and WHATEVER WORKS

First Family Tree:	Getting work
Branch:	**TYPECASTING**
Twigs:	Know your image; Versatility

Second Family Tree:	Screen acting
Branch:	**TYPECASTING**
Twigs:	Be yourself (plus!); Know your image; Versatility

University Courses

Another way in.

It is quite standard for potential professional actors to start off their training at a university, and, in the United States, in Acting 101. In Europe, however, it is more natural for the potential actor to go to a drama school or conservatory.

The great advantage of a university course is that you end up with a degree that can be essential for earning money in other related fields. The disadvantage is that you have to share your training, in its initial stages at any rate, with those for whom the subject is an interesting elective, a course that will enable them to develop their interpersonal skills as future doctors or lawyers. Or it might be just a good course to meet attractive young men and women.

Getting on the university ladder is an obvious career move, and going on from a bachelor's degree to a master's degree is a logical choice, for it will allow you in the future to work in the university field if that route beckons you, but it will take a large chunk out of your early life. Going on to a PhD is again a logical choice if joining the academic life appeals to you, as it certainly will appeal to your bank manager and parents. Working in a university department and acting in the summer months in lieu of writing books or articles is a well-worn path for those who want to mix acting with a responsible life, such as bringing up kids or just having enough money to buy a house.

The Director Says:

I was directing at Southern Methodist University in Dallas, and had a wonderful actor playing a role that he never quite got to grips with—because he was also on a scholarship and needed to keep on the Dean's List (keep his grades up to a certain level). So although I was sad he could not devote as much time to the play as I wanted him to, I could quite see that he had to divide his time carefully. So the actual achievements in university productions can be compromised by other factors.

At university you also can start to get yourself ready for the real world of acting. When Meryl Streep left Yale for New York, she took with her the reputation of being "that actor from Yale who is amazingly versatile." She had used her time there well to set up her subsequent career, going out of her way to tackle those roles that would eventually give her that versatile reputation.

Just as the keenest students in business, law, and medicine use their time with an eye to the future, so should student actors, using their time as part of their eventual careers.

Family Tree:	Training
Branch:	**UNIVERSITY COURSES**
Twig:	Qualifications

Versatility

We all want it—but the world is not so sure.

So, you think you are versatile? You can do masses of different accents and dialects, and you can play straight romantic leads and comedy-character roles? How lovely. How clever. How lucky—however, we are sad to report that the days of versatility are over. They only ever really existed in the mid-twentieth century. In the days when weekly repertory was standard and many towns supported a repertory company, actors' versatility came into its own. Although they would have been engaged by that company as a leading man, juvenile, older character, or character juvenile, with some backstage work required as well, they would certainly have been called on to show their versatility in accents in a range of roles, which simply do not exist in today's theatre.

No, today you are still expected to be versatile, but in an entirely different way. The modern actor is expected to be able to perform in all styles of theatre, of course, but also to perform on television and in films and commercials, do voice-overs, and role-play for training doctors, lawyers, and the like: all the varieties that require performances.

The Actor Says:

I have played Queen Victoria at least three times (did I mention that I was rather short?). Once was as the Queen in a television drama about the pre-Raphaelite painters, once as an older lady in a rocking chair in a TV commercial, and once in an Old Time Victorian Music Hall, when Her Majesty unpredictably broke into a song and dance routine. Each Queen Victoria had to be approached differently (especially the singing and dancing one), according to the style and medium I was working in—what versatility, what a range!

Actors also need to be able to work in a variety of ways, and **that** is the true versatility needed. You need to be able

to perform without any rehearsal at all
to perform the same part the same way for a year (stage)
to perform the same part with different dialogue for many years (television)
to perform with other actors you never actually meet (film)
to rehearse for only a few moments
to rehearse for a week—or two, or three
to rehearse for a very long period of time, including research and lectures
to rehearse using lots of theatre games
to improvise your entire part, or all the others' parts
to improvise the script from scratch
to improvise around tight guidelines given by the author, director, or audience

And so on.

The truly versatile actor has a huge toolbox at his disposal, and he knows how to use each tool. The skill is knowing which tool is wanted for which job and using it effectively to deliver not only what is required but also **more** than could legitimately be expected from the given circumstances.

This means that from the most method-drenched project to the most technically demanding musical, the versatile actor will deliver what is required: a wonderful, believable performance full of richness and invention.

SEE also: METHOD ACTING and NEVER SAY NO and OUTSIDE-IN VERSUS INSIDE-OUT and REHEARSALS (LONG, SHORT, OR NONE)

First Family Tree:	Getting work
Branch:	Typecasting
Twig:	**VERSATILITY**

Second Family Tree:	Screen acting
Branch:	Typecasting
Twig:	**VERSATILITY**

Voice

A most valuable part of your talent.

When you hear "the voice beautiful," you recognize it, you love it, and you never get tired of it. But what is it? Is it the timbre, good diction, clarity, depth of tone, comic intonations, or just good old familiarity? And it is familiar because of constant exposure. Yes, it is possible to be employed because of your popular voice.

Whatever quality of voice you are born with there are things you can do to make it more sought after. In the first place you must recognize any faults or failings, although it is unlikely that friends and family would be so personal. Teachers of voice are much more inclined to identify and do something about speech impediments and so on, so lisps, nasal blockages, and the like will be corrected.

All speech impediments affect the quality of voice, such as the weak "r" sound. If you know you have an impediment, then a speech therapist can help. This means that you can then choose whether to have it, rather than having to always present a weak "r" to your audience. A sibilant "s" is one that produces a slight whistle through the teeth or a splashy sound, and should also be acted on in a remedial way. There is a possibility that no one has ever told you about an impediment, or perhaps people are too polite to mention it. Tape-record yourself and be **really** critical.

How often do you hear these impediments among the actors who are used regularly for their voice alone? Not a lot, so if you wish to join them, you need to do your vocal exercises, take those classes, and put in the time necessary to give yourself the voice that gets you employed.

It is slightly dangerous to put on speech mannerisms such as a lisp or an extreme strange accent. Lisps are particularly dangerous as they become irritating to listen to and can make your character completely unintelligible if you are not very careful.

There are, however, other speech patterns that irritate the listener, especially those who wish to hear their language spoken with a certain degree of correctness.

Some regional accents drop the last consonant sound of a word, and others will stress it unnaturally. As a professional actor, you should be able to use these accents when you need to and be able to drop them when such vocal mannerisms are no longer appropriate.

A voice that people recognize and **want** to hear again is gold dust!

SEE also: SCREEN VOCAL LEVELS

First Family Tree:	Homework
Branch:	**VOICE**
Twigs:	Dialects and accents; Projection

Second Family Tree:	Style
Branch:	Modern contemporary acting
Twig:	Radio acting
Leaf:	**VOICE**

Whatever Works

The ultimate criterion.

The Actor and Director Say:

As this is almost the final article in this book, it should come as no surprise that this is the final conclusion we have come to over acting and all its related techniques—whatever works.

For every actor you can find who lives and breathes the role, you can find one who does it completely technically, and the audience loves them both (or hates them both). For every tried and tested piece of technique, we can find moments of sheer lunacy that work against all logic.

This book should be rather like a tool chest, full of techniques and ideas as to how tools can be applied. Different jobs demand different tools, and different craftsmen use different ways of solving the same problem. Your job as an actor is, we believe, to get skillful at deciding which tool you need and how to use it to get the best results.

It could be that in your toolbox is a technique that is never used, until suddenly at a particular juncture in your career, there it is, ready to be used, and joy of joys you know how to use it. The very techniques that you need to tackle a play by Shakespeare will not instantly be appropriate when performing in a commercial, although there can be interesting links.

Everyone has an image of what an actor is and how she works, whether starring in a role on Broadway or appearing in the latest Hollywood blockbuster, but the actual things you will get up to as an actor will be mindblowing. Playing a tomato advertising a pizza firm (well, someone has to do it)? Being a convincing doctor lecturing on the latest surgical techniques to a roomful of experts? Playing a chicken paid by a candidate's opponents to follow a political figure around all day? Remember the accusation that all those Santa Clauses are usually out of work actors? No, they are not; they are actors in work and giving a good performance. Actors are asked to do the impossible and the outrageous, and you need to be able to adjust to whatever is demanded of you, by using whatever works.

There can, of course, be many other reasons why a particular part came your way, such as an emergency recasting or the simple fact of nepotism, or that without your investment the production would not be happening at all. Whatever the reason, you should not ignore the most valuable acting note—that you are acting the role and that your job is to make it work, using whatever technique seems most appropriate and doable. Remember the valuable old saying that has been a life belt, saving many excellent performances:

Spontaneity comes last!

All through this book we have been giving you lifesaving equipment to help you keep your head above water, but all rules are meant to be broken at some time, and nothing we have said is an absolute. Our lifelines are for guidance, not absolute obedience. Take whatever is useful, store away what might come in handy for the future, and try all things until it works— whatever that might be.

SEE also: VERSATILITY

First Family Tree:	Rehearsing
Branch:	**WHATEVER WORKS**
Twigs:	Acting: What is it?; Truth

Second Family Tree:	The Team
Branch:	You (your other life)
Twig:	**WHATEVER WORKS**

You (Your Other Life)

Most of your time will be here (sorry, we didn't mean to upset you).

In a recent survey of working artists on the east coast of the United States, a troubling statistic came up: of those who called themselves artists, fully 80 percent earned less than 10 percent of their income from their artistic side. In other words, they called themselves painters, musicians, actors, writers, and so on, but they earned their living as, well, you name it, and they will do it. We must assume that the same could be true of you.

Most of the actors we know either have been independently wealthy or are married or partnered to someone who is wealthy or earns a regular wage. This seems to be our modern fate: to practice our craft but not to be able to earn a complete living from it. Because this shows no sign of changing in the future, we must address what it means to you as an actor.

Perhaps you can take turns with your partner in being the regular earner? In any case, you both need to be realistic about the need for finance. Believe in your parents' support of you, do not be proud, and accept all the handouts or loans that are going. Remember, when (you must believe it is going to be a *when*) you appear on the national screens, your parents will get a great kick out of it, and all the neighbors and friends will be informed so that they can watch your first (second, frequent) outing on the big or small screen. Your parents will get a huge thrill and credit for this, so they should pay for this privilege by supporting you more than they would if you were going to be an accountant (we apologize to all accountants, but they probably wanted to be something else—oh dear, not an actor?).

The Director Says:

With graduating drama students, I often ask them to imagine the next year of their lives, and to believe that it will be the best possible year for them as far as acting is concerned. Not that they will immediately star in a Hollywood movie— no—but that they will be in a play, maybe do a couple of commercials, get a small role in a TV drama, perhaps spend a couple of days doing a small part in a film. We agree on what a really good realistic series of jobs would be—and then I work out for them what they would earn from such an ideal year. The money never comes to more than half of what they will need to survive—so I ask them the saddest question: "And so what will you be doing to earn the rest of your living?"

For your artistic yearnings to continue and be nourished, you need to get other work that reflects you, your personality, and your ambitions. If not, if you get trapped into the waiter–supermarket-worker mode (unless those are the very jobs that you find most fulfilling), you will find that the time you take away from acting will be down time, time when your ambitions and talents seem to fade and become less accessible for you. You can and probably will get involved in acting classes, unpaid acting jobs, student films, and the like, but it is important that the job you do to raise the necessary monies to live on should reflect your feelings.

What else do you do, care about, or are skilled at? There are some who avoid these very things, in case they get too settled and do not want to return to acting should it happen, but that will cut you off from part of your passions as well, and that will not be good for your acting. You **will** do other work. You will in all likelihood spend more time (and earn more money) doing your other work than your acting work, so choose something that feeds you financially and artistically. Even if the work is not directly linked with your acting needs, use it as a learning curve to observe and store up what real people do in real circumstances. You never know which of your experiences will be needed in the future for a part.

Stacking shelves is fine when you are young and keen, but it can be soul destroying when you are in your forties, as you **will** be one day. You might spend quite some time in this other work, so take time out to train in it. Then you can achieve more than just a few bucks for what you do, and, much more important, you can keep yourself alive artistically.

To go for an audition when you have been working in a supermarket for nine months straight is not as easy as if you had been, for example,

teaching acting to street kids
working as an assistant to an agent or casting director

working as an interior designer
meeting people as a counselor—of whatever sort
going around to offices, giving the workforce a much needed massage
working as a tour guide or demonstrator
writing freelance articles on restaurants, holidays, or motor cars

Finally, it is so frustrating to meet up with actors whose greatest talent is **not** for acting but who refuse to use their considerable talents elsewhere. It is as if they are punishing the world for not letting them be the frequently working actors they had planned to be. Of course, they are just punishing themselves.

A great many agents, casting directors, directors, producers, news broadcasters, and so on started life in the entertainment business as actors—maybe this will be your pathway too.

Family Tree:	The Team
Branch:	**YOU (YOUR OTHER LIFE)**
Twigs:	Drugs; Jobs requiring acting skills; Qualifications; Rejection; Whatever works

Biographies

Patrick Tucker trained as a physicist in the United Kingdom (BSc from London University) and as a theatre director in the United States (MFA from Boston University). He went into the business as an assistant stage manager and worked in a striptease club, on West End musicals, and with the tour of *Oliver!* Since his first professional production of a murder mystery in 1968, he has directed more than 200 stage plays in all forms of theatre, from weekly repertory to the Royal Shakespeare Company, from the National Theatre in Seoul to the Bob Hope Memorial Theatre, Southern Methodist University in Dallas (where he was visiting professor). He has directed musicals and pantomimes (including *Cabaret* and *Jack and the Beanstalk*), new plays and improvised performances, restoration comedies and promenade productions (including *The Beaux Stratagem* and *The Ambridge Pageant*), and lots of Alan Ayckbourn and Shakespeare. He started directing for the screen in 1978 and has directed more than 150 drama productions, from television soap operas to medical dramas to the feature film *In the Dark*.

He has directed radio dramas for the BBC, exercise videos for children (featuring the infamous *Joggy Bear*), and plays and musicals in Danish, Hebrew, Korean, and Spanish (none of which he speaks). He has lectured to a group of nuns, a class of violinists, a conference of Japanese professors, and trans-Atlantic passengers on the *Queen Elizabeth 2*. He has taught the Kenyans and the Danes how to direct and act in soap operas, and he has developed and taught courses on screen acting and screen directing and on Shakespeare in London, all over the United States, and elsewhere in the world.

He has served on the artistic directorate of Shakespeare's Globe since it was formed. His own Original Shakespeare Company has presented plays at Shakespeare's Globe in London, at the World Stage Festival in Toronto, at the Shakespeare Festival in Sydney, Australia, and at other festivals in the United Kingdom, Germany, and Jordan.

His publications include *Secrets of Screen Acting* (now in its second edition), *Secrets of Acting Shakespeare—The Original Approach,* both published by Routledge, and *First Folio Speeches for Men* and *First Folio Speeches for Women,* both published by LAMDA and Oberon Books, London.

Christine Ozanne graduated from the Royal Academy of Dramatic Art (RADA) in 1958 with an honors diploma and three comedy prizes. Having left school at age fifteen and with five years' experience of amateur dramatics under her belt, she began her professional career in weekly repertory theatres, sometimes playing twice nightly. She was in one company for so long that she did Agatha Christie's *Murder at the Vicarage* twice (once as the maid and then as an aristocrat!).

Her theatrical roles have included a cuckoo, a cow, a tea bag, and Lady Bracknell; in addition, of course, innumerable maids, nuns, landladies, and spinster aunts. She created the role of Mrs. Ebury (a politician) in Tom Stoppard's *Dirty Linen* in the West End, has sung and danced in several musicals, and has flown as a witch in pantomime. She did scores of Old Time Music Hall shows and some cabaret and was a reciter in William Walton's *Facade* as a fund-raiser for the Shakespeare Memorial Theatre at Stratford-upon-Avon.

On television she has played Queen Victoria twice, appeared with top comedians in many situation comedies, and played a bag lady in a hospital drama. She has done her fair share of costume dramas, too, in works by Dickens, Dostoievski, and Sir Walter Scott. She has appeared in more than fifty television and cinema commercials, directed by such luminaries as Alan Parker and Ridley Scott. She made her first and probably best-known feature film, the British comedy *Carry On Nurse,* at Pinewood within six months of leaving RADA. Many small parts followed, and she suspects that her height (or lack of it) played a big part in her comedy career.

It was on the tour of *Oliver!* in 1965 that Christine and Patrick met, and he has directed her in a number of plays and several television dramas (yes, he cast her as the bag lady). Together they cofounded the Original Shakespeare Company, and she was the book holder and verse nurse for most of their productions. She played *Lady Capulet* at the Jerash Festival in Jordan, and she has taught Shakespeare master classes in North Carolina, Sydney, Toronto, and Vancouver and on a regular basis at the London

Academy of Music and Dramatic Art, for whom she helped prepare the *First Folio Speeches for Men* and *First Folio Speeches for Women*.

Patrick and Christine do a one-day Masterclass based on this book: *"From the Folio to the Frame (how professional acting has come full circle)."* They would also appreciate any feedback on the book's contents, either positive or negative; you can e-mail them at: tuckozanne@btopenworld.com